Find more of my work at my blog:

www.theauthorstack.com

Find all my work at my website:

www.russellnohelty.com

BookBub:

https://www.bookbub.com/profile/russell-nohelty

HOW TO LAUNCH YOUR BOOK ON KICKSTARTER

By:
Russell Nohelty

Edited by:
Lily Luchesi

Proofread by:
Katrina Roets

INTRODUCTION

KICKSTARTER CHANGES THE GAME

For years, authors have felt chained to the whims of Amazon algorithms and traditional publishers. Crowdfunding is changing all that. Kickstarter has opened a new frontier where you launch your book directly to readers on your own terms. No more praying that some platform's roulette wheel lands on your book. Instead, even a *modest* fanbase can turn into thousands of dollars of support.

In fact, it's often easier to rally 500 die-hard fans to back your project at $10–$40 each than to find 10,000 strangers to buy a $0.99 ebook on Amazon. I've seen this firsthand: one of my campaigns raised $26,000 in funding from only a few hundred backers, and another cracked $39,000 with under a thousand fans behind it

Brandon Sanderson shattered records with a $41 million Kickstarter, proving that crowdfunding isn't some fringe gimmick, and he did it with only 185,341 backers. That's over $200 per backer.

It's a game-changing launch strategy for authors at every level.

Unlike a traditional retail release, a Kickstarter campaign generates cash flow upfront, buzz, and an interactive community around your book. You're not just selling a book. You're creating an event. Readers who pledge aren't casual buyers; they become invested superfans who feel like partners in your success. They'll cheer you on, share your project, and eagerly anticipate updates. This level of engagement simply doesn't happen when someone one-clicks an ebook on Amazon.

I've been part of close to 100 successful crowdfunding projects myself, raising over $1.2 million, and I can tell you that the energy and goodwill from a Kickstarter launch is incomparable. You get validation that your idea has an audience *before* you spend months or years bringing it to life. You get pre-orders and revenue in hand, which means no more guessing how many books to print or going out-of-pocket hoping people buy later. And perhaps best of all, you get direct access to your readers. Not just their emails, but their feedback and their enthusiasm, too, which is something no retailer will ever give you. In short, a well-run Kickstarter doesn't just fund your book; it builds a fan community that will stick with you for the long haul.

Now, before you start seeing dollar signs, Kickstarter is not a magic money tree or a last-ditch rescue raft. It's a strategy, not a charity drive. If you come to the platform with a half-baked project or no audience to speak of, guess what? Crickets. A Kickstarter campaign will expose the truth of what you've built, or haven't built, faster than any tweet or Amazon launch ever could. If your offer is weak or your outreach is nonexistent, Kickstarter will make that painfully obvious. No fluff, no fairy dust, no "Field of Dreams" delusions that if you simply launch, backers will magically appear. I've seen authors treat Kickstarter as a Hail Mary for a failing series or a way to "get money for marketing" because their book wasn't selling. It never ends well.

Kickstarter won't save a sinking ship. It reflects the groundwork and the trust you've earned with readers. On the flip side, if you *have* put in the work to cultivate even a small but passionate readership, Kickstarter can amplify that like nothing else. Throughout this book, we're going to be brutally honest about common pitfalls and how to avoid them. I'm not here to sell you a fairy tale. I'm here to show you how to put in the work so Kickstarter pays off, and to warn you where you might screw up. Consider this your friendly reality check: if you're looking for a get-rich-quick shortcut, you won't find it here, but if you're ready to hustle and treat your campaign as seriously as a product launch, you can absolutely crush it.

How to Launch Your Book on Kickstarter is structured as a step-by-step journey from the earliest planning stages all the way to post-campaign strategy. Each chapter is packed with tactics. I'll give you motivation, but I'll also give you homework. This isn't a book you plow through passively with a shrug. By the end, you won't just have head knowledge, you'll have a concrete campaign plan on paper. Treat this like a hands-on workshop. I'll be pushing you to actually *do* the exercises, because that's where the real progress happens. This book dishes out some tough love and no-nonsense advice, but it's all in service of getting you across the finish line with a successful, stress-free (okay, *less*-stressful) campaign. So, engage with the material, pause to complete the workbook prompts, and embrace the process.

By the time you turn the last page, you'll have a complete blueprint for your Kickstarter launch from crystallizing your initial vision and deciding on what exactly you're funding, to delivering rewards to your backers and nurturing them afterward. You'll know *exactly* what steps to take and in what order. More importantly, you'll have the confidence to execute.

This is huge. Confidence means you'll approach launch day knowing you have a plan, not just a wish. You'll see Kickstarter for what it truly is: a launchpad, not a gamble. Yes, there's always uncertainty, but with solid preparation, you tilt the odds dramatically in your favor. My goal is that you finish this book feeling empowered and fired up, with any fears left in the dust. We're going to replace any lingering "What if no one backs me?" anxieties with an attitude of "I can't wait to show my readers something awesome." Sound good? Great, because it's time for some tough love and serious strategy. Buckle up, and let's crush it.

WHAT'S NEW

Since we first launched *Get Your Book Selling on Kickstarter* in October 2021, there has been a seismic shift in the way Kickstarter has been perceived in the indie community. With the addition of a new CEO, they have made huge changes in how the platform works.

MINDSET SHIFTS

Brandon Sanderson broke open the fiction category: In March 2022, Brandon Sanderson launched a "secret" Kickstarter that raised over $41 million and became the highest-grossing Kickstarter campaign ever by a wide margin. This showed fiction authors, and especially fantasy authors, that they could make serious money on Kickstarter. Prior to that campaign, it was hard to find 5-10 fiction campaigns live at any one time. Now, you would be hard pressed to find a time when there weren't 100+ fiction campaigns live at any time.

The community grew into something massive and powerful: Whether it's our Writer MBA community, the Kickstarter for Authors Facebook group, Kickstarter specialists that will help you run and fulfill your campaign, or just the general discourse of the indie community, there are exponentially more people who can help you with Kickstarter now than there were in 2021 when we had to introduce the concept to the whole community.

Special edition Kickstarters: Prior to 2021, there were many different varieties of fiction campaign, while now people seem to be using Kickstarter mainly to produce special edition Kickstarter campaigns (which we'll talk about later) with all the bells and whistles. There has been a standardization of what a campaign looks like for both good and bad.

Competition ramped up: Along with Indiegogo, Crowdfundr and Backerkit have emerged as direct competitors to Kickstarter on a global scale, while platforms like Zoop (Comics), Seed and Spark (Movies) and Gamefound (Games) have built category-specific platforms for crowdfunding.

PLATFORM CHANGES

Late pledges: Since the inception of Kickstarter, backers have had to pledge while a project is live, or not at all. Other platforms, like Indiegogo, allow for late pledges after a campaign is over. Now Kickstarter does, too. At the bottom of the basics section of your campaign, you can enable late pledges and allow backers to pledge even after your successful campaign ends. Unlike a live campaign, funds are deducted from backer accounts immediately, and you are paid weekly for any new funds that might accrue. Another nice feature of late pledges is that you can turn them on at the reward level, so if you want certain rewards to keep going and others to end when a campaign is over, you have that flexibility. You can also set a different price for late pledges so that people who back while it's live get the best deal. Finally, I should mention that yes, your campaign has to successfully fund before late pledges work. You can't keep limping along with a failed campaign forever.

Images in your rewards and add-ons: You now have ability to upload imagery in your rewards. It used to be that we had to create clunky lists in our campaign pages, but now we can create graphics (or you can hire somebody to do it for you) where people can easily see what they get in every pledge. This added the newest complexity to a campaign, but overall we think it's a good change.

A redesigned home page: The discover tab (where you look for new projects) used to be on the left and now it's on the right. Additionally, the top menu has every category now, with dropdowns that make it easier to search for projects. This had the effect of basically eliminating the landing page for each category.

Pivot to video: When a backer searches for a campaign, the video starts playing automatically when you hover over the image. This makes a video even more important AND makes the first couple of seconds critical to get attention.

No more total pledges in the Discover tab: You used to see the total amount a campaign has raised when searching for a project. Now, you have to click on a campaign to see how much it's raised, though it will tell you how funded, or overfunded, the campaign is at a glance, making pricing more interesting. Do you make a lower goal so you can be more overfunded?

The new story editor: There is a new editor on the story page, but if you've used any text editor on the internet, you'll probably get a hold of it very easily. The one nice change here is that they now have a navigation pane on the left side that lists out all your headlines for easier backer navigation.

Fully redesigning fulfillment dashboard: Kickstarter completely redesigned the backer survey tool to help integrate it better into the fulfillment cycle for publishers.

They have simplified set-up, improved reporting, implemented SKU generation and improved address collection. Additionally, they have made it easier to update project status (and also constantly send you pop-ups to update your status even if you are just a collaborator on a project and not the one responsible for fulfillment). Instead of just having surveys, you now have a complete fulfillment system under the hood.

The pre-launch page has been beefed up: Now you can see the Project We Love and categories on the page, and you can write a whole blurb or additional marketing information on the page instead of just the one sentence logline.

CHAPTER 1

IS KICKSTARTER IS RIGHT FOR YOU?

Let's start with a simple question: Why do you want to launch a Kickstarter?

Be *specific* and *honest*. Are you crowdfunding a special edition hardcover with fancy swag? Launching a brand new series and testing the waters? Reviving an old project that your readers keep asking about? There are many good reasons to crowdfund a book. "Everyone's doing it now" is not one of them. Neither is, "I heard it's easy money." (Spoiler: it's not.) Your first task is to pin down what Kickstarter can uniquely do for you and your book. For example, maybe you want to raise funds upfront to hire a top-notch cover artist, or pre-sell copies to gauge demand for an unconventional story or build buzz for your series launch by turning it into an event. Maybe it's "all of the above." Great, list those reasons. Be crystal clear about your goals from the outset. This clarity will keep you focused when we get into the weeds of planning.

On the flip side, if you were secretly hoping Kickstarter would just magically create an audience for you out of thin air, consider this your wake-up call. A successful campaign is built on the audience *you bring with you*. Kickstarter's platform can help you reach new readers, yes, but the core momentum comes from people who already know your work or trust you. If you have zero readers right now, we'll discuss how to start building some (don't worry). But understand that Kickstarter is not an "if you launch, they will come" situation. It works *best* when you already have a base to tap into – even a small, enthusiastic one. Focus on what *you* want out of this campaign and what *value* you're going to offer backers. That mindset shift – from "what can I get?" to "what can I give?" – is critical. Know your why, and make sure it aligns with providing something awesome to your audience.

NO BEGGING, NO CHARITY

Kickstarter is not a platform of last resort for failed projects. It's not where you turn after your book didn't sell and you're desperate. If you treat it like a begging bowl, you'll get nothing but pity or silence. Successful creators treat Kickstarter as a deliberate launch strategy for exciting new projects, not as a Hail Mary for something that's already flopped. So ditch any notion that "maybe my series isn't selling, but perhaps it will magically fund on Kickstarter." It won't. I say this with love: Kickstarter is a strategy, not a charity. Backers are not donating out of kindness. They're pre-ordering a product they really want.

This means you need to approach your campaign like a product launch to your customers, not like you're asking for favors from friends. If you show up with a mentality of "please fund my dream," that's going to repel people.

Instead, you want to exude "I've got something amazing for you, and I'm launching it here first!" See the difference? One is desperation; the other is excitement and value.

Now, let's talk about the audience. Kickstarter works best when you already have some readers or a network to tap into. It doesn't have to be huge. Plenty of authors crush it with a few hundred true fans, but you need someone out there who cares. I like to say that if you have 25 backers, Kickstarter will help you find 25 backers, but if you have 0, it won't help you at all.

If you truly have zero audience right now, that's okay, but you're going to need to put in extra work *before* you launch to build interest. A Kickstarter campaign reflects the platform and trust you've built up to that point. It's like a mirror. If you've nurtured a small but mighty email list, engaged with readers on social media, or built any kind of community, the campaign will reflect that with pledges. If you haven't, well, a Kickstarter won't magically drop money from the sky into your lap.

Here's a personal example. Early on, I had a comic book series that people kept telling me they wanted more of. I decided to test that on Kickstarter. I literally told my fans I'd only continue the series if we hit about $16,000 in funding. Essentially, *I challenged my audience to put their money where their mouth was.* And guess what? They did. We hit the goal with that campaign, which proved there was enough interest to justify making multiple new issues. I then ran campaigns for each of those new volumes, and each one met its target as well, and we ended up raising over $93,000 for that series that only existed because I went to my audience.

The key takeaway: Kickstarter can validate demand and launch something new *if* you approach it as a serious, goal-oriented venture. It was not a last resort for me. It was the launch pad that gave my project new life. That's how you need to view it.

Kickstarter is a tool for proactive creators, not a lifeline for passive ones. Treat it accordingly. If you're feeling uneasy about whether you have "enough" of an audience or platform yet, don't worry – Part I of this book will help you get those foundational pieces in place (or at least set realistic goals based on where you're at). Just be prepared to do the work and treat your campaign like the high-stakes product launch it is, not a hopeful shot in the dark.

LOOK BEYOND THE MONEY

Yes, we all know the primary goal. You want to fund your book, but one of the coolest things about Kickstarter is the bonus perks that come along for the ride. A successful campaign can do more than just hit a dollar figure. It can fundamentally change your career trajectory in surprising ways. Here are a few fringe benefits to chew on:

- **Expanded Readership:** Every Kickstarter campaign has the potential to attract new readers who just stumble upon your project on the platform. People who have never heard of you might click because your concept or art catches their eye. These new backers aren't just one-time customers; many of them can turn into long-term

fans. I've had folks discover me through Kickstarter
and then go on to buy all my backlist books afterward.
Crowdfunding can be a great discovery tool.

- **Media and Industry Attention:** A buzzing campaign
  can act like a flare in the sky. Local news, niche
  bloggers, even bigger media outlets sometimes
  spotlight interesting Kickstarter projects. You might
  also catch the eye of industry folks – publishers,
  editors, etc. who see that you've got momentum. I've
  seen authors get approached for opportunities *because*
  their Kickstarter made some noise. Not saying it's
  guaranteed, but it's happened and it's pretty awesome.

- **Community Building:** This is my favorite. When you
  run a campaign, you're not just making sales. You're
  forging a community. The people who back your
  project feel a sense of **ownership** and pride. They're
  not just readers now; they're collaborators who helped
  bring your book into the world. That changes the
  relationship. Suddenly you've got a posse of true fans
  who are emotionally invested in your success. They'll
  comment on your updates, share their excitement on
  social media, and basically become your hype squad.
  This sense of community can be deeply motivating and
  carry well beyond the campaign itself. Your readers
  transform into *ambassadors* for your work. Trust me,
  that feeling is addictive, in a good way.

- **Confidence and Validation:** Writing can be a lonely,
  doubt-ridden endeavor. A successful Kickstarter can
  give you an incredible boost of confidence. There's
  nothing quite like hundreds of people literally **putting
  down money because they believe in your project**. It

validates that you're on the right track. That energy can fuel you through the hard work of finishing the book and beyond. Even if you're a seasoned author, seeing concrete evidence of reader demand is immensely validating.

Now, these benefits come *after* you do the work of creating a strong campaign. But I mention them because they're worth considering when you're deciding whether to launch. Kickstarter can be a transformational experience for your relationship with your audience, but only if you're ready for that level of engagement.

Some authors aren't prepared for a flood of messages, feedback, and interaction. So ask yourself: *Am I ready for readers to really feel invested in me and my work?* It's a great "problem" to have, but it does require you to step up your interaction game. If the idea of readers looking behind the curtain of your process or eagerly awaiting every update stresses you out, take note. You can manage the workload, but you need to welcome that sense of community rather than shy away from it. If you're ready to embrace your readers as partners in this journey, Kickstarter can fundamentally change how those readers see you and how you see your own role as an author. It's no longer just your book. It becomes *our* book in a way. That's powerful stuff, and it's part of what makes crowdfunding so special.

BE READY TO WORK (AND SAVOR THE RIDE)

Running a Kickstarter campaign can be intense. There are plenty of ways to cut down the intensity, but you've probably never launched something like you launch a Kickstarter. I say this not to scare you, but to prepare you. You need to be honest with yourself about your bandwidth and willingness to show up every single day during the campaign period. Are you ready to hustle?

You'll be sending emails, pushing social media announcements, maybe doing livestreams or interviews, thanking new backers, troubleshooting issues, sometimes all in the same day. It's *work*. Fun work, in many ways, but work, nonetheless. And once the campaign ends, if it's successful, you've got fulfillment to handle getting all those books and rewards produced and shipped. We'll get to strategies for managing that workload, but for now, do a gut-check: *Do I have the time and energy to commit to this fully?* If the honest answer is "not right now," then take a beat. It might be wiser to delay your launch until you can clear some room in your schedule or enlist help. The worst thing you can do is launch and then neglect your campaign because life got in the way. Momentum will stall, backers will get concerned, and your results will suffer.

Maybe you have a day job, family obligations, or other projects. That doesn't disqualify you, many creators juggle Kickstarter with a full plate, but it means you'll need to be super organized and disciplined. You might need to recruit an assistant or a willing friend/family member to help with tasks like packing books or moderating comments when you're at work. There's no shame in getting help. The key is to recognize the commitment upfront and plan for it. This isn't a set-it-and-forget-it situation. It's more like running a small business for a few months. You're in charge of marketing, customer service (answering backers), production, and fulfillment.

Now, before I scare you off, it's also incredibly rewarding. Seriously, running a campaign can be one of the most exciting times of your creative life. It's a wild ride watching the pledges come in, interacting with backers in real time, and seeing your vision inch closer to reality every day. It's a thrill, but with that buzz comes the need to stay on top of things. If you go radio silent for days during a campaign, people notice. If a backer asks, "Hey, will this add-on be available?" and nobody answers, you might lose that pledge. So, commit to being present.

If you're reading this thinking, "Well, I can't possibly do that, I'm too busy," then you have two choices: adjust your timeline (launch when you *can* dedicate the effort) or adjust your approach (maybe scale down your campaign goals so it's easier to manage or get help as mentioned). Remember, these are your fans. They deserve your best effort. The good news is, later in this book I'll share plenty of tactics to streamline your workflow and keep your sanity intact. Just know that showing up consistently is non-negotiable for the duration of the campaign.

If you can't commit the time and energy, don't hit launch. Wait until you can. But if you *are* ready to dive in, I promise the rewards (financial and emotional) are worth the grind.

THE MINDSET TO CRUSH IT

Finally, let's talk about the mindset that separates Kickstarter winners from the could've-beens. In a phrase, it's, **"No excuses – only solutions."** Once you embark on this journey, you need to take **full ownership** of the outcome. That means no blaming the algorithm (Kickstarter does have one for project visibility, but don't lean on that), no cursing your luck if pledges slow down, no whining that "people just don't get my art." That mental baggage has no place in a Kickstarter campaign. Instead, adopt a **problem-solver mindset** from Day One.

What does that look like in practice? If your campaign's pitch video isn't converting viewers into backers, you don't throw up your hands. You tweak your video or your page copy and see if it improves. If your $50 tier isn't getting any takers, you don't pout, you investigate why. Maybe the perceived value isn't there, so you spice it up with an extra reward or emphasize it more on your page. If mid-campaign you notice engagement dropping, you don't just hope for the best. You roll out a new update, stretch goal, or marketing push to reignite interest. Every challenge has a response that you, as the creator, can choose to execute.

This mindset also means being adaptive. No matter how well you plan (and we're going to plan the heck out of things in this book), real life can throw curveballs. Maybe your printer raises prices mid-campaign, or a global pandemic hits (been there!), or a key collaborator flakes out. You must be ready to adapt, adjust, and keep moving forward. Think of it like being the captain of a ship at sea –

when a storm hits, you don't get to moan about the weather; you trim the sails and adjust course. The only way you "lose" is if you quit and sink. As long as you keep problem-solving, you're still in the game.

An important part of this mindset is taking **responsibility** for everything that happens. The phrase "the buck stops here" should be your motto. If something isn't working, you look for what *you* can do to fix it, rather than blaming external factors. This doesn't mean external factors aren't real because they absolutely are. It just means you focus your energy on what you can control. You can't control if a backer's credit card fails to charge, but you *can* send a polite reminder via Kickstarter for them to update their info. You can't control if Facebook ads suddenly double in price, but you *can* pivot to a different promo strategy if that happens. Always ask, **"What can I do to improve this situation?"** rather than "Whose fault is this problem?"

Adopting this no-excuses mindset early will save you a lot of heartache because challenges **will** arise. All campaigns hit turbulence at some point, a slower day, a technical glitch, whatever. If you've already decided that you are going to own those challenges and find solutions, you'll ride out the turbulence and land the plane. If not, it's easy to get discouraged and let the campaign falter. We're not doing that. We're here to crush it, and crushing it starts in your head, long before the first pledge comes in. It starts *now*, with the decision that you will do whatever it takes (ethically, of course) to make your campaign a success.

Does that mean you have to be perfect? Nope. Mistakes will happen, but with the right mindset, a mistake isn't fatal, it's just data. We'll iterate and adjust. By deciding *now* that you'll own the process and outcome, you're setting yourself up to adapt and overcome when those inevitable challenges hit.

Alright, pep talk over. You've heard the no-nonsense truth about what Kickstarter demands. If you're still on board (and I hope you are), then you're already showing the resilience and drive needed to succeed. Next, we'll get into specifics: defining exactly what you want to achieve and how we'll measure success.

CHAPTER 2

DEFINE YOUR CAMPAIGN'S VISION AND SUCCESS METRICS

One of the biggest mistake I see with Kickstarter campaigns is that they fail to clearly articulate the what and why of your campaign. Often, it's because they don't haven't looked deep into themselves for a reason beyond "Cuz everyone told me I should do it and I like money."

There is always, and I do mean *always*, a deeper reason, but you haven't just uncovered it yet.

So before we even get to the prelaunch phase, let's define the bounds by which we'll judge the success of this campaign, and what this book means to you.

CRAFT YOUR ONE-SENTENCE VISION

First, we need to distill your entire campaign's purpose into one powerful sentence. This is for *you*, not an advertising blurb for readers. It's a clarity exercise. Ask yourself, *"What exactly am I crowdfunding?"* and answer in a single sentence that would make sense to a stranger. For example,

"I'm crowdfunding a deluxe illustrated hardcover edition of my fantasy novel."

Bam! That's format, genre, and unique angle all in one go.

Maybe for you it's "a new trilogy of cyberpunk thrillers in ebook and paperback" or "an audiobook adaptation of my award-winning short stories" or "a collector's box set of my comic series with exclusive art prints." The key is to be specific and concrete. Include the format (ebook, hardcover, audio, etc.), the genre or vibe if relevant, and any special twist that makes this project exciting.

Why a single sentence? Because it forces you to clarify your focus. Throughout the planning process, you're going to get a million ideas; "Oh, I could add trading cards! And what if I include a bonus novella? Maybe I should also fund an audiobook…" Your one-sentence vision becomes your North Star to judge those ideas. Whenever you're tempted to drift off course with extra goodies or side missions, you look at that sentence and ask, *"Does this new idea fit my core vision?"* If it doesn't, save it for another campaign or a stretch goal (more on those later). This keeps you from experiencing mission creep, that dreaded scenario where your campaign bloats into something unwieldy and unfocused.

Take the time to get this sentence right. Write a draft, say it out loud, see if it feels true to what you want. If it's vague or packed with commas and clauses, tighten it up. Clarity is king. "A graphic novel" is too vague; "a 200-page graphic novel about intergalactic chefs, in both paperback and digital formats" is clearer and more enticing. Don't worry about making it a sexy marketing tagline. We're aiming for clarity for now. Marketing copy can come later. For now, you need to *know* in the simplest terms what you are offering. Everything else in your campaign will build on this foundation.

So, write your one-sentence project vision down on a piece of paper, and don't move on until you have something that makes you go "Yes, that's exactly what I'm doing." When you have that, congratulations, you have just created the guiding light for your entire campaign.

DEFINE YOUR "WHY"

Next, let's dig into your motivations beyond the dollar amount. Sure, raising $X is the main objective, but why do you want to run this campaign aside from money? Identifying 1–3 key objectives that aren't just "get funded" will give your campaign a deeper purpose and story. Think of these as your north stars, the things that will keep you motivated and that you might even share with backers as part of your campaign narrative.

Maybe you want to expand your reader base and reach new folks who haven't heard of you. Maybe you want to gauge interest in a new genre or series before fully diving in – a successful campaign would prove there's an audience. Maybe you're doing this to create a beautiful collector's edition that wouldn't be feasible without upfront funding. Or perhaps you're using Kickstarter as a way to get more direct with your readers and step away from the grind of third-party platforms – basically a statement of independence. It could even be personal, like "I want to challenge myself to step outside my comfort zone" or "I want to resurrect a project I love that got rejected by publishers and let the readers decide its fate."

Write down your top motivations. These reasons matter for a couple of big reasons. One, when you're knee-deep in campaign prep or stressing in the middle of a launch, remembering your 'why' will keep you going. It's easy to get lost in the minutiae of budgets, marketing copy, and reward spreadsheets. Having that deeper purpose will center you. Two, these motivations can actually become part of your campaign story that you share with backers. Readers love to know the *why* behind a project. If they see that you're not just there to grab cash, but you have a passion like "I want to produce a gorgeous hardcover because I believe this story deserves to be on fans' shelves in a display-worthy edition," that *inspires* people. Your enthusiasm and purpose become contagious.

SET YOUR SUCCESS CRITERIA

Time to get concrete. What does success look like for your campaign, *in measurable terms*? This is where we define your success metrics. Think beyond fuzzy feelings and outline specific numbers or outcomes that will mean "I achieved what I set out to do." This might include: a funding amount (e.g., "at least $5,000"), a backer count (e.g., "100+ backers"), perhaps certain pre-order quantities ("50 hardcover editions pre-sold"), or even things like profit margin ("I want to net $2,000 after expenses") or community growth ("200 new email subscribers from the campaign").

It's okay to have multiple success criteria. In fact, I recommend defining a few so you have a well-rounded picture. For instance, you might say: *Success = raise $8,000 + get 150 backers + at least 20 people choose the deluxe tier.* Or *Success = fully fund my print run (minimum $3,000) and reach at least 50 new readers who've never heard of me before.* Maybe *Success = cover all costs and break even and get this book into at least 100 hands.* It's your success, so define it *your* way. There's no one-size-fits-all.

Be realistic but aspirational. Set metrics that are challenging enough to be meaningful, but not so insane that you're setting yourself up for disappointment. If you're a first-time author with no email list, a goal of $50,000 might be unrealistic, but maybe $5,000 is quite doable.

If you have a decent-sized following, maybe $10k or $20k is within reach. We'll refine the funding goal after we do the budget in Chapter 3, so you don't need to finalize the dollar figure yet. But you can set a ballpark or a minimum you'd be happy with.

Also think about backers. Sometimes people get fixated on dollars and forget that the number of backers is a huge indicator of success (and future potential). Would you be happier with 50 backers who each paid high amounts, or 500 backers at smaller amounts? Different strategies yield different profiles. Backer count translates to readers holding your book, which has its own value in terms of reach and word-of-mouth.

As you go through this process, make sure to avoid the "moving goalpost" syndrome. It's easy during a campaign to keep upping your internal expectations ("Well, I hit 5k, maybe I can get 10k... okay 10k, maybe 15k...") and then bizarrely feel *disappointed* if you "only" hit 14k after you mentally hoped for 15k. Human brains are silly like that. By defining success criteria *now, before launch*, you can later ground yourself and say, "Hey, I decided that $5k and 100 backers would make me happy, and I achieved that. So this is a win."

Otherwise, you risk achieving something great and then not even appreciating it because you kept chasing an ever-receding target. Don't rob yourself of the joy. Set the goalposts now and then allow yourself to celebrate when you hit them.

Write these success metrics down ("I will consider this campaign successful if..." fill in the blanks). This will also be crucial after the campaign, when you debrief and evaluate what went well and what didn't. You'll have a clear yardstick to measure against, rather than a vague feeling.

Finally, share these metrics (at least internally or with your team). If you have an assistant, co-writer, or even just a supportive friend, let them know your targets. Speaking them out loud or writing them in big text on your wall gives them power. It shifts your mindset from "I hope I do okay" to "I'm aiming for *this*." If someone asks, "So what's your goal with this Kickstarter?" you can answer with confidence: "My goal is to raise at least $7,500 and get 200 backers on board." That kind of clarity is attractive to collaborators, to your own subconscious, and yes, even to backers who sense that you have a plan.

REALITY-CHECK YOUR GOALS AGAINST REALITY

Alright, you've got a vision, some lofty goals, and success metrics. Now let's apply a dose of pragmatic reality to ensure your aims are ambitious but attainable. I'm all for dreaming big, but not for living in la-la land. So, it's time to ask: *Do my targets make sense given my current platform and resources?* If there's a huge mismatch, better to adjust now than to faceplant later.

Take the funding goal you have in mind and the backer count you'd love to see. How do those numbers compare to your existing audience size? For instance, say you're aiming to raise $40,000 and you figure an average pledge might be around $40 (just a rough industry average for book campaigns with physical items). That would require about 1,000 backers. Do you have anywhere near 1,000 people actively following your work right now? If you have an email list of 200 and a small social media following, that goal might be a stretch. It's not impossible – sometimes campaigns go viral or get boosted by Kickstarter's discoverability – but it's risky to bank on that. Conversely, if you have 10,000 Instagram followers who love your art, a $40k goal might be reasonable. It's all relative.

The point is to align expectations with reality. This doesn't mean you can't outperform your expectations, and many do, but you should plan based on a realistic baseline. If success to you is, say, "deliver my book to 50 enthusiastic readers and cover all my costs," and you achieve that, that's 100% valid and awesome! Don't compare yourself to some other author's blockbuster campaign. This is about you and your situation. It's far better to set a modest goal and exceed it, and enjoy the ride, than to set a sky-high goal, miss it, and feel like crap (not to mention get $0 if you don't hit the minimum, since Kickstarter is all-or-nothing funding).

If your desired goal is looking iffy given your current audience, you can either adjust the scope of your campaign or double down on building your audience pre-launch.

Adjusting scope might mean lowering the funding goal by reducing what you're offering (fewer costly rewards, a shorter print run, etc.), or it might mean splitting your dream into two smaller campaigns (for example, crowdfund Book 1 now, and Book 2 later, instead of trying to fund a whole trilogy at once). We'll get into budgeting in the next chapter, which will provide more clarity on what your goal *needs* to be. But keep in mind, you don't have to shoot for the moon on your first outing. Hitting a smaller goal and overfunding (getting more than 100%) can actually be a fantastic strategy to build momentum and credibility.

On the other hand, if you really want that big goal and you know you're not there yet audience-wise, note that too. That means before you launch, you'll want to focus heavily on audience growth activities. That might involve building your email list, ramping up social engagement, maybe doing a pre-launch publicity push to gather followers on your Kickstarter pre-launch page. Essentially, you can *earn* a bigger goal by putting in more work upfront to enlarge your pool of potential backers. Just be aware of the time and effort that entails.

Use this reality-check phase as a sanity filter. No shame in revising your targets to be more in line with what's feasible. Ambitious but attainable, that's the sweet spot. You want a goal that excites you and pushes you a bit, but not one that's going to require a literal miracle. Save the miracle goals for when you have a breakout hit and a few campaigns under your belt.

COMMUNICATE YOUR VISION (PRACTICE YOUR PITCH)

Now that you're crystal clear on what you're doing and why, try explaining your project out loud in a few sentences. Think of this like your elevator pitch, except it's primarily for your own benefit, though you'll certainly use it externally too. Can you confidently and succinctly tell someone what you're crowdfunding and why it matters to you (and why it might matter to readers)? If you stumble or start rambling into caveats and side notes, that's a sign you need to tighten up your understanding of your own campaign vision.

For example, you might say, "I'm launching a Kickstarter to fund a deluxe hardcover edition of my sci-fi novel. I want to give my readers a special collectible version with gorgeous artwork. My goal is to raise $8,000 to cover printing and pay the artist, and if we hit it, it'll also prove there's demand for more books in this universe." Boom – that's a clear, compelling summary. It includes the *what* (deluxe hardcover sci-fi novel), the *why* (special collectible for readers, plus testing demand for series), and the *goal* ($8k to cover costs and art). If you can convey something along those lines in a few sentences, you're in good shape. If not, refine your notes and try again.

Being able to articulate your vision on the fly will be invaluable. You'll use it when emailing potential collaborators, when posting on social media, when talking to fans, even when crafting your campaign page later. Consistency is key. If you have this core pitch, you can adapt it to different contexts, but it'll always carry the same core message. That cohesion makes your campaign messaging stronger and less confusing.

Also, practice explaining why it matters. Why should anyone care about this project? You might incorporate your deeper why: "I'm doing this to bring this story to life in a way that fans will cherish, and to build a community around the series." That kind of passion is infectious. If you sound unsure or timid about your own project, how can backers get excited? Own it. Speak about your campaign with conviction. It might feel weird to "sell" your idea at first, especially if you're used to just quietly writing and hoping for the best. But consider this training for being the best advocate your book can have, because if you won't champion it, who will?

You should also work on tailoring your pitch depending on the audience. If you're talking to a fellow author friend about your Kickstarter, you might emphasize how you're testing a new funding model or trying to break free of traditional molds. If you're talking to a long-time reader of yours, you'd focus on how this is their chance to get a limited edition and be part of your creative journey. The core vision stays the same, but you highlight different angles for different folks. That's advanced pitching, and you'll naturally get better at it as you talk about your project more.

For now, get a baseline version down pat. You can even write it down in the workbook or on a sticky note: *This is what I'm making, and this is why it's awesome.* When you have that, you not only gain confidence, you also set yourself up to create a campaign page that is clear and compelling. Clarity on your end leads to clarity for everyone else.

Beginning with the end in mind means you're not just launching a campaign and seeing what happens. Instead, you're launching with purpose and a clear vision of success. This mental prep work might feel abstract now, but it will pay off a hundred times over as we move into concrete planning. You're essentially creating the compass that will guide all your next steps.

CHAPTER 3

PRE-LAUNCH PLANNING

Kickstarter campaigns can be chaos, expensive, and draining, but they don't have to be, especially if you build a rock-solid plan *before* you launch. If the last chapter was about define the north star vision to guide your campaign, then this one is about building the plan that will carry you through to success.

We're going to calculate your funding goal based on real costs (no guesswork!), map out a timeline from now through fulfillment, and outline how to build buzz and an audience ahead of launch. By the end, you'll know exactly how much money you need, when every major task needs to happen, and how to ensure people actually show up on launch day. This is the unsexy prep work that 90% of Kickstarter success is built on. Let's get into it.

LOCK IN YOUR RETAIL PRE-ORDER BEFORE YOU HIT "LAUNCH"

One of the easiest ways to keep post-Kickstarter chaos at bay is to schedule your wide-platform pre-order **before** the

Kickstarter ever goes live. This is because your Kickstarter will bring excitement to people, but they all won't want to buy on Kickstarter. So, giving them the ability to buy on their platform gives you a lot more buzz, and the ability to gather that interest wherever it is.

I used to say not to do this, but I've come around after seeing that Kickstarter sales didn't seem to be very affected by retailer sales, while retailer sales could be positively affected by having a campaign live.

So, I recommend setting the retail pre-order date at least 90 days *after* you expect Kickstarter fulfillment to be finished. Make sure to use the retailer cover instead of the Kickstarter exclusive one (if applicable).

Why 90 Days?

1. **Buffer for the Unpredictable.** Even the best-run campaigns can hit a snag—printer delays, freight slow-downs, or an unexpected round of proof corrections. A three-month cushion protects you from angry retail readers who pre-ordered on Amazon and wonder why the release date had to slide.
2. **Backer Exclusivity.** Your Kickstarter supporters paid first and waited longest; they deserve to unbox their copies well before the book pops up in the wild. Ninety days is enough time for them to feel special, post photos, and stoke buzz that will roll straight into retail launch.
3. **Marketing Flywheel.** As soon as backers start sharing photos, embed those images in your retailer A+ content, social ads, and newsletter funnels. By the time the

Amazon/Apple/B&N date arrives, you'll have a wave of organic social proof ready to convert fence-sitters.

Scheduling the retail pre-order this way turns your Kickstarter timeline into a neat relay race: backers get the baton first, retail readers grab it next, and you never have to sprint to push a date because the printer hiccupped.

BUDGETING 101: KNOW YOUR NUMBERS OR GO HOME

Nothing will sink a campaign faster than fudging the numbers. We need to know, down to the dollar, what it's going to cost to deliver your project, and therefore what your funding goal should be. Far too many creators set an arbitrary goal ("$10k sounds nice!") only to realize later that, even if they hit it, they'll lose money because they underestimated expenses. Not on our watch. We're going to build your budget from the ground up, so your funding target is grounded in reality and ensures you won't be eating ramen for a month because you forgot about shipping costs.

Start by listing all your costs. I mean all of them. Grab a spreadsheet and break down every expense your campaign will incur:

- **Production Costs:** This includes anything required to produce the core product and rewards. For a book, that's editing, cover design, interior layout, printing and binding the books (get quotes for how much each copy costs and multiply by the number you plan to produce), plus any extra goodies like artwork, stickers, bookmarks, etc. If you're doing an audiobook, include narrator fees or studio costs. If you promised an exclusive bonus story, include editing for that too. Don't forget *manufacturing* costs for merch. If you're making enamel pins, t-shirts, or other swag, get estimates for those items. Essentially, if it's something you have to pay for to create what you promised to backers, list it here with a dollar figure.

- **Shipping & Fulfillment Costs:** This one is huge and often underestimated. For shipping, consider the cost of postage per package for each type of reward (domestic and international). If you're shipping 100 books domestically at $5 each and 20 internationally at $25 each (just an example), that's $500 + $500 = $1,000 in postage. Packaging materials are also a cost – boxes, mailers, tape, bubble wrap, labels. They may be cheap each, but it adds up. If each mailer costs $1 and you send 150 packages, that's $150. If you're using a fulfillment service or warehouse to ship for you, include their fees. And don't forget digital delivery costs if any (maybe negligible, but if you need a bigger Dropbox or a shipping software subscription, etc., factor it). *Tip:* A good practice is to make a mini table of all reward levels and how much shipping each one will require, then sum it up according to your backer count projections. We'll also talk more about how to charge for shipping. Kickstarter lets you charge it separately, but for budgeting, account for it now so you're not caught off guard.

- **Marketing Costs:** Are you planning to run Facebook ads for your campaign? Paying for a promotional newsletter spot, like a Kickstarter-centric promo service? Printing flyers or posters to promote locally? Any paid marketing activities should be tallied. Even if you're just boosting a few Facebook posts for $10 a pop or running a small giveaway, list an estimate. It might be $0 if you intend to only use free methods (social media, email, word-of-mouth), which is fine, many do, but I want you to consciously decide that and note it. If you have a budget for ads, put that in. It's easy to think "I'll throw some ads in if needed" and then suddenly you've spent $300 on ads you didn't budget for. Plan it now.

- **Kickstarter and Payment Processing Fees:** Kickstarter will take 5% of whatever funds you raise right off the top. Payment processors (Stripe for Kickstarter) will take around 3–5% more (it's usually ~3% + $0.20 per pledge). Altogether, it's safest to assume roughly 8–10% of your total funds will go to fees. This means if you raise $10,000, you actually net about $9,000 after fees (give or take). It's not optional or avoidable, so include this in your budget. E.g., if your raw costs add up to $5,000, you'd actually need around $5,500 to cover everything + fees. Earmark 10% for the Kickstarter gods and you'll be safe.

- **Taxes:** I'm not a CPA but know that Kickstarter funds are usually considered income. Depending on your country and situation, you might owe taxes on the profit or revenue. While we won't delve deep into tax planning here, keep in mind that if you want to be extra safe, you could set aside a portion for taxes if you expect to have significant profit. Many creators ignore this in planning because if you're spending most funds on delivering the project, the actual taxable profit might be low. Just a note for completeness – consult a professional if needed. One thing I will say is that if you live in the US, inventory you don't sell the same year you buy can't be deducted from taxes. It's called carry-over inventory, and it sucks.

- **Contingency Fund:** Things go wrong. Packages get lost and need resending, costs fluctuate, you might need to order a few extra books, or any of a hundred little surprises. I strongly recommend adding a 5–10% contingency on top of your total estimated costs. It's like a buffer for the unknown. If you don't need it, great, that becomes extra profit or wiggle room. If you do need it, you'll be so grateful it's there. This prevents the "Oh crap, I'm $300 short because shipping rates went up" scenario.
- **A Little Treat:** Budget a little money to get yourself something to celebrate. It might be dinner or a new hat, just something to say, "I did a hard thing."

Now, sum up all those costs. This gives you your Total Estimated Cost to fulfill the project. Look at that number. That's the minimum amount you need to raise in order not to lose money. It might be higher or lower than you expected; that's okay. This is why we do the math. A lot of creators, if left to guessing, would set a goal too low and then get burned by expenses. You're not going to be one of them. You're going to know that if you set a goal of $X, it covers everything.

Once you have the total cost, consider if you want to pad the goal a bit above that or not. Many creators set the Kickstarter goal at just about the break-even point or slightly above, with the *intention* (or hope) of exceeding it. Why? Because Kickstarter is all-or-nothing. If you set the goal too high and fall short by even a dollar, you get $0. That's a brutal outcome. Sometimes a lower, reachable goal is smarter, because you can always raise more (so-called "overfunding") once you hit the goal. There's a psychological effect where backers are more likely to jump in on a funded or close-to-funded project too, so a reasonable goal can help you gain momentum.

For example, if my total costs are $5,000, I might set the goal at $5,500 or $6,000 to have a tiny buffer and then aim to surpass it. But I likely *wouldn't* set it at $10,000 unless I had a solid reason and the audience to match. Remember, you can still get to $10,000 by starting with a $6k goal and then exceeding it. Kickstarter doesn't shut you off at your goal; it lets you keep raising until the campaign ends. So often the strategy is: set a conservative goal, hit it, then ride the wave of overfunding as high as you can. We'll talk about stretch goals (extra targets beyond the initial) later in the book. But for now, decide on a funding goal that covers your needs and feels achievable given your earlier reality-check on audience size.

One more reality check: Compare your funding goal to those success criteria you set. If you told yourself "100 backers would be success," and your goal is $5,000, that means you need an average pledge of $50 per backer to hit it (because $5,000/100 = $50). Is that plausible with the pricing you have in mind? If your main product is a $15 ebook, averaging $50 per backer might be optimistic. But if you have juicy $100 tiers and lots of add-ons, $50 average could be reasonable. Use these comparisons to sense-check your plan: funding goal, backer count, and pricing all have to mesh together realistically. Don't worry, we'll dive into pricing in Part II. Just keep it in mind: audience size × average pledge = total funding. All those variables influence each other.

Try not to set a goal lower than your true need out of wishful thinking. If the bare minimum to print and ship your book is $3,000, setting a $1,000 goal "to be safe" is a recipe for pain. You might fund, but you'll be in the red fulfilling promises. Conversely, don't bloat your goal out of ego. Nobody cares if you *asked* for $20k. They care what value they're getting. A smaller, successful campaign beats an ambitious failure every time. And if you do blow past your goal and rake in more, that's icing (and perhaps extra profit or extra goodies for your backers).

That said, failure isn't bad. If you don't hit your goal then you don't have to deliver on a project that nobody wants, and that's okay, too. It's not great, especially if you love your project, but you can always redesign and relaunch.

MAP YOUR TIMELINE

With your budget in hand, it's time to timeline everything. A Kickstarter isn't just about hitting the launch button; it's a full lifecycle: pre-launch preparation, the live campaign, and post-campaign fulfillment. Planning each phase will save you from last-minute scrambles and ugly surprises. Let's break it down.

THE THREE PHASES

Think of your campaign in three chunks – **Pre-Launch, Campaign,** and **Post-Campaign**. Each has its own tasks and milestones. Visualize it as a roadmap:

- **Pre-Launch**: this covers all the weeks (or months) leading up to your launch day.
- **Campaign**: the period (often 30 days or so) when your Kickstarter is live and collecting pledges.
- **Post-Campaign**: after the campaign ends, where you produce and deliver rewards, and continue engaging backers.

We're going to fill in what happens in each phase and when. Trust me, seeing it laid out on a calendar will both relieve anxiety ("oh good; I do have time to get this done") and instill urgency ("ah, I really *don't* have time to procrastinate that task"). Both are helpful realities to grasp.

PRE-LAUNCH PREP

Choose a tentative launch date for your campaign (you can adjust later but pick something to aim for). Now, working backwards, list all the tasks you need to complete *before* that date, and assign them timeframes or deadlines. Some key pre-launch tasks include:

- **Finish Your Book (or have it near-final):** This is huge. If you're crowdfunding a book, ideally the manuscript is complete or in final editing by launch.

Why? Because backers expect you to deliver relatively soon after the campaign. If you haven't finished writing, you risk major delays. At the very least, have a solid draft. (If you're funding something like cover art or illustrations, those can sometimes be done after, but the core content should be in hand or nearly so.) So, one task might be "Complete final manuscript – by [date]," perhaps a few weeks or months before launch. On top of that, it's really hard to launch a second campaign until you've fulfilled the first, and we should always be planning for the future. You want a career, not just a successful project, right?

- **Complete Your Budget & Set Your Goal:** Hey, you're doing that now! This is a pre-launch task and you're on it. By the end of this chapter, you'll have that goal set.
- **Create Your Campaign Page Content:** This includes writing the project description (the story section of your Kickstarter page), designing graphics, perhaps shooting and editing a promo video. These tasks take time. For instance, if you need to film a video, you might set a task "Script and film video – 4 weeks before launch; Edit video – 3 weeks before launch." For page graphics, maybe "Design header image and reward graphics – 2 weeks before launch." If you're not a designer, you might hire someone, which means budgeting time to find and brief them.
- **Plan Your Marketing (Build Buzz):** In pre-launch, you should be warming up your audience. Key tasks might include: ramping up your email newsletter frequency, posting teasers on social media, doing a

cover reveal or sneak peeks of artwork, reaching out to any partners or influencers who can help promote, preparing a press release if applicable, etc. One specific and powerful pre-launch step is creating a **Kickstarter pre-launch landing page** (Kickstarter lets you do this once your project draft is made – it's basically a "Coming soon, notify me on launch" page). You'll want to drive people to click "Notify me on launch" on that page in the weeks leading up. So a task might be "Set up Kickstarter pre-launch page – 6 weeks before launch and promote it regularly." Also consider scheduling some **preview** or beta reader feedback: some creators share their campaign page with a few trusted folks or a small group for feedback a week or two before going live, just to catch any confusing bits or improve the pitch. You could pencil that in too (soft launch to friends – 1 week before launch, for example).

- **Finalize Rewards and Pricing:** Before launch, you'll need to settle on all your reward tiers, pricing, and shipping approach. That's Part II of this book, so we'll get there. Just note it as a pre-launch milestone: "All reward tiers decided and page listings written – [date]." Often this is about 1–2 weeks before launch so you have time to input everything on Kickstarter and double-check.

Pretty much anything that isn't actually collecting pledges or fulfilling rewards belongs in pre-launch. It's a lot, I know. To avoid feeling overwhelmed, spread these tasks out over the weeks you have. If you're four months out, great, you can assign maybe one major task per week. If you're four weeks out, well, that's going to be more intense (and you might consider pushing launch back if too crunched). A common pitfall is underestimating how long things take, especially if you're waiting on others. For example, printing advance copies or proofs of your book. Do you need one to make photos or a video? Order it early. If shipping from the printer takes 2 weeks, plan for that. By mapping out timelines now, you catch those needs. Another example: if you're ordering custom merchandise for the campaign (like sample swag to show off), that could take 4-6 weeks to manufacture. You'd want to have designs ready, and orders placed well ahead of launch if you intend to have them in hand for marketing. These are the details a timeline helps reveal.

My personal practice is to create a calendar (could be Google Cal, a spreadsheet, or sticky notes on a wall) from now until a couple months after the campaign's end. Mark launch day and an end date (if you know the campaign length – e.g. 30 days). Then fill in backwards and forwards: when to execute each step. If you see any task uncomfortably close to launch, try to move it earlier. Nothing important should be left to the last 48 hours pre-launch, because inevitably something unexpected will demand your attention then (it always does). By two days before launch, you want to be mostly set, just doing final sanity checks and getting a good night's sleep, not writing your campaign story frantically.

So, set those deadlines: finalize tiers by X date, finish video by Y date, etc. This level of planning might feel pedantic, but it's the cure for pre-launch panic. With a roadmap, you wake up each week knowing what chunk to tackle, rather than freaking out about everything at once.

CAMPAIGN DURATION – CHOOSING LAUNCH AND END DATES

How long should your Kickstarter run? Typical campaigns run **30 days** (give or take). It's long enough to gather momentum and not so long that backers lose interest. That said, my favorite launch window is **17 days.** It's just enough time for me to build and lose excitement, with very little downtime until it's over. On the other side, I also like really long campaigns, but only if you can stomach having a campaign live that isn't doing much. I like to have things live for a while because then people can find it at their leisure and the pressure is off of me. That said, I'll only run a really long campaign if I have the marketing to back it up. Remember, I have a 50,000 person audience, so there's a lot of things I can do that just don't make sense to most people. If you don't have a big audience, aim for the shorter side. I really like 17-21 days.

For now, decide roughly, and mark your **Launch Day and End Day** on the calendar. E.g., Launch on March 1, end on March 31 (pro-tip: ending at the same time of day you launched, e.g., 9am launch -> 9am end, because Kickstarter counts exact days).

Consider external factors: Avoid launch or end dates that conflict with major holidays, personal events, or known dead zones. Don't end on Christmas Day or during a big convention you're attending where you can't be online much. Also, think about what day of week and time to launch. Many creators launch on a **Tuesday or Wednesday morning** to maximize visibility (start of a workday when people are at computers, not lost in weekend stuff). The final 48 hours of your campaign are critical. That's when Kickstarter sends a reminder to all who clicked "notify" and there's a natural urgency spike. So, ending on a weekday around midday can be smart too, when people are active. For example, launching Tue 9am and ending Thu 9am four weeks later is a solid window. Jot these down.

Within the campaign, mark a few special milestones:

- **Day 1 (Launch Day)** – you'll want a big push here.
- **Mid-campaign checkpoint** – often the middle of a campaign slows down, so around the halfway point (Day 14 for a 30-day) you might plan a special event or promotion.
- And the **Final 48 hours**.

You'll likely do a last big marketing push here and maybe update frequently as the clock counts down. By planning these now, you can think ahead: maybe schedule a live Q&A or a fun stretch goal reveal at the midpoint to inject energy, and a "closing party" livestream in the final 2 days, etc.

Write these ideas on your timeline: e.g., "Day 1: Email list at launch + social media blitz + personal messages to close contacts." "Day 15: mid-campaign live reading event on YouTube." "Final 3 days: daily countdown posts, personal thank-yous, etc." We'll refine marketing tactics in later chapters, but having placeholders is good.

Also, be mindful of your own schedule during the campaign. If you know you have a week where you'll be less available (say a day job crunch or a family thing), perhaps avoid launching or ending in that window. Or adjust campaign length around it. You need to be present and energetic, so plan around any known energy sinks.

POST-CAMPAIGN FULFILLMENT – PLAN THE AFTERMATH

 After the campaign ends, the real work begins: **delivering everything you promised**. A shocking number of creators plan the campaign but not the fulfillment, leading to delays and chaos. Not you, though, you're going to plot it out now. Look at the timeline beyond your end date and map the key steps from campaign finish to rewards in backers' hands.

Key post-campaign steps typically include:

- **Backer Surveys:** Once the campaign ends, you'll send out surveys (via Kickstarter or a pledge manager) to collect things like shipping addresses, each backer's variant choices if any, t-shirt sizes, name spelling for acknowledgments, etc. Mark "Send backer survey" about 1–2 weeks after campaign ends (Kickstarter lets you prepare it and send it when ready). I usually send surveys about a week after, to give time for Kickstarter to charge cards and for me to prep the survey. So, e.g., "Campaign ends Aug 1, send surveys by Aug 8."

- **Finalize Counts & Place Orders:** Once you have survey data (like how many of each item you need and confirmed addresses), you'll order the production of everything. That means sending your book to the printer with the quantity, ordering the merch (pins, posters, whatever) in the amounts needed, etc. Figure out how long each production takes. For example, your printer might need 4 weeks to print and ship books to you. Custom merch might need 6 weeks. If you're hand-making something, account for your time. Plot "Order books by Aug 15, expect delivery by Sep 15" etc. Also line up your vendors early, maybe even during the campaign get quotes and tentative schedules.
- **Production Time:** Mark how long each thing takes. If editing is still happening, note that timeline. If you promised a December delivery but printing itself takes until January, you've got a problem. So, adjust now if needed. It's *much* better to promise a later delivery and deliver early than vice versa. Remember: under-promise, over-deliver. So if you think you can ship by October, maybe promise November to be safe, etc.
- **Receiving & Quality Check:** When the books and items arrive from printers/vendors, you might need a few days to inspect them, sign books, etc. If something's wrong, you'd have to reprint; hope not but build a little cushion. Mark when you expect to receive inventory.
- **Packing & Shipping Rewards:** This can be a beast or a breeze, depending on volume and help. If you have 50 backers, you can probably pack in a day solo. If you have 500, you might need a week or two and some

helpers. Plan accordingly: e.g., *"Books arrive Oct 1; Packing takes Oct 2–7; Ship everything by Oct 10."* If you're using a fulfillment company, you might say "Send files/list to fulfiller by X date, they ship by Y date." Either way, set a target for when all rewards will be out the door.

- **Digital Rewards Delivery:** Don't forget to schedule sending of ebooks or other digital goodies, often earlier than physical if those are ready. You might deliver PDFs as soon as the campaign money is collected (as a thank-you while the physical is printing) or at least set a date.
- **Follow-up/Customer Service:** Mark a time for handling any stragglers: packages that get returned or lost, backers who fill surveys late, etc. For instance, you might say "Keep an eye on tracking and resolving issues throughout October-November." It's ongoing, but good to note that you'll need bandwidth for it.

Now, look at the timeline you mapped. Does it *seem realistic* given your promised delivery date to backers? If you told backers "Books will ship in June" but your timeline shows them arriving to you in June and needing 2 weeks of packing, you're already late. Better adjust the promise *now, before launch*. Kickstarter makes you estimate a delivery month for each reward tier. Use your timeline to pick a safe date. If in doubt, push it a bit later. Backers generally don't mind waiting a reasonable time if you communicate, but they do mind broken promises. So set yourself up to beat your deadline.

For example, if everything suggests you could fulfill in October, put November on the campaign as the delivery month. Then if you ship in October, you're a hero who delivered early. If you slip to early November, you're still on time. *Everyone's happy.* If you say October and slip to November, some folks will grumble. Little psychological difference, big effect.

Also consider if any part of your timeline feels *too tight.* Maybe you realize you promised a custom art piece to each backer and that means drawing 50 sketches in a month – ouch. Either adjust the offer or timeline or plan help. If you see a bottleneck (e.g., everything hinges on you finishing writing the last chapter by X date), double-check that. Basically, sanity-check the whole flow.

By planning fulfillment now, you also highlight any resource gaps. Need a friend to help pack boxes in exchange for pizza? Pencil that in and maybe ask them ahead of time ("Hey, late October, are you around to help me for a weekend?"). Need to hire a virtual assistant to handle surveys and data? Flag it now. Need to budget for a postage label printer or tons of printer ink for labels? Add to the budget. This is why we plan – to avoid the, "Oh no, I didn't think of that," later.

COMMUNICATE TIMELINES TO BACKERS

This is slightly looking ahead to when your campaign is live, but relevant now: Backers love to see that you have a plan. On your campaign page and updates, you'll likely share a high-level timeline ("Editing done by May, books printed by July, rewards shipped by August," etc.). Because you've mapped everything, you can confidently communicate dates. This instills confidence in backers that you're organized and reliable. Throughout the campaign and after, you can then update backers with progress relative to the timeline ("Book is at the printer on schedule, we expect to ship next month," etc.). All of this reduces anxiety for everyone. Many backers are used to creators being late or vague – you're going to be a breath of fresh air by being on top of things.

BUILD YOUR AUDIENCE NOW

We touched on audience earlier, but it's so critical it bears repeating here in the planning phase: "If you build it, they will come" only works if *they know about it*. A huge part of pre-launch is making sure you have people to launch *to*. So alongside timeline and budget, you should have a strategy for audience building in the weeks or months leading up.

Ask yourself: who are the people most likely to back this project, and how can I reach them and excite them before launch? The core is usually your existing readers/fans. If you have an email list, plan out email content teasing the project. Perhaps a monthly countdown: "Coming soon: My first illustrated hardcover!" with maybe a behind-the-scenes snippet to whet appetites. If you have social media followers, start posting concept art, progress updates, or polls ("Help me choose between these two cover designs!") to engage them. Essentially, you want to turn passive followers into interested prospective backers. By launch day, some folks should be thinking "Finally, I've been waiting for this!" because you seeded that anticipation.

If you're starting from a near-zero audience, don't despair, but do hustle. This might mean joining some communities (Facebook groups, subreddits, Discords) related to your genre and genuinely engaging (not just spamming your link – be cool, contribute, then let them know when something big is coming). It could mean running a lead magnet campaign: e.g., giving away a prequel story or sample chapters in exchange for emails, so you can build a mailing list of interested readers. It might involve old-fashioned networking: reaching out to author friends for signal boosts, maybe doing a blog tour or podcast appearances to talk about your upcoming project, which subtly advertises it.

Plan at least one channel that you'll focus on. Email is king in my opinion – it converts well. So if you have even a tiny list, nurture it. If not, consider building one now. Even getting 50 people on a list who are enthusiastic can make a difference on Day 1. One thing I do: in the lead-up, I'll send an email to my list with something like "I'm launching a Kickstarter in two weeks – here's why I'm excited and why you should be too." I share some details and include the "notify me on launch" link. That way, those truly interested click it and are practically guaranteed to come on Day 1 (because Kickstarter will remind them).

Also, leverage the Kickstarter pre-launch page I mentioned. It's basically a landing page with a button "Notify me on launch." You can share that link everywhere – on social media bios, in your email signature, on forum posts, etc. Collect those followers (Kickstarter will show you how many you have to give you a nice little barometer of interest). Typically, a decent chunk of those who click notify will back on day one or two. So, the more you have, the stronger your launch.

If you already have readers on other platforms (say a Patreon, or a Facebook reader group, or a Wattpad following), formulate a plan to convert them into Kickstarter backers. Often, it's education + incentive. Some might not know what Kickstarter is ("Do I have to pay now? What is this?"). Educate them ahead of time: "Kickstarter is a platform where you pledge support for my project; you only get charged after the campaign if it's successful. It's basically a pre-order with extra perks!" Many authors even do a little Q&A post or video like "Wondering what Kickstarter is? Here's the deal…" to alleviate confusion. That's a good pre-launch task if your audience is new to crowdfunding.

And think about incentives: maybe let your audience know that Kickstarter backers get the book first or with exclusive goodies. The idea is to make them feel like being a backer is special (which it is). You're building a tribe, not just conducting a transaction.

Finally, schedule some personal outreach. Identify your super-fans – those 5 or 10 people who always support you. Maybe a couple of family members or friends who believe in you. Plan to personally message or email them on launch day (or launch week) to ask for their support and shares. That direct touch can go a long way. You'd be surprised how many people are happy to help if asked but might not act if they only saw a general post. Line up your "street team," even informally.

All these audience efforts should be on your timeline as tasks: "Post cover reveal on Instagram – 3 weeks before." "Launch pre-launch page and email link to list – 4 weeks before." "Weekly countdown tweets starting 4 weeks out." "Guest on X podcast – 2 weeks before." Whatever fits your strategy. If you see you have nothing in place to gather interest, make that a priority task *before* you launch. It can significantly impact your Day 1 success, which often sets the tone for the whole campaign.

THE 1,000 TRUE FANS FALLACY

Kevin Kelly wrote a piece on his blog in 2008 called " 1,000 True Fans," which became one of the definitive pieces on building an audience with its claim that if an artist can find one thousand people willing to spend one hundred dollars a year on their work, then they can successfully make a living on their art. Even though I have issues with this theory, I hope we can all agree that generating $100,000 in income would make a successful year. The idea is that if you can find 1,000 people willing to give you $100/yr, then you have a six-figure business. You'll need close to 2,000 people willing to pay you $50/yr to make $100,000 in revenue, not profit. Let's talk about that number for a minute, though, because to find 2,000 people willing to pay you $50/yr, you need to "kiss a lot of frogs," as they say, not everyone is a possible fan, which means you probably need to spread your message to 10x more than that to attract enough people to make these numbers work. ***That's between 500,000 and 1,000,000 people to find 1,000 buyers.***

In my own business, 30-50% of buyers will buy again, and 10% will become superfans. ***That means now I need to find 10,000 buyers to find 1,000 superfans and, thus, talk to 5-10 million people.***

I talked to a creator recently who related a story from a company he worked with, where they gathered 4,000,000 to find 100,000 engaged fans and 1,000 of them to become buyers.

They were selling a wildly expensive enterprise product of some type, but even as an extreme example, it's instructive.

The fallacy inherent inside the 1,000 True Fans parable is that you will need to talk to more than 1,000 people to find enough people who resonate with your message to financially back you.

AUTHOR KICKSTARTER LAUNCH CHECKLIST

Use this as a quick reference to track your progress. You can check items off as you complete them. The tasks are grouped by phase:

PRE-CAMPAIGN PREPARATION (PLANNING & SETUP)

- **Build your budget** – Calculate all costs and set your funding goal.
- **Fill out the One-Page Campaign Worksheet** – Develop your pitch, story, and content for the page (Module 3).
- **Record your video** – Script and film a short, engaging campaign video (if doing one).
- **Choose imagery for your campaign** – Gather all graphics (cover art, author photo, reward images, etc.) and upload them to your page.
- **Set up the basics** – Input project title, category, goal, duration on Kickstarter.
- **Create reward tiers** – Enter all your reward levels and descriptions on Kickstarter.
- **Plan early bird perks** – Decide on any limited-time/quantity rewards for early backers and set them up
  .
- **Design stretch goals & bonus perks** – Outline stretch goals and any weekly or flash bonuses for backers.
- **Write pre-launch and launch announcement emails** – Draft the emails you'll send to your list on launch day (and perhaps a teaser before).
- **Write your marketing copy (sideways sales letter)** – Plan out your marketing messages/posts sequence (the "story" you'll tell over the campaign).

- **Network with other creators** – Reach out to fellow authors for potential cross-promo or advice.
- **Brainstorm "emergency" rewards** – Prepare a couple of extra reward ideas to add mid-campaign if momentum slows.
- **Plan weekly update themes** – Decide how you'll keep the campaign fresh each week (new talking points, reveals).
- **Create a pre-launch landing page** – Publish your KS pre-launch page and share it to gather followers.
- **Final review of campaign page** – Proofread all text, check images, ensure reward details and shipping are correct. Maybe have a friend test-read it.
- **Submit for Kickstarter approval** – Do this a few days before launch to be safe (if not auto-approved).
- **Launch date prep** – Announce your launch date to your audience a few days prior.

LIVE CAMPAIGN (LAUNCH TO CLOSE)

- **Launch your campaign** – Hit that launch button! Then execute your Day 1 promotion blitz.
- **Share to social media** – Post the project link and announcement on all your platforms (and repeat as needed).
- **Send a launch email** – Email your newsletter or contacts with the big announcement and link.
- **Message backers as they pledge** – Thank individuals (especially higher-tier backers) with a quick personal note via Kickstarter (optional but leaves a great impression).
- **Monitor and respond** – Answer any comments or messages from backers promptly.

- **Post first update** – Within the first 1-2 days, post an update celebrating the launch, thanking backers, and sharing next steps.
- **Track and adjust marketing** – Watch where pledges are coming from; adjust your outreach if some channels are lagging.
- **Mid-campaign promotions** – Continue regular social posts, consider a mid-campaign event or live stream.
- **Deploy emergency rewards if needed** – If funding stalls, add that new reward or bonus perk to re-energize interest.
- **Backer update swaps** – Share an update about a fellow creator's project (and they share about yours) if arranged.
- **Weekly backer perk (if promised)** – Deliver any weekly bonuses to backers (via update or message).
- **Engage community** – Keep answering comments, maybe run a fun poll or prompt in an update to involve backers.
- **Final week countdown** – 5 days out, 3 days out, etc., ramp up the reminders and highlight any last-minute incentives.
- **Final 48-hour push** – Leverage Kickstarter's reminder email – post updates and social reminders "last chance!".
- **End-of-campaign update** – When the campaign concludes, post an update thanking everyone and confirming the success (or next steps if not funded).
- **Celebrate!** – You did it. Take a breath but remember the fulfillment phase is next.

POST-CAMPAIGN FULFILLMENT

- **Send "thank you" update** – Immediately after the campaign, thank backers and let them know what's next (survey timing, etc.).
- **Collect backer info (surveys)** – Prepare and send Kickstarter surveys or set up the pledge manager to gather addresses, choice selections, names for thank-you page, etc..
- **Address failed payments** – Contact any backers whose payments errored (Kickstarter will list them) to help resolve within 7 days.
- **Lock orders/final counts** – Finalize how many of each item you need based on survey responses.
- **Order merchandise and books** – Place orders with printer and merch suppliers for all physical rewards.
- **Order packing materials** – Purchase boxes/mailers, tape, labels, etc., if not done already.
- **Plan postage** – Decide and acquire postage (buy online postage or set up USPS pickup).
- **Digital reward delivery** – Send out any digital rewards that are due (ebooks, etc.).
- **Receive and organize inventory** – Once books and merch arrive, organize them for fulfillment (sign books if needed, bundle sets, etc.).
- **Quality check** – Ensure items came out correctly (flip through a book, test an item).
- **Pack and ship rewards** – Package all rewards securely and mail them out to backers.
- **Mark orders as shipped** – If using a pledge manager or even a manual list, note each backer's package has been sent.

- **Update backers – shipped** – Post an update when the majority (or all) packages have been shipped, detailing expected delivery times and asking backers to confirm receipt or report issues.
- **Handle any issues** – If any backer reports a lost/damaged package or missing item, arrange a replacement or solution promptly.
- **Debrief your campaign** – Analyze the results and jot down lessons learned for next time.
- **Add project to Indiegogo InDemand (if desired)** – Keep funding open for late backers (optional).
- **After ~90 days, add to retailers** – Once backers have had their exclusivity period, publish or sell the book through other channels (Amazon, bookstores).
- **Stay in touch with backers** – Invite them to join your newsletter or follow you elsewhere, so they know about your next release.

CHAPTER 4

TESTING ON KICKSTARTER

Most authors launch their books with no real data about how their readers prefer to buy. They price their books based on market averages, package their editions based on what's common, and hope that readers will respond well. But hope isn't a strategy, and launching without testing is a recipe for lost revenue and missed opportunities.

Kickstarter eliminates this uncertainty. Instead of blindly setting a price on Amazon or designing a direct sales offer based on guesswork, authors can use Kickstarter as a real-world testing ground. The platform provides hard data on what readers are willing to pay, what formats they prefer, and what upgrades they're most excited about, all before the book ever reaches retail or direct sales.

Traditional publishers spend months conducting market research before releasing a book. They test covers, experiment with pricing, and gauge audience demand long before a book ever reaches shelves. Every decision, from packaging to distribution strategy, is backed by data. In contrast, many indie authors skip this step entirely, going straight to launch without any real validation. They finalize covers, set prices, and choose formats based on intuition rather than actual reader demand.

Kickstarter offers indie authors a built-in market testing system that eliminates the guesswork. Instead of launching blindly and hoping a book will sell, authors can use a crowdfunding campaign to gather real-world data before committing to production decisions. The platform allows authors to experiment with different pricing structures, test packaging options, and gauge interest in special editions, all while funding the book in advance.

Through Kickstarter, authors can see exactly which price tiers perform best, giving them insight into how much readers are truly willing to pay for different formats. They can test demand for paperbacks versus hardcovers, standard editions versus collector's editions, and determine which options are worth producing at scale. Add-ons, stretch goals, and exclusive content provide another layer of insight—revealing what readers value most and what they are willing to pay extra for.

This kind of real-time market research is invaluable. Instead of guessing what will sell, authors can let their audience decide, ensuring that every future launch is optimized for maximum revenue and engagement. Used like this Kickstarter isn't just a funding platform. It's a powerful tool for shaping the most profitable and reader-driven version of a book launch.

TESTING PRICING

One of the biggest challenges authors face is knowing how to price their books. Charge too much, and readers won't buy. Charge too little, and the author leaves money on the table.

Kickstarter solves this problem by allowing authors to test multiple price points in real time. By setting up different reward tiers, authors can see exactly what readers are willing to pay, not just for the book itself, but for exclusive editions, signed copies, and premium add-ons.

For example, an author might structure their tiers like this:

- **$10** – Digital Edition
- **$25** – Paperback Edition
- **$50** – Signed Hardcover + Bonus Content
- **$100** – Collector's Box Set + Exclusive Art Print

If the $50 tier far outsells the $25 tier, that's a clear signal that readers are willing to pay more for premium experiences.

TESTING PACKAGING

Every author wrestles with decisions about which formats to offer. Should they invest in hardcover editions? Do readers even want signed books? Will special packaging options actually sell?

Instead of making these decisions blindly, Kickstarter allows authors to offer multiple formats and see which ones backers prefer. If a limited-edition hardcover gets strong support, it makes sense to offer that format in future direct sales. If a particular reward tier struggles, it might not be worth producing in bulk.

What Packaging Variables Can Be Tested on Kickstarter?

- **Paperback vs. Hardcover Demand** – Are readers willing to pay more for a premium edition?
- **Special Editions vs. Standard Releases** – Is there demand for collector's versions?
- **Signed vs. Unsigned Copies** – Are readers paying extra for personalized books?
- **Exclusive Add-Ons** – Do readers want bookmarks, slipcases, or art prints?

TESTING ADD-ONS

Many authors assume that books are the only thing readers care about, but Kickstarter often proves otherwise. Readers frequently want more than just the book. They're interested in behind-the-scenes content, exclusive merchandise, and unique collector's items.

Or at least they say they do. Kickstarter allows authors to test which extras resonate most before investing in large production runs. Instead of guessing what readers want, authors can see real purchasing behavior in action.

Some of the most popular extras include:

- Exclusive bonus stories or novellas.
- Limited-run artwork or illustrated editions.
- Merchandise like mugs, t-shirts, or enamel pins.

- Behind-the-scenes access (author Q&As, live chats, digital perks).

By testing these extras as stretch goals or add-ons, authors can identify the most profitable options before scaling them in direct sales.

KICKSTARTER AS A HIGH-VALUE MARKETING ASSET

Many authors think of Kickstarter purely as a way to raise funds for a single project, but the real benefit goes well beyond one campaign. Each Kickstarter you run can be used to create evergreen marketing assets that help propel your career for years to come. Yes, building a campaign can be time-consuming and sometimes expensive, but that's because building marketing assets is exhausting. If you do it right, you can build these assets now and use them in the following pieces of the stack, which is another reason why Kickstarter comes first.

When you invest in crafting compelling rewards, writing polished sales copy, building emails and creative content, and networking with potential backers, you're not just funding a book, you're laying the groundwork for all your future marketing. From the Kickstarter page itself to the behind-the-scenes videos, bonus content, and stretch-goal ideas, these materials form a library of assets that can be reused and adapted for:

- **Future Book Launches:** The same polished copy or exclusive materials can migrate to your direct-sales website or be recycled as special-edition bundles later.
- **Email Marketing and Automations:** The email sequences you create to nurture backers can be tweaked for new subscribers who discover you after the campaign.
- **Social Media & Ads:** The teaser images and videos you made for the Kickstarter become ready-made content for Facebook, Instagram, TikTok, or anywhere you run ads.

Running a Kickstarter campaign demands more front-loaded work like planning rewards, crafting a compelling page, filming videos, and managing backer communication. There may also be added costs for things like professional design, promotional materials, or higher-quality reward items, but this upfront investment is work you will eventually have to do anyway. So, you might as well get paid to do it from your campaign.

MINE THE PUBLIC DATA GOLDMINE

Every Kickstarter campaign is a fully transparent case study sitting in plain sight. Click on any campaign, successful or not, live or archived, and you can see things like how many backers pledged, which reward tiers they chose, what they spent, and exactly when momentum spiked or stalled. Pair that with free tracking tools like Kicktraq or BiggerCake and you can export pledge curves, average pledge values, and backer-count velocity for any project in any genre, no scraping required.

- **Reverse-engineer winning rewards.** Sort a successful campaign's reward table by popularity: note the price breaks, format mixes (digital-only, print, deluxe), and how each tier nudges buyers to climb the value ladder. Do the same for under-performers to see where complexity, poor pricing, or irrelevant add-ons killed conversion, then adjust your own ladder accordingly.
- **Study update cadence and content.** Mine the updates and plot which posts coincide with pledge spikes. You'll quickly spot patterns that reignite momentum. Borrow the cadence, not the copy: match their rhythm to your voice and audience size.
- **Time your launch window.** Kicktraq's daily breakdown shows which weekdays and hours deliver the highest pledge velocity in your niche. If the top three campaigns in your genre all funded 30% on a Tuesday morning, you have a data-backed clue for your own Day-One blast.
- **Benchmark realistic goals.** Filter campaigns by category and funding level, then average the top ten. You'll know whether a $10K ask is ambitious or conservative for a 300-page fantasy hardcover and you can price rewards to hit that number without guesswork.

Treat Kickstarter like a public lab notebook: every success and flop is open-source intelligence. Spend an afternoon dissecting campaigns before you build your own and you'll skip months of trial and error—launching with data-driven confidence instead of hopeful hunches.

CHAPTER 5

PROVEN PLAYBOOKS THAT WORK

Often, the hardest part about getting somebody to use Kickstarter is having them envision what kind of campaign to run. It can be overwhelming, but it doesn't have to be. In this chapter we'll unpack the **four baseline playbooks** every author should know. For each, you'll get:

- **Core concept**: What you're really selling.
- **Recommended reward ladder**: Plug-and-play tiers that convert.
- **Marketing angle**: The psychological hook that grabs backers.

When you come to a new platform, it's all about testing, and these playbooks allow you to test and validate with proven products that already work. This gives you the best chance to see whether Kickstarter is right for you without investing a ton into the process, either monetarily or with your time.

Run one of these playbooks cleanly and you'll look like a Kickstarter genius. Combine them over multiple launches and you'll build a compounded revenue engine that keeps spitting out profitable projects year after year.

PLAYBOOK #1: ANNIVERSARY BOOKS

Take a book that's already written, loved, and profitable, wrap it in an irresistible package, and charge a premium price. Think sprayed edges, variant covers, foil stamping, interior art, ribbon bookmarks, maps, the works. You're selling **bragging-rights editions** to superfans who will proudly display them on Instagram.

WHY IT WORKS

- **Unlimited price ceiling**: Deluxe hardcovers routinely fetch $60–$80; with leather, metal, or hand-done edges you can go well past $150.
- **Instant profit**: The manuscript is done; Kickstarter funds pure production.
- **Fast cash-flow**: Money hits your bank in 14 days, not 60 days like Amazon.
- **You know that it works:** This is a book that's already successful and you already know your audience loves, so the odds it will work on Kickstarter is very high.

RECOMMENDED REWARD LADDER

Most campaigns open with a **$5-$10 digital version** for casual readers, then step up to a ten-dollar "deluxe ebook" that bundles audio commentary or bonus scenes.

$25 usually buys a signed paperback for readers who want a hold-in-hand copy without the luxury price tag.

The heart of the stack is the hardcover, often priced anywhere from **$40-$80** depending on upgrades.

Above that you offer experiential tiers, perhaps a **$50-$100 live Q&A, a low-end book box in the $125 range, and a high-end box at $200-$300** that adds extra merch and maybe a leather or metal variant.

One final prestige tier of **$500+** lets a superfan commission a cameo character, snag the last test print, or join you for a private dinner at a future convention. Each rung makes sense, each upgrade feels worth it, and the high tiers are intentionally limited so you don't drown in bespoke commitments.

Pro Tip: Start simple. Offer one killer upgrade (foil or sprayed edges) plus a ribbon. Add interior art only if you *enjoy* managing artists or can leverage AI. Complexity is the enemy of timely delivery.

PRODUCTION & MARGIN NOTES

Expect to pay **$3-$5** dollars per book if you outsource sprayed edges, and roughly **fifty cents to a dollar per copy** for foil or spot gloss. Ribbon bookmarks cost mere pennies, while full-color interior art bumps print cost by a few dollars if you're using POD services like BookVault that charge per color page. A branded slipcase or book box will set you back **$3-$5** dollars apiece at a run of 250 units. The point: pick two or three enhancements, price the book to leave at least a forty-percent margin after print, packaging, and Kickstarter fees, and you'll do fine. Don't let enthusiasm push you into twenty different upgrades on a first attempt. Complexity kills schedules.

MARKETING HOOK

Lead with scarcity and luxury. "A numbered, never-to-be-reprinted anniversary edition with custom foil and edge art." Glamour shots of the shimmer and stencil sell the fantasy. The campaign story is half retail pitch, half behind-the-scenes documentary of book-making nerdery. Readers aren't just buying a novel; they're buying a display piece and a ticket to watch you geek out about paper stock and metallic inks. This one is all about celebration.

PLAYBOOK #2: SECOND-CHANCE PAPERBACKS

You've got a backlist title that hardcore fans adore but that never found a wide audience (maybe the Amazon rank languished). Kickstart a **reformatted, slightly upgraded edition** and price it high enough to actually make money this time.

- **Minimal new work:** Light interior refresh, maybe a new cover or larger trim.
- **Charge what it's worth**: $25-$30 signed paperback vs. $15 Amazon.
- **Built-in testimonials**: Use rave reviews from existing readers as social proof.
- **You know it has a fandom:** your core fans love it, so you know they'll likely buy it if you show it some love. Plus, you get to introduce it to new fans.

RECOMMENDED REWARD LADDER

Kick off with a **$5-$10** rerelease ebook, followed by **a $25 signed paperback** that includes the updated digital. Many creators add a **$45 "before and after" bundle** containing both the original paperback and the refreshed edition for collectors.

If you've got multiple forgotten gems, bundle them, **a trilogy set at $75,** for instance. Then, the $50-$100 VIP call and some top level tiers to close it out. The beauty is simplicity: four or five tiers tops, nearly all print-on-demand, so cash risk is near zero.

This playbook monetizes **existing assets**. Your hard cost is mostly printing + postage. Because you're re-selling a finished product, fulfillment is straightforward, and margins stay fat.

PRODUCTION & MARGIN NOTES

Updating interior layout costs may be a couple hundred dollars at most, and re-covering would be perhaps three to six hundred. Printing a POD paperback runs three to four dollars per copy; selling it at twenty-five leaves a fat margin even after shipping. Because everything except the cover already existed, your biggest investment is time, not cash.

MARKETING HOOK

Frame it as a redemption arc. "This underappreciated gem finally gets the gorgeous treatment it deserves, and you can be the reader who rescues it from obscurity." Fans feel heroic funding a book the market overlooked. Sprinkle in past five-star reviews and heartfelt commentary from early readers to make the emotional appeal irresistible.

PLAYBOOK #3: BRAND EXPANSION & WORLD-BUILDING

Leverage an established IP to spin off **new product lines** that deepen the reader experience. It could be board games, enamel pins, short-film adaptations, card decks, plays, art books, cookbooks, world-building guides, or anything that lets fans live in the universe beyond the page. Please note, this should really only be done if you have a fandom, or you see an opportunity to bring in a new fandom, like a fantasy novelist who makes an RPG because the audience is huge for them already.

WHY IT WORKS

1. **Huge average pledge**: Physical or experiential add-ons push pledges well above $100.
2. **Cross-market appeal**: Game players find the book; readers try the game; total addressable market grows.
3. **IP flywheel**: Each spin-off feeds attention back to the core series.

RECOMMENDED REWARD LADDER

Start with a **$10 digital-art bundle** for casual supporters who just want pretty wallpapers or a lore PDF. Then, **$25**

might net an enamel-pin set. At $40, you add the art book. Then, $60 gets the core board game. A **$100+ might be the "Universe Box"** that crams in every physical product, game, book, pins, maps, stickers. For super-fans, offer a cameo card in the game art or a producer credit around **$200-$400 dollars**, and a top-tier **$1,000+** experience (private play-test session or dinner with the creator). Each tier stacks logically, and the higher ones stay limited to prevent overwhelming fulfillment.

PRODUCTION NOTES & MARGIN WATCHOUTS

Board-game manufacturing requires tooling costs; pins demand MOQs of one-to-two hundred pieces; heavy boxes balloon postage. Partner with experienced vendors (PandaGM, PrintNinja, Quartermaster) and build freight duties into your margin. For international shipping, budget for EU/UK VAT or use third-party hubs so backers aren't slapped with surprise fees.

MARKETING HOOK

"Step inside the world you love." Backers aren't just reading—they're eating recipes from your cookbook, shuffling cards with character art, wearing the story on a pin. Pitch the collection as a passport that lets them live in your universe.

PLAYBOOK #4: THE NON-FICTION STACK

This is the stack we used at Writer MBA all the time. Non-fiction backers don't just want a pretty book on the shelf.

They want **results**. They're paying for the shortcut your expertise provides. The Knowledge Stack layers multiple levels of access to that expertise, so every budget has a logical next step up the ladder. Because most deliverables are digital (a PDF, a Zoom call, a recorded workshop), your hard costs stay tiny while perceived value skyrockets. It's the most margin-rich stack we've ever run: one manuscript becomes a book, a masterclass, and a live cohort, each tier feeding the next.

WHY IT WORKS:

- **Scales infinitely**: digital products + your time.
- **Excellent profit margin**: print cost is tiny relative to price.
- **Upsell ladder**: Each tier naturally leads to the next.
- **Authority positioning**: Teaching establishes you as the go-to expert, fueling future book sales.

RECOMMENDED REWARD LADDER

The entry point is a **$10 ebook**, cheap enough for the merely curious. At **$25-$30** you upgrade to the signed paperback plus the digital files.

Around **$50**, you invite backers to a private VIP Q&A or live webinar, easy for you, high perceived value for them.

At **$100-$150**, you offer a two-hour masterclass that walks through your framework step-by-step and includes a replay link. You prepare the deck once, record it, and it becomes evergreen content you can resell forever.

The golden tier sits at about **$300**, a four-to-six-week live cohort where you meet weekly on Zoom, assign homework, and give direct feedback. Because the masterclass session doubles as Week 1 and the VIP Q&A doubles as the final week, you're really committing to four extra live calls, a manageable workload with massive value. Above that you can float a **$500-$1,000** consulting tier (one-on-one sessions) for the handful of backers who want bespoke attention, and a **$2,500-$5,000 VIP day** for true high rollers. Even if only one person bites, you just covered a chunk of print and shipping costs.

If you write how-to or business books, this playbook is almost mandatory. Readers are actively seeking solutions; give them multiple levels to engage, learn, and pay.

PRODUCTION & FULFILLMENT NOTES

Physical fulfillment is painless: a single paperback printed POD, shipped Media Mail. All higher tiers are digital or time-based, so your "manufacturing" cost is essentially Zoom Pro and an email platform. Record every live session; the replay becomes a bonus upsell later. Automate delivery: after surveys close, drop a Google Calendar invite and a Zoom link into each qualifying backer's inbox, then send a reminder the morning of the call. For cohorts, host replays in a private YouTube playlist or Thinkific classroom—low tech is fine as long as access is gated. Budget wise, ninety-plus percent of pledges hit your account as profit once the book print run is paid.

MARKETING HOOK

Sell **transformation**. The book is the blueprint, but the masterclass and cohort are the guided sprint to implement that blueprint. Your copy should read: "Read the book in a weekend, attend the live masterclass to clarify questions, then spend four weeks actually building your system with me looking over your shoulder." Prospective backers instantly grasp the escalation of support, and the escalated results.

Testimonials from beta readers who increased newsletter revenue or doubled their audience seal the deal. Fear of missing out is real here: if they wait for the retail edition, they'll pay the same for the paperback but lose the chance to interact with you live.

WHY THIS STACK WORKS

The Knowledge Stack leverages your single scarcest asset, **your time**, at premium tiers while keeping lower tiers affordable. Every hour you spend on the cohort is multiplied across dozens of participants, so your effective hourly rate climbs into triple digits. Better yet, every interactive session creates new assets (recordings, worksheets) you can bundle into future launches. And because students often get real wins, they return for your next course or book, becoming lifelong patrons of your brand.

Remember, you can cycle through playbooks across campaigns. Use a Second-Chance relaunch to revive backlist, then follow up with a Special-Edition box set of your bestseller, then drop a Brand-Expansion art book or game. Each campaign feeds the last, compounding audience size and credibility.

Now it's your turn.

Pick on, commit, and run it. The playbooks in this chapter aren't hypothetical. They're **battle-tested blueprints** that have funded millions of dollars in books, merch, and creative upgrades. Now they're yours. Take the one that fits your goals, tailor the reward ladder to your audience, and watch your next campaign fund faster, grow bigger, and deliver more profit than you thought possible.

CHAPTER 6

NAIL YOUR OFFER

Think of your Kickstarter offer as a **ladder of escalating awesomeness**. Each rung (tier) has more value than the one below it, enticing backers to climb as high as they're comfortable. A common structure for publishing campaigns goes like this:

- **Low-Dollar Entry Tier ($1):** This is often a simple "tip jar" or thank-you level, or perhaps a digital short story or sampler. It's for people who want to support you at a token level or just get a small taste. Not every campaign has a $1 tier, but if you do, it might be something like "$1 – Thank You! Get an outline of the book at this tier." The point is to give something meaningful, but easy to deliver, to entice people to buy. The hardest thing to do in marketing is to get something to go from spending $0-$1. Once they do that, then you're just negotiating on how much value.

- **Ebook/Digital Tier ($5–$15):** If you're offering a book, the **ebook** is usually the next rung. Often around $10 (give or take) for an ebook or digital copy of the book being funded. This tier is *essential* because some backers only want digital, and it's also the tier with no shipping or production cost for you. It might include all ebook formats (PDF, ePub) of the novel. Some creators set it at $5; others at $10 or $15, depending on length and their audience. Many backers see $10 as fair for an early, maybe Kickstarter-exclusive ebook. If you have bonus digital content (like an exclusive short story), you might bundle it here or in a slightly higher digital tier. I recommend having a "bare bones" version for $5 and a special edition one for $10, with an audio commentary and the exclusive cover, plus maybe some early drafts. The $5 one gets the retailer cover.

- **Paperback/Softcover Tier ($20–$30):** Next up is the **physical book in paperback** (if you have one). A very common pricing is $20 or $25 for a signed paperback + the ebook. Backers at this level get a tangible copy. Always bundle the ebook with physical books (there's no reason not to; it costs nothing and adds value). The paperback tier is often the most popular for book campaigns. Many readers still love a physical book but might not splurge for hardcover. So, ensure this tier is solid value. If $25 gets them a signed paperback + ebook + name in the thank-yous, that's a sweet deal many will jump on. If you're charging shipping after the campaign then $20 is probably the sweet spot. Since I feature all in pricing, I go with $25.
- **Hardcover/Special Edition Tier ($40–$60):** If you're doing hardcovers or some kind of premium edition (foil cover, extra art, etc.), that's a higher tier. Commonly $40–$50 for a signed hardcover + all the digital formats + maybe an art print or small bonus. This is for collectors and superfans. If your project is specifically

about a deluxe edition (like a special illustrated hardcover), this might actually be your *core* tier that you expect most to take. Price it to cover your costs amply – hardcovers are pricier to print and ship. Backers at this tier are willing to pay a premium for something special, so don't undersell it. $50 is not uncommon for a signed, limited-run hardcover with nice bells and whistles.

- **The Special Thanks Tier ($50):** This is easily the most profitable tier on any campaign because the margin is 100% profit. All you have to do is create a page at the front of the book and list the people who supported. It takes a few minutes, and it could make you a lot of money without a lot of cost.
- **Deluxe Bundle Tier ($75–$100):** Here's where you combine multiple items into a bundle for those who want *everything*. For example: **$99 – Deluxe Bundle**: *signed hardcover, paperback, ebook, audiobook (if available), plus swag like bookmarks, stickers, maybe your signature on a bookplate, and their name in a special thanks section*. This tier piles on the value. It's for your biggest fans who want the complete experience. The price should be at a slight discount compared to buying all those items separately, to encourage people to go for the big bundle. Also consider limited extras here like "exclusive art print only in this tier" to make it distinct. A $100 tier often performs well if you have a dedicated fanbase; many people love to treat themselves to the ultimate edition.
- **Superfan/Collector Tier ($150–$300+):** This is the top-of-the-ladder, usually limited quantity, for the true

die-hards. Could be $150, $250, $300 or more, depending on what's included. Ideas for this tier: **everything in the deluxe bundle plus something personal or rare.** For instance, "Your name as a character in my next book" is a popular high-end reward (usually limited to a few slots). Or a one-on-one Zoom call with the author. Or a custom short story written for them. Or original artwork. Something that you can't mass-produce, hence the limited nature. Price these according to the effort and rarity. If you're offering to write a custom flash fiction for them, factor your time (and maybe limit to 5 slots or whatever). People will pay a premium for unique experiences or contributions. Another example: a **premium patron** tier: "Everything plus you'll be listed as a Producer in the book, and I'll take you out to dinner at the next con" (if that's something you'd do). Make it fun and exclusive. Not everyone will go for these, but one or two backers at $250 can significantly boost your total. And even if nobody takes it, it makes your $100 tier look more reasonable by comparison – classic price anchoring.

These are just examples. **Your ladder should be tailored to your project.** Maybe you have only digital and hardcover, no paperback. Maybe you have multiple books (like a series set) to bundle at higher tiers. The key is that each tier **ascends in value and price logically**. If I look at your tiers from lowest to highest, I should never think, "Huh, why does that higher tier have less stuff?" Each step up should include everything below (in most cases) plus extra. Typically, physical tiers include digital automatically. Higher tiers often include lower-tier items unless there's a reason to separate (some campaigns do separate digital-only vs physical-only, but even then, a big bundle might include both).

Take your reward item list and distribute items into tiers in a way that feels like a natural progression. Picture a backer climbing: "If I add $20 more, I get a hardcover instead of paperback and an art print. If I add $30 more beyond that, I get the bundle with swag." It should feel like a **value-add at each step**.

Go ahead and sketch out a tier ladder now: Write down, say, 5–7 tier levels you plan to offer and list what's in each. Something like:

- $10 – Digital Only (Ebook + name in thank you)
- $25 – Paperback (Paperback + Ebook + Name in book)
- $50 – Hardcover (Hardcover + Ebook + Name + bookmark + art print)
- $75 – Hardcover + Paperback Bundle (for collectors who want both + all above goodies)
- $100 – Deluxe Bundle (Hardcover + Paperback + ebook + art print + sticker pack + your name in special thanks section)
- $200 – Be A Character Tier (All deluxe rewards + name a character in my next book, only 3 available)

This is just an example; yours may differ. But notice how each higher tier includes the previous items (except maybe that $75 one where I gave both books, which inherently includes the content of lower tiers). **No backer should feel punished for upgrading** – they shouldn't lose something by going to a higher tier. Commonly, each higher tier = everything from before + more. If for some reason you have parallel tracks (like a merch-only tier vs book-only tier), consider combining or clearly differentiating them. Simplicity is your friend (more on that later).

Once you have a draft ladder, sense-check it: Does it cover different price points to fit different budgets? Do you have a logical entry for digital-only folks, a mid-tier for most people, and a spicy option for high rollers? If your tiers are too close in price or too far, adjust. E.g., having $20 and $25 and $30 tiers might be overkill – you could combine some. Conversely, jumping from $50 to $200 with nothing in between might leave money on the table – maybe add a $100 option. Aim for no huge gaps unaddressed (like a $50 gap with no tier). This gives backers smooth stepping stones.

PRICE YOUR TIERS FOR VALUE *AND* PROFIT

Now let's talk **pricing strategy**.

We use something called **the double 50** to design our campaign, which means that every tier is at least 50% profit and delivers 2x the value of what somebody could buy on the open market. Sometimes you can't make every tier have a 50% profit margin, but the whole campaign should have a 50% profit margin.

The way we beef up value is to **add digital, not physical rewards,** to increase the value. An exclusive audio commentary is something that takes very little time to record, for instance, and significantly increases the value of the perk. Adding additional ebooks, or other things from your back catalog is another way.

The goal here is to understand that revenue is not profit. So often people plan their rewards including shirts and mugs and all sorts of things that might be high revenue, but very low profit. It doesn't matter how much money you make. What matters is how much money you keep, and the value readers perceive.

When I look for items to produce during a campaign, for instance, I'm looking for a 10x profit margin, which is why I love pins. You can make a pin for $1-$2 and sell them for $10-$20. Plus, the perceived value is high, so they check all the boxes.

Pricing your tiers is part art, part math. You want the price to feel like a good deal to backers *and* cover your costs with some margin. Here are some guidelines:

- **Cover Your Costs:** At **minimum**, the price of a tier must cover the cost of producing and delivering the items in that tier (including a share of your fixed costs, overhead, etc.). We already budgeted all costs, so you have a sense of unit costs. For example, if a paperback costs you $5 to print and $4 to ship (domestic average) and maybe $1 for the share of editing/cover cost per book, your total cost per paperback reward might be ~$10. So pricing it at $25 means you get $15 margin on each (less KS fees), which is decent. Pricing it at $15 would barely break even after fees – not good. Always leave margin because unexpected costs or higher international shipping can eat into it. **Never price a tier**

at near cost. You're not running a charity; you need some profit to make this worth your time and effort.

- **Consider Perceived Value:** Backers aren't thinking about your costs; they're thinking, "Is this worth $X to me?" Factors include uniqueness, exclusivity, and how it compares to retail. For instance, an ebook is usually $5–$10 in retail, but on Kickstarter you might charge $10 because it's early access or includes bonus content. A signed paperback might be $15 retail; on Kickstarter $20–$25 is common because it includes the signature, maybe a thank-you mention, and the excitement of the campaign. Backers *expect* to pay a bit more on Kickstarter than the absolute cheapest retail price, because they're getting more (and supporting you directly). So don't undersell out of fear. If you give away hardcovers at $20 which cost you $15 to make + ship, you might get backers, but you'll regret it when you see slim profit.
- **Psychological Pricing:** Small tweaks like ending in 5 or 9 can affect perception. $29 feels slightly less than $30. $50 vs $49, similar. Some use these tactics, others go with clean numbers ($25, $50) for simplicity. Up to you. On lower tiers, $9 might seem more approachable than $10. But honestly, for books, round numbers are fine. People aren't *that* price sensitive over a dollar in this context. It's more about the tier structure as a whole.
- **Best Value Tier:** Think about which tier you expect or want most backers to choose. Often, it's a mid-high tier that gives the best bang for buck (like your $50 hardcover that includes extras). You might even label it

"BEST VALUE" on your campaign page. Price that tier so it's attractive compared to those around it. For example, if $25 gets a paperback and $50 gets a hardcover + goodies, many will think "double the price, but I get way more than double the goodies – yeah, I'll go for $50." That's what you want. Make the jump to your preferred tier a no-brainer. I often see the $50–$60 tier being the sweet spot in book campaigns (lots of value, and people feel they're getting a premium experience without breaking the bank). Design that tier carefully: load it with value (without destroying your margin) and consider highlighting it visually.

- **Fill the Gaps:** As mentioned, don't leave giant price gaps without a tier. If someone has, say, a $30 willingness and your next tier after $25 is $60, you might lose them. Maybe a $40 tier could catch them (like paperback + some swag). On the other side, if someone might go up to $150 but your highest tier is $100, you might be leaving money on the table – offering a $200 tier gives them an option to spend more if they really love you. Some backers actively look for higher tiers to support more generously *if* it comes with something cool.

- **Everything Should Stack:** As best as possible, your rewards should include everything in the previous tier. This makes it easy for people to upsell themselves during the campaign and move to increasingly higher and higher tiers. If they have to give something up to make that move, they usually won't.

- **Limited vs Unlimited Pricing:** If you do limited tiers (like only 5 available), sometimes creators price them a bit higher due to exclusivity, or sometimes lower as early-bird. Early-Bird discounts (time-limited or quantity-limited lower prices) can spur quick action – e.g., "Early bird hardcover $45 for first 50 backers, then it's $50." Use these judiciously. If you include early birds, have a plan for the regular tier price after. The early bird should be a nice bonus, but not so much cheaper that people who miss it feel bad. Often a $5 discount is enough to reward early supporters without angering later ones. We'll discuss early-birds more later but just consider if you want to incorporate that into pricing now.

- **Don't Race to the Bottom:** Kickstarter backers are generally **willing to pay a premium** for exclusive or early access content. They know they're supporting creation, not bargain hunting. So resist any urge to undervalue your work. In fact, many backers perceive lower prices as a red flag ("Is this author going to lose money? Will they be able to deliver?"). Reasonable, confidence-exuding prices can actually boost credibility.

Let's check an example pricing set with logic:

- $10 Digital (basically pure profit, fair price for ebook + name credit)
- $25 Paperback (covers production ~$10, leaves ~$15 margin, fair for a signed book and ebook)
- $45 Early-Bird Hardcover (limit 50, a little thank you for early backers, still covers hardcover cost maybe $15 and leaves good margin)
- $50 Standard Hardcover (after early-birds gone)

- $75 Hardcover + Merch Bundle (adds maybe $10 worth of merch – art prints, bookmark – which costs you $3 to make; giving backer a deal compared to buying separately, and you net extra margin)
- $100 Mega Bundle (paperback + hardcover + all merch + maybe an extra ebook of another book if you have; perceived value maybe $130 if bought individually, so $100 feels like a deal; your cost maybe $30, so still good margin)
- $250 Ultimate (all the above + limited custom reward like name a character or 1-on-1 call; mostly profit aside from your time; only 3 available)

From these, you can see you're making a profit on each tier, and the more someone spends, the more total profit (even if margin % might be a bit less on higher bundles because you throw in more stuff, but it's fine since absolute $ is higher). E.g., $25 tier profit $15, $50 tier profit $30, $100 tier profit $60, $250 tier profit maybe $200. This scaling is good for you and them.

One more thing: **shipping**. Many Kickstarter projects (especially now with new tools) charge shipping separately in the pledge manager or via Kickstarter's survey tool. This is recommended to simplify pricing, and because shipping rates vary a ton by country.

On your tiers, you'll typically list something like "(Shipping will be charged after the campaign through BackerKit, see shipping section for estimates") or if using Kickstarter's shipping feature, you input shipping costs per country per tier. Regardless of how you charge shipping, make sure **backers know** if shipping is separate.

We'll cover communication of that in the campaign page section. For planning, decide how you'll handle shipping fees.

If this is confusing: short answer, you can charge shipping after, so price tiers as product value. If you choose "free shipping worldwide" you better have padded the tier heavily and know what you're in for (rarely a good idea). Shipping strategy aside, just keep it in mind as you price.

MAKE YOUR TIER DESCRIPTIONS CLEAR AND ENTICING

Each tier on Kickstarter has a title and description. Clarity here is crucial. When a backer scrolls your page or the sidebar of tiers, they should immediately grasp what they get at each level. Some tips:

- **Use a Naming Convention:** Many creators label tiers with the main item. E.g., "Digital Edition," "Paperback Tier," "Hardcover Deluxe," "All-In Superfan." A short title helps backers scan. You can even add a bit of flavor ("$50 – **Dragon Hoard Bundle** (Hardcover + Goodies)") but ensure the core is understandable. I generally hate these cute titles because it makes things harder to understand, so use them with caution.
- **List What's Included:** In the description, there is a place to add all the items included in your pledge. I like to add the items in the description AND also list out the items since it's often confusing how Kickstarter lists the items when you are quickly scanning.

- **Be Precise:** If something is unsigned where another is signed, note it. If the hardcover is a special edition, highlight it. If prints are 8×10 art prints, mention the size. Essentially, answer any question a backer might have by looking at the tier description. **No surprises**. For example, if shipping is not included, you could add "(shipping charged separately)" in fine print. If the tier is limited, say it so urgency is clear.

- **Match your Fulfillment Plan:** Make sure you can deliver what you promise. If a tier says "free bookmark" but you didn't account for printing bookmarks in budget, fix that now (either add it to budget or remove it). If a tier offers a "name in book," be sure to include that in your timeline to gather names before printing.

- **No Gaps or Conflicts:** Double-check that when you say "includes X" it actually does. For instance, if someone could interpret that a tier includes two copies of the book because you said "Includes paperback and hardcover" make sure that's intentional. I'd clarify "1× Paperback and 1× Hardcover" if both are included, or if it's choice of cover or something, state clearly.

- **Call Out Special Perks:** If a tier has something unique (limited slot, custom reward, etc.), highlight it. For example: "BECOME A CHARACTER: Your name (or a name you choose) will appear in Book 2 as a character! Plus everything in the Deluxe Bundle. (Limit 3)". The excitement is in the unique bit, but listing the rest ensures they know they also get the book and all that.

Clarity in tiers prevents confusion and customer service headaches later. Imagine a backer pledges and later says "Oh, I thought this tier included X because it wasn't clear." We want to avoid that.

One more thing, as you craft the offer: **keep the number of tiers manageable**. There's a temptation to make a tier for every slight variation ("one for international? one for just a hardcover without the ebook? one with this swag, one without?"). Too many choices can overwhelm backers, leading them to indecision (or choosing a lower tier because they're unsure). I'd say aim for around 5 to 10 tiers total (not counting add-ons or stretch stuff, just base tiers). If you have more than 10, see if you can consolidate. For instance, do you need separate tiers for paperback vs paperback + ebook? Probably not – just make the paperback tier always include the ebook. Do you need a tier for two copies? Possibly, but you could also handle multiple copies via add-ons instead of separate tier (Kickstarter's add-on system allows "add an extra book for $X"). Many creators used to make a tier like "Retailer pack – 5 copies" but now they might just tell retailers, "Pledge at $1 and we'll handle a bulk order offline," or use add-ons. Simplify where you can. Each additional tier is another thing to explain and manage.

PLAN FOR UPGRADES: EARLY BIRDS AND LIMITED REWARDS (OPTIONAL)

We touched on this: early-bird specials (time or quantity limited lower prices) can encourage fast pledges. Limited rewards (only X available) can drive urgency or manage your capacity (like only 5 custom sketches because you only have time to draw 5). If you decide to use an **early-bird tier**, plan it now. Usually it's the same as a regular tier but maybe $5–$10 cheaper or with a small extra goodie for those who pledge in the first 48 hours or so. For example, "Early-Bird Hardcover – $45 (save $5, only through the first 2 days!)". Alternatively, you set the quantity (like the first 50 backers). If time-based, you'll just close it after 2 days. Early-birds are optional. Some creators swear by them for momentum, others skip to avoid FOMO backlash. If unsure, you can skip – plenty of campaigns fund fine without early-bird discounts.

For **limited high-tier rewards**, decide the limit number and reflect that in the tier creation. E.g., "Limit 3" on that character name tier. Limited tiers will show "0 of 3 left" when they fill, which also creates excitement.

If you do have limited tiers, consider what happens if they sell out quickly. It's a good problem (you got money!), but sometimes others want that reward too. You could potentially add another similar tier if demand is there (like one more slot or a slightly different offer). But try to set limits according to your true capacity or exclusivity promise. Don't say "limit 3" then later make it 5, that might annoy those who thought it was ultra-exclusive. Better to maybe have a second tier like "Character Name – Round 2" with maybe a slightly higher price if you really want to extend it. But that gets into campaign management tactics; initially, stick to your plan.

TEST THE FLOW

Now that you have tiers and pricing drafted, do a mental walkthrough: If I were a random backer, what choice would I make and is everything logical? You can even ask a friend to look at the tier list (when your preview page is ready) to see if they find it clear and appealing. If everyone selects the same tier in your informal poll, check if other tiers are not attractive – maybe adjust value. If folks are confused about the difference between two tiers, maybe combine or clarify. This feedback loop helps ensure your offer is solid.

Remember, you can search every previous campaign and see the most popular tiers, then use that distribution to plot your own campaign for testing.

To summarize designing your tiers: **make it easy for backers to give you more money** by offering progressively cooler stuff, and **make sure you're happy no matter which tier they choose** (because every tier yields profit and helps your goal). If you find yourself secretly hoping no one picks a certain tier because it's not great for you – either improve that tier or remove it.

You've essentially designed the blueprint of your Kickstarter storefront. This is what will make you money, so it's worth the time to get right.

You now have the skeleton of your Kickstarter offer. In the next chapter, we'll flesh it out by brainstorming all the **specific rewards and goodies** that will populate those tiers and discuss which ones truly attract backers (and which to avoid). You've built the ladder; now let's decide what shiny things to hang on each rung to entice climbing.

CHAPTER 7

CRAFT COMPELLING REWARDS

The core of your campaign is your book. That's why people are here. So, we begin by ensuring you offer your book in all the formats your readers might want. Common formats to consider:

- **Ebook:** The entry-level reward for readers who prefer digital or are international and avoid shipping. Offering the ebook is a must. Make it available in common formats. This likely goes in your lowest content tier and is included with all higher tiers by default. Ebooks cost you almost nothing to deliver (just some time to format), so it's pure value-add.
- **Paperback (Softcover Print Book):** If you have a paperback version, that hits the sweet spot for many readers who want a physical copy but don't want the expense of hardcover. Plan to offer a paperback as a reward. If this is a new book, you'll likely print via POD or short run after the campaign – budget accordingly. If it's an existing book, you might have stock or use POD per order. In any case, **signed** paperbacks are a great draw on Kickstarter. The signature (and maybe a personalized message) adds a

collectible aspect beyond a normal retail copy. Highlight that aspect: it's not just a paperback, it's a signed paperback just for them.

- **Hardcover (possibly Special Edition):** Hardcovers are premium, and many fans love them. If you can produce a hardcover, even if it's a short-run or premium POD like IngramSpark's case laminate, consider it for your higher tiers. You might also spice it up to justify the Kickstarter – e.g., a **Kickstarter-exclusive hardcover edition** with a variant cover, foil stamping, maybe interior illustrations or better paper. Something that won't be available later in stores (or at least not in the same form). This creates a collector's item and urgency to back now. Hardcovers carry higher cost, but fans often happily pay $40–$80 for a special one. If your campaign is specifically about a special edition (like an omnibus or illustrated edition), this *is* your main product. Offer the hardcover, possibly numbered or limited if that fits your strategy.

- **Audiobook:** If you have an audiobook or plan to create one, that can be a nice higher-tier or add-on item. Audiobook production is costly, so only promise it if you're prepared to produce it (maybe campaign funds contribute to it). Some campaigns use audiobooks as a stretch goal – "if we hit X, I'll produce the audiobook and all backers $25+ get it". That's an option too, but if you already have one or are confident, you could include it at a mid-tier (for example, $25 gets Ebook + Audiobook for the audio lovers). Audiobooks widen your audience (some backers only listen, not read). Delivery is digital (through BackerKit or send codes), so no shipping. It's a great bonus if feasible. Just be mindful of time; producing an audiobook can take longer than print. If this is a new element, be clear about the timeline or deliver it later to backers if needed (they'll usually understand). Alternatively, you can create an AI audiobook, which we've done a bunch of times, and people seem to like it just fine. Also, it gives you an additional proofreading pass as you listen to it.

- **Other Book Formats:** If applicable, consider things like a **graphic novel** version (if your project has one), or a **serialized email version**, or whatever unique format. Most campaigns stick to the basics: digital, paperback, hardcover, audio. But if you have something like, "collector's box set of 3 books" or "loose-leaf edition" (just making that up), that could be a special reward. Use if relevant.

For series or backlist: Are you launching book 3 of a series? Many new backers might want Books 1 and 2 as well. Consider a tier or add-on for the previous books (digital and/or print sets). If it's the full series, it's better to put [Book 1-X] than just [Book X], so people can catch up on the full experience.

You can snag bigger pledges by bundling the series. Just be sure to price and account for those extra books' costs. If you have multiple works, one popular strategy is an "ultimate library" tier – all my ebooks or all my paperbacks in one bundle. This can entice newcomers who want your whole catalog.

In summary, **cover all reader preferences**. Some only read on Kindle, some want a signed paperback for their shelf, some die for that deluxe hardcover. By offering multiple formats, you maximize your potential backer pool.

Also, offering multiple formats naturally creates an upgrade path: "Oh, you just wanted the ebook? But look, for a bit more you can get the print copy." It helps bump people up.

MERCHANDISE & SWAG: FUN EXTRAS (BUT CHOOSE WISELY)

Beyond the book, think of swag or merchandise that complements your project and would delight your fans. There's a huge range of possibilities, but let's brainstorm a few popular ones for authors:

- **Bookmarks:** Practically a no-brainer for book campaigns. Custom bookmarks are cheap to produce and very relevant (who doesn't need a bookmark?). You can design them with your cover art or characters. They're lightweight to ship (often can slip into the book). So nearly all print-backers could get a bookmark included. Cost is low (a few cents each in bulk). Just watch out. Glossy, fancy bookmarks might stick together or scratch books, but that's a very minor concern. Bookmarks are great freebies or tier sweeteners.
- **Art Prints:** If your story has cool visuals (fantasy world, characters, maps), art prints or posters can be a big draw. These could be postcard-sized up to full posters. Many authors commission an artist to create a special piece (like a map of the world, a character

lineup, an alternate cover art) and offer it as a print. Cost varies by size and paper, but 5x7 or 8x10 prints on card stock are relatively cheap (maybe $0.50-$1 each). Posters 11x17 or bigger are trickier to ship (require tubes or folding), so consider smaller prints unless you're prepared for tube shipping. Backers love artwork, especially in speculative genres (fantasy, sci-fi) or even for romance (character art). And if you do a signed art print, that's extra special. One thing that's really popular is Vellum inserts for books, especially with romance authors.

- **Stickers:** Custom vinyl stickers (of your book's logo, characters, a witty quote) are inexpensive and fun. You can throw a couple in as freebies at higher tiers. People like slapping them on laptops, etc. Just ensure the design appeals (maybe your book cover chibi-fied, or a cool symbol from the story). Stickers typically cost $0.20-$0.50 each at quantity. Easy add.

- **Enamel Pins:** Very popular in crowdfunding. If your book has an iconic symbol (a crest, a dragon, a cute monster, etc.), an enamel pin can be a coveted collectible. These cost more (typically $2-$3 each to manufacture a 1.5" pin with custom mold, depending on run size). They also add weight for shipping and some complexity (packing pins so they don't damage books). But fans absolutely adore pins – they're shiny, durable, displayable. If you think your audience is the type to enjoy fan merch, an enamel pin as a mid/high-tier bonus or add-on can drive interest. Maybe limit to one design to keep cost manageable, unless you're doing really well. I've seen campaigns where a nice pin design actually gets people to jump tiers just for the pin.

- **Posters/Maps:** If your book involves a map (common in fantasy), a folded map insert or rolled small poster is a hit. Or a series poster. People like visual immersion. Keep size moderate or plan for shipping tubes which ups cost. Alternatively, a **cloth map** or **playmat** style can be rolled with books – that's advanced but very cool (also more expensive to produce).
- **Character Cards or Stickers:** Could be art trading cards of characters, or sticker sheets. Fans of series love character art. If you have artistic skills or can hire it, a set of 5 character mini-prints or cards can be a neat reward. Not too costly if printed on card stock. They also serve as keepsakes and conversation pieces.
- **Lanyard:** You would be surprised how much people love a good lanyard, and how many people need them. Most professionals who go into an office have a badge, and so they are always looking for ways to support their unique vibe while being a cog in a machine.
- **T-Shirts/Apparel:** T-shirts are classic, but I often caution against them unless you have a sizable campaign. Why? Sizing complexity (you'll need to collect sizes, and possibly stock extras if sizes run out), higher cost ($7-$12 each unless huge volume), and shipping weight. They can still be done (some creators love doing a shirt with a catchy phrase from the book). If your brand is strong and folks would proudly wear it, go for it, but if you're not sure, this might be a headache. Consider doing it as a stretch goal or special add-on later if demand surfaces. If you do shirts, try to

use print-on-demand for fulfillment or at least get a quality vendor. Nothing worse than cheap shirts backers won't wear.

- **Mugs/Totes etc.:** These are bulky and heavy to ship, often not worth the hassle unless you have a very merch-driven audience. They also have breakage concerns (mugs). If you go this route, factor shipping separately (maybe offer them as add-ons for those willing to pay extra shipping). I'd generally say skip heavy items like mugs unless it's a stretch goal or you know a lot of local pickup fans.
- **Exclusive Content:** Not all rewards are physical! Consider **exclusive digital content** like a bonus chapter, a short story tie-in, a behind-the-scenes PDF ("Author's notes or world guide"), or even a video thank-you. These cost mainly time, not money, and can add a ton of perceived value. For example, "All backers $25+ get a bonus short story set in the world, exclusive to this Kickstarter." Or "behind-the-scenes making-of video series." Be mindful of your time, but digital exclusives are fantastic because they delight fans and cost you nothing to deliver (except the effort to create). And they make backers feel like insiders. One of my favorites is **audio commentary.** You open the book and basically do a director's cut of your book. Other people really love **annotations,** but I find them tedious. Readers love them though.
- **Personalized/Experience Rewards:** These are things like a **one-on-one Zoom call** with the author, a critique of their writing (if you offer that), a custom poem/story written for them, etc. These aren't physical items but

experiences. They can justify high tier prices because they're unique. But only promise what you're comfortable delivering. If you hate phone calls, don't offer a call. If you can write a short flash fiction about any topic, that could be a cool $300 tier reward for a few backers, something truly personal. These are best kept limited (due to your time). They can be crowdfunder gold if you have super fans who want that personal touch. Also, **name a character** in the next book is sort of in this category, called Tuckerization. It's like they pay to be part of the creation. We mentioned that earlier as a high-tier option. Doesn't cost money, just a cameo, but huge perceived value for some.

- **Collector's Box/Bundle:** If you have multiple items, sometimes the swag itself can form a special reward. For example, you might do a **Collector's Box** – a branded box containing the hardcover + all swag (bookmarks, art, pin, etc.). The box can be custom printed (costly at low volume though) or a nice craft box with a sticker. This is a flashy high-tier concept (some Kickstarters do "book boxes" now because of the trend in book subscription boxes). It's a lot of assembly though. Only attempt if you have a sizable campaign and help. It does present really well, though, in unboxing videos and social media buzz.

- **Letter(s) from the universe:** Letter writing campaigns have been very popular recently, and if you have a story that can be told in letters, you might add an upgrade (or even base a whole campaign) around sending letters "in universe" for a month or even a year. Maybe people base their whole author business on these, and I know people making seven-figures just on letter writing stories.

- **Name In Book / Acknowledgements:** We talked about this above, but I would be remiss not to mention the simplest reward, listing backers in the book's acknowledgments or on a special thank-you page. This is straightforward, costs nothing, and makes backers feel included. You can do this for all backers or a specific tier and above. Many campaigns say, "All backers $5+ will be thanked in the book." It's nice but consider volume; if thousands back, that's a lot of names – but a good problem. Usually it's fine to promise, just get a proper spelling list after. Some do only $25+ get in thanks to make it special. Up to you. If you want to differentiate, maybe a general thank-you list for regular backers and a "Super Special Thanks" section for high-tier backers. In any case, include some kind of shout-out; people love seeing their name in print.

Now, **caution**: It's easy to brainstorm a ton of swag and want to do it all. But every item is something you have to produce, possibly design, and fulfill. It can complicate logistics significantly. The key is to balance excitement vs complexity. For first campaigns or smaller operations, lean towards fewer, high-impact items rather than a million tiny things. A well-designed enamel pin might have more appeal than a bundle of five mediocre trinkets. And each item's cost adds up – remember your budget.

A good rule: *if you're a first-timer, pick maybe 3 merchandise items max* (besides the book itself). For example, decide: "I'll do a bookmark, an art print, and a sticker." That's enough to spice up the tiers without overwhelming you. If you're more experienced or have help, you can expand that list.

Also consider **minimum order quantities**. Things like pins or shirts often require ordering 50-100 minimum. If you have only 10 backers who want the pin, you still have to order 50. That's fine if you plan to use leftovers for later sales or promos but keep it in mind. Items like prints and stickers you can often print exactly the quantity needed (or small extras).

Now think: Which of these items would *your* readers actually love? Genre can guide this:

- Fantasy readers go bonkers for maps, pins of magical symbols, art of characters, maybe even custom dice or coins themed to the world.
- Sci-fi readers might dig blueprint schematics of your starship as an art print, a patch of the space fleet, etc.
- Romance readers might love character art prints, maybe a playlist or recipes (digital content can be thematic too).
- Mystery/thriller readers might not care for merch as much except maybe a cool prop replica or a dossier of clues (just brainstorming).
- Kids/YA books can have fun stickers, buttons, etc.

Always ask: **Does this reward enhance the reader's connection to the book?** If yes, it's worth considering. If it's random (like throwing in a fidget spinner with your book's logo just because), maybe skip.

Also, mind the **cost vs appeal** ratio. Some items sound cool, but few will pay extra for them. Example: keychains. You could do it, but will it draw someone to pledge more? Possibly not unless it's very unique. Focus on those with strong appeal: art, world immersion, personal touches.

One more category: **Digital rewards for higher tiers**: Some creators make things like a **digital artbook**, or a **video reading of a deleted scene**, or a **soundtrack** if they have musical talent or commissioned music. Those can add value especially for those who can't get physical items (like international backers who might stick to digital tiers to avoid shipping). Think if there's any cool digital-only perk you can add to mid/high tiers. For instance, "All backers $50+ get access to a private livestream Q&A or writing workshop". Experience again.

PERSONALIZED & EXCLUSIVE ITEMS: MONEY CAN'T (USUALLY) BUY

We touched on some in merchandise, but to reiterate, personalized and exclusive items are often the most coveted rewards. These justify premium tiers:

- **Name a Character / Cameo:** It's popular and easy to implement (just keep it reasonable: a minor character or naming a place/pet is safer than promising they'll be the protagonist). That said, I had a minor character who became a major character, and that fan was able to keep appearing in every book.

- **One-on-One Time:** A Skype/Zoom chat, an invitation to dinner if they're local or you meet at a con, a chance to be in a book club meeting with you. These interactions can mean a lot to fans.
- **Manuscript Critique or Coaching:** If your backers include fellow writers, offering a critique of their short story or a 1-hour coaching on crowdfunding or writing can be valued.
- **Physical exclusives:** E.g., a handwritten thank-you letter with doodles or a signed & sketched bookplate (if you have art skills or can get artist to do quick headshot sketches in a few copies), or a polaroid of your writing desk (hey, some super fans might find that charming!). The idea is something that feels one-of-a-kind.
- **Limited Editions:** Could be as simple as numbering the first 100 hardcovers and signing them with a special ink. Or including a piece of original art (like you have the original cover painting? One backer can buy it). I have sold lots of original art from my comics this way. Or maybe you wrote a short story by hand on nice paper. One backer can own that. Think outside the box for unique items.

These things "money can't normally buy" are where Kickstarter shines. It allows creators to offer special experiences that you can't get on Amazon or in a bookstore. They are often low-cost to you (besides time or creativity) but high value to fans.

However, only do **what fits your personality and capacity.** If you're camera shy, maybe not a Zoom call tier. If you hate drawing, don't offer sketches. Pick something you'd actually enjoy doing for a fan. If you enjoy connecting, a call or meet-up is great. If you prefer writing, offer a custom poem. If you like crafts, maybe make a one-off craft item related to your book to give at a high tier.

DON'T OVEREXTEND YOURSELF

Every item you add is something you must produce, pack, and ship. While it's tempting to throw in the kitchen sink to attract backers, too many distinct items can become a fulfillment nightmare, especially if you're doing it solo.

Some practical guidelines:

- **Limit the Variety:** If you have 10 different merch items, that's 10 different things to source/manufacture. The coordination and possibility of something going wrong multiplies. Try to reuse designs across items (e.g., same artwork on bookmark, print, sticker – then you only commission one art). And consider bundling items so not every tier has a unique combination.
- **Shipping Realities:** More items mean heavier packages, larger boxes, and more complexity in packaging. **It also means not being able to ship media mail.** Are you ready to mail tubes for posters and separate book packages? If not, maybe do folded maps that can go in the book or skip the poster. Consider items that fit easily with the books in one package. Flat items like prints and bookmarks are easy to include.

Odd shapes (mugs, figurines) may require separate handling or risk damage to books if thrown together. **Minimize fragile or bulky merch** unless you're prepared to handle it (or to charge extra shipping accordingly).

- **Suppliers and Minimums:** Do you have reliable places to get these items made? Research ahead of time. E.g., know where to print bookmarks (plenty of online print shops), where to make pins (there are known pin makers), etc. And note their turnaround times. Some items (like custom pins from overseas) might take 2 months lead time. Work that into your timeline. Don't promise you'll ship in a month if pins will arrive in three.

- **Costs and Waste:** If an item is expensive and only a few backers end up wanting it, you may regret it. Example: you offer a t-shirt at a high tier, but only 5 people choose that tier. You might still have to print 20 shirts (if that's a minimum) and handle sizes. That's wasted money and leftover stock. So either ensure items have broad appeal (so many backers will take them) or that you can produce very low quantities. A solution: some items can be offered as *add-ons* after the campaign to gauge demand. For instance, you might not have a specific tier for a t-shirt, but after funding, in the pledge manager, you ask "Want to buy a shirt for $25?" If enough choose it to meet print minimum, you proceed; if not, you cancel and refund that add-on. This is a bit advanced, but it's a strategy to reduce risk on borderline items.

- **Fulfillment Help:** If you end up with lots of merch, consider using a fulfillment service or at least recruit friends/family to help pack. It can be fun for them one afternoon to do a packing party with pizza, but if you have 500 packages to fill with 8 items each, that's a heavy lift. Keeping item count manageable ensures you can pack faster and error-free. Remember, each distinct combo is a chance to mess up an order (oops, forgot their pin!). The simpler, the fewer mistakes. Fulfillment houses used to only work with you if you had a ton of orders, but there are several set up specifically for indies now and I use a few different ones.

A note on first-time creators: *I've had campaigns where I included like 15 different items. It's doable but boy is it a ton of work.* If this is your first rodeo, you might be better served focusing on making the core product amazing (the book) and adding just a sprinkling of extras. You can always expand in future campaigns once you have experience and maybe a system.

THINK FROM THE FAN'S PERSPECTIVE

When deciding on rewards, put yourself in your fan's shoes. Ask: *If I were a big fan of this book/author/genre, what would make me squeal with excitement?* That's your north star.

For instance, if your book is a space opera and you have a fictional spaceship, maybe a schematic poster or a patch of the ship's crew insignia would tickle a fan's geeky heart. If you write cozy mysteries, maybe a cute enamel pin of the pet cat that's in your story would charm readers. If it's an epic fantasy, a beautiful map or a sword-shaped bookmark... you get the idea.

Genre and story elements give clues. For fantasy, art and maps are huge. For sci-fi, techy swag or concept art. For romance, anything that evokes emotion or connection to characters (like art prints of the couple, or maybe a playlist of their songs). For horror, perhaps a small prop or a unique packaging (I recall someone did a "blood-stained" signed page). Tailor to what *you* as a fan of your own work would love to have.

Also consider your existing readers. If you have some, what have they responded to? Do they rave about a particular character? Maybe make a reward around that character (like a chibi sticker). Did they say they want hardcover editions? That's a sign to do that.

Excitement is contagious. If you're genuinely excited about a reward item, that will show in how you present it, and backers will get excited too. Conversely, if you're only offering something because you feel you should, but you're meh on it, that might also come through. So choose items that you're **proud and happy to deliver**.

One method: come up with a big brainstorm list of all possible rewards, then circle the ones that make you go, "hell yeah, that'd be so cool!" Those likely align with what fans will think is cool. Then cross out ones that seem like more trouble than they're worth or are just filler.

Even better? If you have fans, ask them, just don't necessarily expect them to be "right." There's a difference between what they think is cool and what they will buy.

A quick mention: **Digital-only backers** – often international fans might stick to digital (to avoid shipping), but they still want some of the fun. Offering **digital equivalents** or extras can make them feel included. For instance, if you have art prints for physical, maybe offer a digital art gallery PDF for all digital backers, so they see the art. Or a printable bookmark PDF. It's not the same, but at least they get something. Also consider offering to ship merch internationally separately for additional cost as an add-on, if you have demand (some int'l might pay, others not – tricky, so usually it's easier to make digital goodies to compensate).

HOW WE TEST REWARDS

We don't guess. We launch, watch, and adapt.

When we're testing reward tiers, we're looking at **backer behavior in real time**. This means tracking *which tiers convert*, *when people back*, and *what patterns emerge over the first 48–72 hours*.

PRE-LAUNCH TESTING

Before the campaign goes live:

- **Look at previous campaigns**: What were the top 3 most-selected tiers last time? Start from there.

- **Ask your audience**: In your email list or social group, run a quick poll: "If I offered X, would you prefer A, B, or C?"
- **Use past performance as a forecast**: Did the $60 bundle dominate your last launch? Don't reinvent the wheel. Improve it.
- **Preview Page Feedback**: Send your Kickstarter preview page to 5–10 trusted readers and ask where they paused, got confused, or hesitated.

LIVE TESTING (ONCE THE CAMPAIGN LAUNCHES)

- **Watch pledge velocity**: If Tier 3 stalls while Tier 2 and Tier 4 move, that's a sign Tier 3 needs a clearer value bump or repositioning.
- **Create urgency with mid-campaign bonuses**: Add "early bird ends tonight" or "bonus art print added to all $40+ tiers this week" to test how people respond to FOMO.
- **Run an update with a new offer**: "Hey, we're adding a new $75 tier that includes all three hardcovers and the limited-edition sticker pack." Then watch what happens over 24 hours.
- **Message backers** who chose the $1 tier and ask what held them back. Sometimes you'll get product gold from their answers.
- **You can't delete a tier once somebody backs it,** but you can sunset it so that it gets buried at the end of the rewards.

POST-CAMPAIGN REVIEW

- Sort your backer report by revenue and tier.
- Highlight:
- Which tiers overperformed?
- Where did most people drop off?
- Did expensive tiers bring in the volume—or just big numbers from a few whales?

This isn't just analysis, it's planning for the *next* launch. What worked once usually works again. But don't assume anything. Use your last campaign to sharpen your next one.

Kickstarter is a laboratory. Every tier is an experiment. The good news? The results come with receipts.

To sum it up, your campaign rewards should feel like a celebration of your book. They turn a simple book launch into an experience. By carefully picking rewards that add genuine value and joy, you'll not only attract more backers but also leave them delighted they joined your journey. A delighted backer becomes a repeat backer for your future campaigns, so it's worth the effort now to wow them.

You've now got the list of what you're offering and how it fits into tiers. In the next chapter, we'll take these items and structure them into those tiers and fine-tune pricing, plus talk about making the campaign page visually appealing. But first, make sure you're satisfied that the rewards you chose are ones you can deliver and that your fans will adore. You're curating an experience here as much as selling products.

CHAPTER 8

DESIGN FOR DELIGHT

A Kickstarter campaign isn't just a list of tiers. It's a story page that convinces people to back you. Visuals play a huge role in capturing attention and conveying professionalism. Here's how to design for delight on your campaign page:

- **Campaign Header Image:** This is the banner or thumbnail that represents your project (the one people see on Kickstarter browse and at the top of your page). Make it count. It should clearly show your book or something iconic from it, plus your project title. Aim for an image that's high-quality and on-brand. I use DepositPhotos when I don't have a cover yet, or Bookbrush, or BookGraphix to build my mockups. If you have cover art, that's usually front and center. You might combine it with some text like "A New Fantasy Novel" or a tagline, in an easy-to-read font. Keep in mind thumbnails are small; clear, bold imagery works better than clutter. If you're not a designer, consider hiring one or use simple tools to put text on your cover image nicely. The header is like the cover of your campaign – it should entice and inform at a glance. If this is your first time, test a couple with your fans to pick a winner.

- **Project Video (Optional but recommended):** Kickstarter stats often show projects with videos do better. A video gives a personal touch – backers see the creator and connect. If you're comfortable, a 1-3 minute video of you introducing the project, maybe intercut with images of art or previous books, can be powerful. It doesn't need Hollywood production; authenticity and clarity matter more. If video isn't your thing, at least do a nice slideshow with voiceover. But seeing your face excited about your project can win hearts. Pro tip: caption your video (many watch without sound initially). If you absolutely don't want a video, it's not a deal-breaker, but make sure your visuals elsewhere do a lot of heavy lifting then.

- **Page Graphics for Rewards:** A huge new feature in recent Kickstarters is the ability to include **images in reward descriptions and add-ons**. You can create a graphic that shows each tier's contents visually – like an image of the book + icons of each item included, perhaps with tier name. Many creators make a nice table or infographic of their tiers for the story section. This way someone scrolling can see, for example, pictures of "Ebook" tier (just a tablet icon), "Paperback" tier (book icon + tablet icon), "Deluxe tier" (hardcover + pin + art print images, etc.). Humans process images faster than text, so this helps them quickly grok your offer. You can design these in Canva or Photoshop. It's an effort, but worth it. Kickstarter's interface also now shows images within the sidebar if you upload them to each tier, which is great. Plan to create or commission some graphics for your rewards and add-ons to make them crystal clear.

- **Use Mockups and Photos:** People love seeing what they're going to get. If you have physical proofs or previous books, photograph them nicely and include them on the page. If not, use mockup generators (there are tools where you can place your cover onto a 3D book image). Show the cover in 3D, show an interior page or illustration sample if you have. If you're offering merch like pins or art, include concept sketches or sample images. Did an artist make character art? Display it proudly. The more tangible you can make the rewards look, the more backers can imagine owning them. For example, if you have a hardcover with foil, maybe show a mockup with a shiny effect or an image of similar foil books. Visualization helps conversion.
- **Campaign Story Layout:** Organize your page with clear headings and sections. Common sections: *Introduction* (what the project is, a quick pitch), *About the Story/Book* (synopsis or background), *Rewards* (explain tiers or highlight special ones), *Add-Ons* (if using, describe how), *Stretch Goals* (if you plan any, maybe mention them or at least "more will be revealed"), *Timeline* (show key dates for production/fulfillment), *Funding Breakdown* (maybe a pie chart of where money goes, shows you're responsible), *Team* (if multiple collaborators, give credits), and *Thank You*. Use graphics for section headers or thematic imagery as separators – e.g., a graphic of a decorative line or an emblem from your

book. But keep things legible: use Kickstarter's built-in
header styles for text where needed so it's readable on
mobile (Kickstarter story pages have H1, H2 etc. – use
them for headings "The Story", "Rewards", etc., to
break up text).

- **Page Theme / Aesthetics:** Match the vibe of your
book. If it's a dark horror novel, maybe black
background images or blood-red highlights. If it's a
bright children's book, keep colors fun and images
playful. Maintain a consistent color scheme and font
choice in your images so the page looks cohesive. You
don't want 10 totally different-looking graphics from
different sources – it should feel like one branded
package. If you have a cover, you likely have a color
palette – use those colors in your headings or accent
graphics. Little things like that subconsciously elevate
the page quality.

- **Keep it Scannable:** Many backers will scroll quickly.
Use bullet lists (like for reward content, you will list
items). Keep paragraphs short and to the point (like we
aim for 2-3 sentences in a chunk). **Bold key phrases.**
People often skim, so ensure that key info (like "Free
bookmark with every paperback" or "Ships in June
2025") is easy to spot. Also, consider an FAQ at the
bottom or use Kickstarter's built-in FAQ section to
answer likely questions (like "Is the book finished?",
"Can I get previous books?", "Why Kickstarter?"). That
transparency also adds trust.

- **Mobile-Friendly:** A good chunk of users browse on the
phone. After you draft your page, preview it on a phone
screen. Make sure images aren't tiny text that's

unreadable on mobile. If you have text in images (like in those tier graphics), ensure it's big enough. Usually a 12pt font on a desktop image becomes too small on mobile if the whole image shrinks. You may need to simplify text on images or also repeat key info in text below. It's fine to have redundancy: e.g., a graphic showing tiers and then below it a text table summarizing – catch all preferences.

Remember, a polished, visually appealing page gives the impression that this project is professional and well-thought-out, making backers more comfortable to pledge. It shows you care (and if you care about presentation, likely you care about delivering quality too).

PLAN ADD-ONS TO BOOST PLEDGE SIZES

Add-ons are extra items backers can opt to buy on top of their chosen tier. Kickstarter has a built-in system for this now. Add-ons are great for offering additional goodies without complicating your tier structure. For instance, maybe you decided not to have a separate tier for "2 paperbacks" or "paperback + audiobook" – you can just let someone pick the paperback tier and then add-on the audiobook or an extra book.

Common add-ons for authors:

- **Additional copies of the book** (many backers might want one for a friend or both paperback and hardcover): You can set an add-on: "Extra paperback copy – $X" and/or "Extra hardcover – $Y". This way you don't need a specific "2 book tier"; they can build it.

- **Previous books in the series or other titles you have rights to sell:** If this is book 3 and you have stock or POD for books 1 and 2, list them as add-ons. Or if you have unrelated novels, you could offer them digitally or physically as an upsell (just ensure delivery timeline aligns – if they're ready to go, fine).
- **Merchandise as add-ons:** maybe some people at lower tiers still want the enamel pin or the art print without going to the high tier. You can list "Art print – $5" as an add-on, etc. International backers who go digital might even add some physical add-ons if they're willing to pay shipping. So this allows flexibility. That said, gauge carefully: offering every piece of merch as a separate add-on does mean you could end up fulfilling lots of little orders. Try bundling: e.g., "Swag pack: includes bookmark, sticker, and print for $10" instead of separate $3, $2, $5 items. This simplifies things (the backer either gets all swag or none).
- **Digital add-ons:** Kickstarter also allows digital add-ons. So if someone at a physical tier didn't automatically get the audiobook, they could add it. Or perhaps an extra digital short story for $2, etc. It's delivered easily via digital distribution. Usually, I include all digital to everyone anyway, but if you have distinct separate digital products (like a related novella that not everyone might want), you can upsell it.

Just note, **digital backers only see digital add-ons, while physical backers see all add-ons**. If you have a bunch of options, you can add a "build your own bundle" tier for $10 (or whatever shipping will be), and then let people build their own bundle, while keeping the reward tiers clean. Just make sure to set it for physical, not digital rewards.

Plan logistics for add-ons: Each add-on item you offer, ensure you have inventory or can produce to meet unknown demand. For example, if you allow unlimited extra hardcover add-ons, in theory you might need to print a lot more if many choose. That's okay as long as you know and can afford it (since they paid for it). But consider constraints: do you want to allow an add-on that could be very popular but difficult to fulfill in large quantity? E.g., offering personal sketches as a $20 add-on unlimited – that could backfire if 100 people buy it. You'd have to draw 100 sketches unexpectedly. So, only allow add-ons of items that are straightforward to fulfill in quantity or that you set a stock limit for (Kickstarter add-ons can have quantity limit too). Usually physical products like extra books or pins are fine to produce more of if the demand is high, just watch the timeline.

Also, **shipping for add-ons**: Make sure not to forget shipping costs. While you will likely use the same box for all rewards, if somebody gets 10 books, then you might have to seriously rethink your shipping and pricing. Take all that into account.

Communicate add-ons clearly on the page: Many backers may not be familiar. Often campaign pages have a section: "Add-Ons: After choosing a tier, you'll have an opportunity to add these extra items...here's how." Show pictures of add-on items, with prices. e.g., an image of your other book covers with "Previous books – $10 each" or a mockup of the swag pack. Make it enticing and clear. Backers then know they can mix and match a bit.

Add-ons are like a mini menu of extras. They can significantly increase your average pledge if done right because people who already decided to back might say "Ooh, I'll throw in an extra $15 for that cool pin and extra ebook."

From a creator standpoint, they are also a way to offer items that you didn't want to include in every high tier but still want to make available (like not everyone might want a t-shirt, but those who do can get it via add-on). This prevents forcing things into tiers that some backers don't care for.

Just be sure you don't rely on add-ons for your core funding goal. They are a bonus. Design tiers such that even without add-ons, you'd meet the goal. Add-ons then hopefully push you beyond.

STREAMLINE FULFILLMENT FOR DELIVERY EASE

The campaign's success isn't just measured in dollars, but in delivering on promises. **Happy backers = future supporters,** and you being not burned out = willingness to do this again. So let's talk fulfilling efficiently:

- **Lock in Your Fulfillment Plan Early:** As you set up rewards, you should already have an idea how you'll deliver each. For books, have you chosen a printer? If doing POD like KDP or Ingram for some, or offset printing for a large run? Know the timelines. For merch, which vendors? Perhaps order samples during the campaign to check quality. After the campaign, you'll likely use a pledge manager (like BackerKit or Kickstarter's own surveys) to collect addresses and let late pledges if any. Research those tools now so you're not scrambling. Many creators love BackerKit as it helps manage add-ons and shipping well (though it costs money). Others use Kickstarter's built-in system if the campaign is small/simple. Decide what you'll use. Knowing this helps you inform backers and streamline the process.

- **Batch Your Workflow:** Plan to fulfill in stages. E.g., week 1 after funds: finalize surveys, week 2: order all books/merch, weeks 3-4: wait for production (meanwhile finalize digital rewards), month 2: receive stuff, month 2-3: sign/pack, etc. When packing, batch tasks – sign all books one day, fold all posters next, assemble boxes in advance, etc. Have a dedicated space for fulfillment (your dining table? garage?). It's easier when organized.

- **Prep Shipping Materials Early:** Order your mailers, boxes, labels, tape in advance so you're ready when items arrive. For books, flat mailers or bubble envelopes? Know what fits what (e.g., hardcover might need a box instead of envelope to be safe). Buying in bulk saves money. Don't skimp on packaging. A damaged book due to thin envelopes is no fun. But also don't overspend on fancy boxes unless your brand warrants it. Plain sturdy mailers work.

- **Consider hiring help or fulfillment service:** If you ended up with hundreds of backers beyond expectation, consider bringing in a pro. There are companies that handle shipping for you. They charge but might be worth it if volume is high and you value your time. Alternatively, recruit friends/family for the packing party as mentioned. Many hands make light work, and you can make it fun. I personally find some zen in packing (authors often say it's meditative), but doing 500 solo is a lot. So plan accordingly.
- **International Backers:** Plan how you handle these. Shipping from the US (if you're in the US) abroad is expensive and sometimes unreliable. Some creators choose to restrict some pledge levels to certain countries or charge higher shipping (which you should). If you have a significant international audience, consider using fulfillment partners in regions (like printing books in the UK for EU backers to avoid customs). That's complex and usually only done for big campaigns. At least be upfront with international folks about shipping cost and that customs/VAT may apply. Better to have a few informed, willing international backers than many surprised unhappy ones. I recommend using PirateShip's simple export rate, as it's less than half of other options on the market or was last time I checked.
- **Keep Backers Updated:** A huge part of smooth delivery is communication. Sharing timeline with backers sets expectations. If the timeline slips, let them know early and honestly. Backers are generally cool with delays if informed and if they see progress. The

worst is silence. So, plan to send updates at key points (e.g., "Books have been ordered from printer!", "Swag arrived, look at the photos", "Shipping begins next week!"). This not only reassures them but also makes them part of the journey – which they enjoy.

- **Address Collection & Verification:** Use surveys to get addresses and any info (like name spelling for thank-you page, T-shirt sizes if you do shirts, etc.). Then *double-check* addresses, especially expensive shipments. There are tools or pledge managers that validate addresses. It saves returned packages. Before shipping, maybe send a "last call to update address" update (people move, or input wrong initially). This can save headaches.
- **Trial Run:** If you can, do a test pack of a full tier. Assemble one full package with all items, weigh it, see how it fits, how you'll label it. This can reveal issues (like "oh the print is slightly too large for this box" or "with the pin and book together, better put the pin in a small bag so it doesn't scratch the book"). Solve these before doing 200 of them.
- **Keep it Fun and Personal:** While efficiency is key, remember each package is a touchpoint with a fan. Some authors add a small personal touch like a little thank you note or doodle on the package. Only do this if feasible (doing 500 handwritten notes might kill you). But maybe you print a generic thank-you postcard and just sign it for each. That's scalable. Little touches can turn a one-time backer into a lifelong superfan. When I was less chronically ill, I found packing meditative and fulfilling because it's a tangible accomplishment. I

viewed it as part of the relationship building, not just a chore. That shift in mindset can make it a more positive experience.

- **Expect the Unexpected:** Something will likely go awry, whether a vendor delays, or you miscounted and need extra books, or postage rates suddenly change. That's where your contingency planning and mindset come in. You padded the budget; you gave yourself a timeline cushion. Use those buffers as needed. If something truly outside control happens (like a global pandemic lockdown), communicate honestly and adapt. Most backers are understanding if kept in loop.

Remember, **fulfillment is the endgame**. The campaign isn't a success until every backer has their reward and is happy. Planning for it now ensures that when you get to that stage, it'll go as smoothly as possible, and you won't be overwhelmed or caught off guard.

Hopefully by now, you have your introduction and mindset solid, your foundation planned (goals, budget, timeline), your offer structured (tiers and rewards), and the extra pieces (visuals, add-ons, fulfillment) ready.

The next steps are for executing: building that campaign page, pressing launch, and then running the campaign day-to-day (marketing it, updating backers, etc.). Those topics (like how to hustle during the live campaign, handle mid-campaign lulls, push in final days, etc.) would be beyond this initial scope but are crucial. When you reach that stage, remember all the prep you did. Trust your plan but stay flexible.

Remember to design your campaign experience with the end in mind, a delighted backer opening a package and feeling it was worth every penny. If you keep that vision at the forefront, you'll make decisions that lead to an excellent campaign and fulfillment. And that is the best marketing for your next launch. Happy backers become evangelists for you.

CHAPTER 9

HOOK THEM FAST

Before a visitor even *scrolls* your Story page, Kickstarter shows four things in search-browse results: the project title, your headline, the thumbnail image, and, if you have one, the run-time of your video. Nail these four and you'll win more clicks, higher browse-rank, and better Kickstarter SEO. We talked about the main image above and will talk about the video below, but let's talk about the other two now.

AN SEO-FRIENDLY HEADLINE

The single most influential line of text on your entire Kickstarter page is the hyperlink that appears in every share card, every search-browse bar, and every mobile notification: **your project title**. Kickstarter's discovery engine scrapes that line for context clues before it decides whether to slot you beside the hottest fantasy novel or bury you on page five of "Other Projects." Search-friendly readers skim it just as ruthlessly. If the words aren't specific, the click never happens, and your beautiful campaign lies unseen.

Think of the title as a compact slug line that must satisfy three masters at once:

1. **Kickstarter's category algorithm,** which indexes the first few words most heavily.
2. **Google's crawler,** which pulls the full string into its preview snippet.
3. **A scrolling human thumb,** which grants you maybe 1.2 seconds of attention.

To land that click you need a hierarchy of information that reads like a miniature sales pitch. Here's how that hierarchy works in a single line.

1. LEAD WITH THE PRIMARY KEYWORD (GENRE + HOOK)

There are two schools of thought here. One is that you should put your title first and your SEO second. The other is to do the SEO bit first, then the title second. There is no doubt that you need both things, though.

The wisdom is that something like "Epic Fantasy Dragon-Heist Hardcover" front-loads the most searchable, most clickable phrases right where the bots, and fantasy diehards, expect them, but I'm not sure it matters much either way. What matters most is that you have both. For our purposes, let's build it with the SEO first and the title second.

- **Weak:** *Chronicles: A Novel*
- **Strong:** *Dragon-Heist Epic Fantasy Hardcover – Chronicles of Solar Fire*

Notice how the potent terms **dragon, fantasy, hardcover** punch first, and the series title rides shotgun.

2. FOLLOW WITH SERIES OR EDITION BRANDING

Once you've grabbed algorithmic relevance, layer in the flavor text that matters to *existing* fans. That might be a familiar property name (*Chronicles of Solar Fire*), a season (*10-Year Anniversary Edition*), or a volume tag (*Book Three*). Doing so tells past readers, "Yes, this is the universe you love," while newcomers have already been caught by the genre hook.

3. END WITH AN OPTIONAL KICKSTARTER-SPECIFIC LURE

If you still have room—you only have 60 characters total—drop in the most seductive production promise: *Foil Edition, Metal Variants, Signed Deluxe Hardcover, Collector's Box*. This signals that what you're offering cannot be replicated at retail.

Put those layers together and your title does triple duty:

Dragon-Heist Epic Fantasy Hardcover — Chronicles of Solar Fire (Foil Edition)

- It signals to the **algorithm** exactly which audience bucket you belong in.
- It tells **Google** that you're offering a premium physical edition (searchers type "Dragon hardcover edition" surprisingly often).

- It whispers to **fans** that this is a celebratory collector piece, not a plain reprint.

Aim for 45–60 characters. That range reads cleanly on Kickstarter's mobile cards, slides neatly into a Twitter preview, and still leaves enough space to breathe. Use en-dashes or em-dashes to separate clauses; they visually cue the reader that each chunk is discrete, digestible information. Avoid wasted filler like "The Amazing Tale of…"—every character either wins a click or gets trimmed.

MICRO-EDITING CHECKLIST BEFORE YOU CLICK "SAVE"

1. **Does the very first noun–adjective pair scream my genre?** ("Dragon-Heist Fantasy," "Retro Space-Opera," "Cozy Witch Mystery").
2. **Can a total stranger tell if this is an ebook, paperback, or deluxe hardcover?**
3. **Does it sound like a headline or a filing-cabinet label?** Rewrite until it sings.

Nail those questions and your project jumps several rungs in organic discovery before you even start paying for ads or cross-promos. Your tagline, header image, and video can now lean into emotion and visuals because the title has already done the heavy lifting of *findability*.

WRITING A TAGLINE THAT CLICKS, STICKS, AND SELLS

If your project title is the neon sign that stops traffic, the **tagline** is the hushed elevator pitch that seals the deal during the six-second ride to your Kickstarter page. It lives directly under the blue title link on desktop, appears in every social preview, and becomes the first full sentence Google lifts into its meta description. Done well, it compresses *genre, premise,* and a *promise of value* into a single breathless line that makes browsers think, *"Ooh— tell me more."*

Think of a perfect tagline as a three-ingredient cocktail:

1. **A vivid snapshot of the core hook** (what makes *this* book irresistible).
2. **A targeted genre cue or keyword** (to confirm fit and feed the algorithm).
3. **A reader-centric benefit** (why backing now matters).

Let's unpack those ingredients in action:

- **Example (bland):** *A steampunk adventure with dragons and daring explorers.*
- **Example (magnetic):** *Two estranged sisters steal a dragon-powered airship to break a blood-oath curse.*

1. LEAD WITH A CINEMATIC IMAGE

Open on the single most cinematic moment in the story. Something a reader can *picture* instantly. In the strong example above, we see sisters hijacking a dragon-powered airship. That visual frames both the stakes and the novelty in fewer than a dozen words.

Ask yourself: *If Netflix bought my book tomorrow, what would be the trailer's opening shot?* Use that shot as your tagline's first clause.

2. THREAD IN GENRE-PROOF KEYWORDS

Next, embed one or two unmistakable genre anchors. These aren't random buzzwords. They're the labels your ideal reader actually types into a Kindle search bar: **cozy witch mystery**, **grimdark epic**, **cyberpunk heist**. Slip them in naturally. Never as a list, always as narrative texture:

*"In this **cozy witch mystery**, a garden-store owner must outsmart a talking raven and a vengeful ghost..."*

Kickstarter's internal search engine catches those phrases, and so does Google. You've simultaneously courted the algorithm and signaled to genre diehards that they've found home turf.

3. CLOSE WITH A PROMISE OF VALUE

End the sentence by telling the prospective backer *why pledging now* is better than waiting for a retail release. That incentive could be format exclusivity, early delivery, a bundle of extras—anything that makes "Kickstarter" translate to "special."

"...all wrapped in a limited, edge-sprayed hardcover available only to backers."
"...plus every pledge unlocks a free digital art-book companion."
"...shipped six months before the bookstore edition hits shelves."

The promise transforms curiosity into urgency. You only have 130 characters, though. So you have to do this all in very little space.

A REPEATABLE FORMULA

[Cinematic visual hook] + [precise genre keyword or comp] + [Kickstarter-only payoff].

*"An immortal librarian races clockwork assassins through a crumbling sky-city—perfect for fans of **Mistborn**, in a numbered leather edition you'll never find on Amazon."*

That thirty-word sentence checks every box:

- action-packed visual (immortal librarian vs. clockwork assassins)
- genre keyword (sky-city hints at steampunk fantasy)
- comp title for instant point-of-reference (Mistborn)
- exclusivity (numbered leather edition, not on Amazon)

Read it aloud. If it excites you, odds are it will excite strangers scrolling past at midnight.

MICRO-EDITING CHECKLIST

1. **Trim passive verbs**—use *steals, hunts, races,* never "is about."
2. **Limit to ~30 words**; anything longer gets truncated in many share cards.
3. **Front-load the wildest noun** (dragon-powered airship > mysterious vessel).
4. **Avoid inside-baseball lore names**; no one cares that it's "The Skywolf Splinter" unless they already read the book.
5. **Read it as a tweet**—would you click RT? If not, punch harder.

THE THREE QUESTIONS

Before a single tagline or splash image, start your Story section by asking readers **three ultra-specific, one-line questions** that almost guarantee a string of silent yeses. The aim is to force an immediate mental handshake between your ideal backer and the project:

• *Do you crave epic fantasy laced with forbidden dragon-fire magic?*
• *Have you been waiting for a heroine who outsmarts gods instead of marrying them?*
• *Ready to hold a limited, foil-stamped hardcover that will never hit big-box stores?*

If a visitor internally answers "yes… yes… yes…," they're primed—emotionally and cognitively—to keep reading. Psychologists call this the "foot-in-the-door" sequence: tiny commitments pave the way for the larger one (your pledge). Choose questions that:

1. **Echo the book's core fantasy or promise.**
2. **Signal scarcity or exclusivity** (Kickstarter-only angles).
3. **Invite ownership** ("ready to hold," "want to be first," "eager to claim").

Keep each query under ten words. They should read like a volley of friendly jabs, not an interrogation. Visually, place them in large type with generous line spacing so mobile users see all three before scrolling.

SIGNAL YOUR AUDIENCE

Right after your three questions, include a sentence that essentially says: **"If you're a fan of X, Y, and Z, then this book is for you."** Fill in X, Y, Z with references your target readers will recognize – comparable authors, popular tropes, or genre touchstones. This acts as a dog whistle for your ideal backer:

- **Example:** *"If you love witty witches, slow-burn romance, and misty coastal towns with secrets, then **Luna's Last Secret** will be your next favorite read."* In one sentence, this signals the genre (paranormal romance with witches), the tone (witty, slow-burn, mysterious), and the setting (misty coastal town). Readers who adore those elements will perk up and think *"Hey, that's my kind of story!"* Those who aren't into it will scroll on—and that's okay. You want the **right** people hooked, not just anyone.
- **Be specific over generic:** Saying "if you like fantasy books" is too broad. Instead, call out the unique mix that defines your book. Think of popular works your audience loves: "If you're into *The Expanse* and *Blade Runner*, check this out" immediately conveys a space opera meets cyberpunk vibe. Don't worry about scaring some folks off; a campaign that tries to please everyone often convinces no one.

AN OPT-IN SAMPLE

One of the best things about Kickstarter is that it can bring a ton of new people into your ecosystem…but they might not all be ready to buy. Because of this, I usually like to have an opt-in to a sample story or something they can download and read. I will say something like *"Click here to get the first 10 chapters,"* or something similar, and I'll often put that right at the top of my Kickstarter page above anything else.

Some campaigns can get hundreds of new subscribers, even if they don't raise that much money.

CRAFT A COMPELLING OPENING BLURB

Now that you've hooked them with a tagline and signaled the target audience, follow up with a short **blurb** that expands on what the book is and why it's special.

Many authors dread writing blurbs, often spending weeks or months agonizing over them or procrastinating entirely. The key to overcoming this paralysis is understanding what a blurb is - and more importantly, what it isn't. A blurb is not a summary of your story; ***it's an emotional hook designed to make readers desperate to know more.***

Writing an effective blurb can feel overwhelming, but having multiple approaches in your toolkit makes the task more manageable. Let's explore ***three distinct methods*** for crafting blurbs that grab readers' attention and drive sales.

The Story Core Method approach, developed by Libbie Hawker, breaks your story down to its essential elements:

1. Identify your main character
2. Define what they want
3. Establish what prevents them from getting it

4. Show how they struggle against this force
5. Hint at whether they succeed or fail

Using *The Matrix* as an example: "Neo, a computer programmer, wants to understand the truth about reality. The machines controlling humanity prevent him from breaking free. When a mysterious group offers him the chance to see the truth, Neo must risk everything to fight against the system - if he can survive becoming humanity's last hope."

This method works particularly well for character-driven stories where the protagonist's journey is central to the narrative.

The ***Three-Hook Structure*** approach uses a series of escalating hooks followed by deeper context:

1. Open with three ultra-short descriptions (3-6 words each)
2. Follow with 1-2 paragraphs expanding on the core conflict
3. Include who will love the book
4. End with a call to action

For *The Matrix*: "Reality is a lie. Humanity sleeps in chains. One man can wake us all.

Thomas Anderson has always sensed something was wrong with his world. When he discovers humanity is trapped in a vast computer simulation, he must become more than human to set them free.

If you love reality-bending action, profound philosophical questions, and heroes discovering their true potential, this book is perfect for you.

Get it now."

The ***Machine Gun Method*** uses a rapid-fire combination of setting, emotion, and character: [Setting] + [Verb/Emotion] + [Character] + [Description] [Second Character] + [Description] + [Stakes] [Three Questions]

For *The Matrix*: "A simulated world. Controlled. A hacker discovering everything he knows is a lie. A mysterious rebellion. Fighting impossible odds. With humanity's freedom hanging in the balance. Can he accept the unbearable truth? Will he become something more than human? Is he truly The One?"

Each method serves different types of stories better:

- The Story Core works best for character-focused narratives
- The Three-Hook Structure excels for high-concept or genre fiction
- The Machine Gun Method shines with action-packed or thriller-style stories

Consider writing your blurb using all three methods and seeing which resonates most strongly with your story. ***Sometimes, you might even combine elements from different approaches.*** For instance, you might use the Machine Gun Method's setting introduction, followed by the Story Core's character focus, and end with the Three-Hook Structure's target audience statement.

Remember the core principles that apply *regardless* of method:

- Keep it between 100-250 words
- Focus on emotional connection over plot summary
- Leave questions unanswered to create intrigue
- Speak directly to your target audience

The best way to master blurb writing is to practice all three methods. Try rewriting your favorite books' blurbs using each approach. This exercise helps you understand how different structures can highlight different aspects of the same story.

BUILDING EXCITEMENT

Now that you've got the hooky stuff out of the way, we need to cover the basics while amping up excitement:

- **What is the project?** State the format, genre, and a one-liner of the plot. *"**The Sunken Kingdom** is a 400-page epic fantasy novel that blends African mythology with a modern treasure hunt. When two estranged sisters inherit a cursed map, they must team up to break an ancient spell—or doom their world."* Here we give the scope (400-page epic fantasy), the flavor (African mythology + treasure hunt), and the core conflict (sisters on a quest to break a curse).
- **Why Kickstarter / what's special?** After the plot tease, immediately tie in what makes this campaign exciting. *"This Kickstarter will fund a gorgeous, illustrated hardcover with full-color maps and artwork to truly bring this world to life."* See how that works?

We moved from the story to the project's purpose. You want backers to think, *"Not only does the story sound cool, but this campaign offers something unique I can't get elsewhere."* Maybe you're funding a **limited edition**, an audiobook production, or a spinoff that only exists if the campaign succeeds – say that here.

- **Keep it concise and vivid:** In a few sentences, convey the essence of the story and the campaign's goal. Show your passion – let them feel that this is a labor of love, not just a product. Avoid vague hype like "This will be the best book ever." Instead, use concrete imagery and specifics so they can *picture* what they're backing. If you have series information (e.g. "first in a new series" or "a standalone tale"), you can mention it in passing to set expectations.

By the end of this blurb, a visitor should understand: *What* you're making (book type, genre, plot teaser), *why* you're making it on Kickstarter (the special things like artwork, edition, or community involvement), and *why they should be excited*.

CONVEY URGENCY AND EXCLUSIVITY UP FRONT

Remember, Kickstarter campaigns are limited-time offers. You need to instill a bit of **urgency** — the sense that *"this is a one-time opportunity, don't miss out."* In your intro section (either at the tail end of the blurb or right after it), hint at why backing *now* is better than waiting for a retail release:

- **Kickstarter-only perks:** If your book or edition won't be available later (or will cost more later), say so. Phrases like *"By backing now, you'll get the book months before it's available anywhere else, plus exclusive extras only for Kickstarter backers,"* or *"This limited hardcover won't be sold on Amazon – it's exclusive to this campaign,"* do wonders. Scarcity and exclusivity encourage readers to act rather than procrastinate.
- **Personal stakes:** If this project is deeply personal or a "passion project," share that sentiment. *"This book is my love letter to the folklore of my ancestors, and I'm thrilled to share it directly with readers through Kickstarter,"* for example, adds authenticity. People back creators who are genuinely passionate. Let your enthusiasm shine through in these lines – it's infectious.
- **Deadline reminders:** Even subtle mentions like "Join us in this 30-day journey" or "Only until [Campaign End Date]" can remind readers that there's a ticking clock. You don't need to plaster "Only X days left!" at the top (Kickstarter's interface already shows a countdown) but weaving in a reminder that *now* is the time helps prevent the "I'll come back later" syndrome.

TOP-SECTION VISUALS: MAKE A GREAT FIRST IMPRESSION

While this chapter focuses on text, note that the **visuals** at the top of your page carry equal weight. Many visitors will first notice the images before they read a word. Ensure the area "above the fold" (what's visible without scrolling) is visually engaging and relevant:

- **Show your book's cover or a key graphic prominently.** If you have cover art ready, display it near the top. A striking cover can stop a scroller in their tracks. It should be high-quality, clear, and set the tone (no tiny thumbnail—make it large enough to see details).
- **Banner or header image:** Some campaigns use a branded banner image across the top. This can include the title, tagline, and an eye-catching background. Just make sure it's not so tall that it pushes important text off the top.
- **Complement text with visuals:** If your tagline mentions "cursed coins and sisters on a quest," having the cover or an illustration that hints at that (e.g., two characters with a magical map) reinforces the story. Consistency between what they see and what they read makes the hook more powerful.
- **Keep it polished:** Blurry or pixelated images will hurt you here. It's worth investing in decent graphic design for the top section. First impressions form in seconds.

By the time someone has read your tagline, audience call-out, and intro blurb, and glanced at your top images, they should be *hooked*. If they're your target reader, they'll be nodding along, intrigued and ready to scroll for details. That's the goal of the above-the-fold content: to convince the right people that *"This is the story you've been waiting for, and this campaign is the event you can't miss."*

CHAPTER 10

STORY THAT CONVERTS

Now that you've pulled people in with an enticing opening, it's time to answer their burning questions and convert their interest into support. The middle of your page should do these things: inform, excite, and reassure. Let's break down the crucial components.

PROVIDE BOOK DETAILS AND SPECS

Once you've hooked them, ensure you cover the **practical details** about the book itself. The kind of information readers want to know before they commit money:

- **Book specifications:** Tell them the planned format, length, and any notable features. Is it a paperback, hardcover, or ebook (or all three)? How many pages (or word count, if pages aren't set)? Are there illustrations, maps, or special formatting? For example: *"The hardcover will be 6x9 inches, approx. 400 pages on archival-quality paper, with a custom foiled dust jacket."* Specifics like this paint a picture of the final product.

- **Completion status:** Let backers know how far along the project is. Is the manuscript finished, edited, in progress? This is crucial for credibility. A backer is more likely to pledge if they know the novel is 100% written and just awaiting printing, versus only a rough draft done. Be honest but reassuring: *"The novel is fully written and currently in its second round of editing. Interior illustrations are 50% complete. We're on track to send to print immediately after the campaign."* If you haven't finished writing, you can still earn trust by outlining your plan: *"The first draft is done; I've scheduled the editor for July and the cover artist is booked for August,"* etc. Show that you have a handle on the timeline.

- **What the funds cover:** Though you'll detail budget transparency later, it's good to give a quick summary of why you need funding. *"Your pledges will go toward hiring the cover artist, printing a high-quality hardcover, and shipping these books to you."* Readers get that books cost money to produce; highlighting the main expenses justifies your goal and shows you're business-minded. (A more detailed breakdown can live in the FAQ or risks section later, but a one-liner here is effective.)

Presenting these specifics serves two purposes: it **informs** backers exactly what they're signing up for, and it **builds trust** by demonstrating professionalism. You're showing that you've thought through the production of your book.

If you have a lot of specs or features, consider using a bullet list or a small table/chart on the page for clarity (for instance, a list of "What's included in the Deluxe Edition: 400 pages, ribbon bookmark, 10 interior illustrations," etc.). Clarity is king. Don't make people hunt for basic info about your book.

EXPAND ON THE PROJECT STORY

Every Kickstarter project has a narrative beyond the book's plot. This is where you share **why you're doing this project** and why it's exciting for both you and the backer. Essentially: *"Here's the story of this project, and why you should be a part of it."*

- **Project background/inspiration:** Briefly tell the origin story of this book or project. Did the idea come to you during a unique moment? Are you fulfilling a childhood dream of creating a deluxe edition? For example, *"I wrote The Sunken Kingdom over 5 years and poured my soul into it. After hearing readers ask for a hardcover edition, I knew I had to create something truly special."* This gives a personal touch and shows your passion.
- **Why crowdfunding?** Explain why you're on Kickstarter instead of (or in addition to) traditional routes. *"I chose Kickstarter because it lets me include fans in the journey from the start – and produce editions and goodies that wouldn't be possible otherwise."* Perhaps you want to do a beautiful, illustrated print run that needs upfront funding, or you want to gauge interest for a niche genre. Spell it out. People respect transparency, and it can convert a

skeptic into a supporter when they understand your motivations.

- **Highlight the unique value:** Emphasize what backers get by joining you. *"Backers will not only get the first-ever hardcover, but also exclusive behind-the-scenes updates, their name in the acknowledgments, and the satisfaction of helping bring this world to life."* Make them feel like *partners* in the creation, not just customers. This emotional investment is key to converting readers into backers.

Through this narrative, you're answering the question: *"Why should I, the reader, care about this project's success?"* A compelling story that goes beyond *"I wrote a book, please fund it"* gives depth to your campaign and helps backers feel connected to you and your mission.

SHOWCASE YOUR CREDIBILITY

Credibility converts. By this point, a backer knows what you're making and why. Now they need to trust that *you can deliver*. In the mid-page content (or woven into the story), include a section that boosts your credibility:

- **About you (briefly):** Include a short bio or credentials note. One to two sentences can suffice. *"I'm a USA Today bestselling author with five novels published in urban fantasy,"* or *"I've successfully fulfilled two previous Kickstarters for comic anthologies, so I know how to deliver on my promises."* Don't be shy—this isn't bragging, it's reassurance. If you're a first-time creator with fewer credentials, focus on your commitment: *"I've spent 10 years honing this story and teamed up with industry veterans to make this book a reality."* The key is to show you're serious about your craft.

- **Track record:** If you have prior successes, mention them. This is where I highlight my own track record in his campaigns. I'll note something like, *"This is my 19th crowdfunding project. My previous campaigns have all delivered rewards to over a thousand backers."* Such statements immediately put backers at ease – they know *this isn't your first rodeo.* Even if you're not a veteran, maybe you can highlight related experience: *"As a project manager by day, I'm no stranger to coordinating complex tasks and meeting deadlines – skills that will ensure this book ships on time."* It all builds confidence.

- **Social proof or accolades:** If your book or writing has any accolades (awards, notable reviews, a popular blog, etc.), or if you have well-known contributors (foreword by a famous author, cover art by a known artist), drop that in. *"Early beta readers have called this 'Pirates of the Caribbean meets Black Panther' – which is exactly the vibe I was aiming for!"* If an author or influencer has praised your work, a short quote can be gold (make sure you have permission to use it). For example, one sentence testimonial: *"'An adventure packed with magic and heart' – Jane Doe, author of XYZ."* Such proof points can tip fence-sitters into believing your story will be worth it.

Sprinkle these credibility elements judiciously. They can be a standalone section (like "About the Author" or "Why

You Can Trust Me") or integrated into the narrative ("After delivering two successful comic anthologies that each raised over $25,000 on Kickstarter, I learned a ton about printing and fulfillment – this new project will benefit from that experience"). The goal is to silently answer the question in a backer's mind: *"Can they really pull this off?"* The answer you're delivering is *"Yes, and here's why."*

OUTLINE OPTIONS CLEARLY

While Part II covered designing an attractive reward structure, on your campaign page you need to **present the rewards in an easy-to-digest way**. Many potential backers will scroll looking for "What do I get for backing?" If this info is hard to find or confusing, you might lose them. Mid-page is a good place to summarize:

Reward overview section: Consider adding a section titled "Rewards" or "Pledge Levels" where you list the core tiers and what's included. This can be a simplified list or graphic. For example:

- **$10 – Ebook Edition:** Ebook (PDF/EPUB) + name in backer thank-you page.
- **$25 – Paperback:** Signed paperback + Ebook + name in thank-you.
- **$50 – Deluxe Hardcover:** Signed hardcover + all of the above + limited art print.

And so on. Keep each description brief here; full details will be in the sidebar where Kickstarter normally lists rewards, but duplicating highlights on the page ensures nobody misses it.

- **Use visuals if possible:** A popular technique is to include a **reward bundle graphic** – an image that shows a spread of all items in a tier. For instance, an image of the hardcover, plus the art print, plus a bookmark, neatly arranged with labels. This visual makes it immediately clear what's in the box.
- **Emphasize the value:** In text, you can call out any particularly great deals. *"Best Value: The $50 tier gets you over $70 worth of books & merchandise – a huge discount for backers only."* Don't overdo marketing speak, but if a tier is a sweet spot, point people to it.

The reward summary not only informs backers but can entice them to upgrade their pledge. Someone might have come in thinking "I'll just grab the ebook," but when they see the $25 paperback also gives them a signed copy and swag, they might go for that instead. Make it easy for them to justify a higher pledge by being clear and compelling about rewards.

Honestly, this is less important if you can make the reward images look great, but I still like to pull out any special tiers and rewards that people can scroll quickly.

STRETCH GOALS

If you plan to use **stretch goals** or other campaign enhancements (those were discussed in Chapter 6), you might mention them briefly on the page once you've hit the initial basics. It's not mandatory to include stretch goals in the initial page content. Some creators add them later via updates. But if you do mention them:

- **Tease future excitement:** *"We have some fun stretch goals planned – like bonus artwork and an audiobook edition – to unlock as we surpass our goal. Stay tuned!"* This tells backers that the campaign can become even more exciting after funding.
- **Don't overshadow the main goal:** Keep the focus on the primary product. Stretch goal info should be secondary. A simple list or graphic of stretch goal milestones (with locked/unlocked icons) works if you have it ready. But avoid promising too much too early; only list what you're confident you can deliver.
- **Campaign updates:** You can note that you'll keep backers posted: *"We'll be posting regular updates throughout the campaign, revealing new bonuses and behind-the-scenes content as we go."* This gives a sense of an active, engaging campaign (backers love feeling like things are happening).

My rule is that even if I have stretch goals planned, I don't announce them until after the campaign is at least on day 3. This allows me to see the velocity of the campaign, and adjust any goals based on how the campaign is funding.

While you're designing them, note that you should have two types: one reliant on backer number and the other on funding goal. This will always give you an attainable number to hit without excitement ever waning because the next goal is so far away.

WEEKLY AND DAILY PERKS

Stretch goals can be nice tentpole moments for a campaign, but the *fabric* that keeps the whole circus lively is a steady trickle of daily or weekly perks. Think of them as micro-rewards or content drops that fire between major funding thresholds. They cost almost nothing, yet they keep your update feed buzzing and your backers checking in "just to see what today's bonus is."

Daily perks are tiny, self-contained treats you reveal whenever your campaign is either sagging and needs a burst of excitement or is going gangbusters and you want to continue momentum. Maybe a downloadable phone wallpaper, a character sketch, a short audio reading, a blooper reel, a Spotify writing playlist. They're a reason to ping your people and give them something cool for acting right now.

Weekly perks are slightly beefier: maybe a 5-page side-story PDF, a behind-the-scenes video tour of your writing cave, or a live AMA on Friday night. None of these require a funding threshold; they're scheduled in advance to maintain momentum regardless of where the total sits. By having them, you always have a reason to reach out to your audience to either open or close perks.

Stretch goals create **vertical** excitement (big spikes tied to funding). Perks create **horizontal** excitement (a consistent hum of daily engagement). When used together:

1. **Stretch goals set the macro narrative**: "Help us unlock the audiobook at $25 K."

2. **Perks set the micro rhythm**: "Day 6 bonus: printable map of the Sky-City."

Backers feel something is *always* happening, even during the inevitable mid-campaign plateau.

PRACTICAL GUIDELINES

- **Front-load low-effort perks.** Early days are hectic; schedule digital goodies that require zero extra production (e.g., desktop wallpaper).
- **Escalate before weekends.** Thursday or Friday drops can reignite social chatter right as weekend browsing kicks in.
- **Tie perks to engagement, not money.** Example: "If yesterday's update gets 50 comments, tomorrow I'll unlock a deleted-scene PDF." This spurs activity without pressuring for dollars.
- **Keep each reveal bite-sized.** A perk should be consumable in minutes, not hours; backers feel an instant dopamine hit and move on.
- **Archive for late pledges.** After the campaign, bundle all digital perks into a single "Backer Vault" folder so newcomers buying a late pledge don't miss out.

Stretch goals move the meter; daily and weekly perks keep the pulse. Marry the two and your campaign never feels stalled—even when the funding graph flattens, your comment thread and share-metrics will keep jumping.

END WITH A CLEAR CALL-TO-ACTION

As you wrap up the story section of your page, end by **encouraging the reader to take action**. This might sound obvious (Kickstarter has a big "Back this project" button always visible), but a direct invitation from you can be powerful:

- **Express gratitude and excitement:** *"Thank you for checking out my campaign – it means the world to me. I hope you'll join me on this adventure and grab your copy of **The Sunken Kingdom**!"* A warm thank-you plus an encouraging nudge can make people feel appreciated and part of something.
- **Remind them what's in it for them:** *"By backing today, you'll be among the first to read the book and you'll get that exclusive art print as a bonus."* Summarize the benefit once more in a sentence as you conclude the page content.
- **Use positive, inviting language:** Instead of "I need your help" (which can sound desperate), frame it as *"I'd love to have you on board"* or *"Let's make this book a reality together."* It's a collaborative tone— creators and backers working as a team.

At this point, your potential backer has all the info they need: they know what the project is, what they get, why it's special, and that you're a credible creator. A friendly call-to-action is the gentle push that says, *"Go on, hit that pledge button – you won't regret it."*

CHAPTER 11

CAMPAIGN PAGE WORKSHEET

Now is your chance to go step-by-step through each component of a strong Kickstarter book page. You can write your answers in the spaces provided (if printed) or in a separate document. Each step builds the content that you will later format and input into Kickstarter's editor for your project page. When complete, you should have a cohesive draft of your page.

(Note: These steps assume a fiction project, but if you're a non-fiction author or have a project that doesn't fit the mold, you can adapt the prompts. For example, if it asks for characters and you're doing a memoir, you might instead highlight key topics or real figures in your book. Always tailor things to suit your book!)

HOOK YOUR AUDIENCE

The top of your Kickstarter page needs to grab attention immediately. Many potential backers will only read the first few lines before deciding whether to scroll further or leave.

Step 1: Tagline – Write a one-liner that hooks readers, ideally referencing your genre or a compelling aspect of the story. Think of it like a movie tagline or a hook you'd put on the book's cover. *Example:* "**Three cursed coins, two estranged sisters, one epic quest.** Dive into an African-inspired fantasy adventure in *The Sunken Kingdom*." This line should make someone curious to read more. (It doesn't literally have to be one sentence but keep it punchy and front-loaded with intrigue.)

_____

_____

_____

_____

_____

_____

_____

_____

_____

Step 2: Audience Connection – Identify your target reader with a simple phrase: "If you love X, Y, and Z, then this book is perfect for you." Fill in X, Y, Z with things related to your book's appeal – could be comparable authors, genres, or tropes. *Example:* "If you love **witty witches, slow-burn romance,** and **misty coastal towns with**

secrets, then *Luna's Last Secret* is the perfect book for you." This helps readers self-select ("Oh yes, that's me!").

_____

_____

_____

_____

_____

Step 3: Hook Questions – List three captivating questions or statements that draw people into your story's premise. These should pique curiosity about the plot or world. *For instance:*

- *"Do you love X?"*

- *"Are you a fan of Y?*

- *"Is Z irresistible to you?*

_____

_____

_____

_____

These questions set the stage for your book's conflict and stakes without giving spoilers. They make the reader think and want answers – which (hopefully) prompts them to back the project to eventually read the book! Write 2-3 hook questions for your book.

By now, you should have a snappy tagline, an "if you love this, you'll love my book" sentence, and a few hook questions. These elements together form the **introduction section** of your page. They immediately signal the genre, tone, and core conflict to the reader.

SHOW THE BOOK

Next, you want to show people what they're backing. This means **cover imagery** and a **blurb** (book description). Kickstarter pages allow images and text, so we'll plan accordingly:

Step 4: Cover Image – You should display your book's cover prominently. Insert the image below.

Step 5: Book Blurb – Write the description of your book (the kind that would go on the back cover or Amazon page). This is the narrative text that tells readers what the story is about, introduces the protagonist, conflict, and

stakes, and leaves them wanting more. Aim for 2-3 short paragraphs.

_____

_____

_____

_____

_____

_____

_____

_____

_____

_____

_____

_____

_____

_____

_____

_____

Step 6: Book Mockup Image – A 3D render of your book (like a paperback or hardcover image) can make the project feel tangible. You can create a simple mockup using templates or online tools.

Insert your image below.

At this point, your page will have: Hooking intro text, and the book's cover & description section. The reader should understand what the book is about and see what it looks like.

SHARE YOUR PASSION AND PROJECT DETAILS

After the blurb, it's time to share more personal and detailed information to further convince backers of the project's value and legitimacy.

Why This Book? (Author's Note) – Backers love to know the story behind the story. Write 2-4 paragraphs about why you're passionate about this book. Answer questions like: *Why did you write it? What themes or personal experiences does it draw on? Why are you excited to share it with readers?* Your enthusiasm can be infectious. For example, *"I've poured my love of ancient mythology into this novel.*

As a child, I dreamed of warrior queens – and now I've written one. I'm bringing this book to Kickstarter because I believe it deserves a beautiful collector's edition for fellow mythology geeks!" Be genuine – let your voice shine. This section essentially says, *"I love this project, and here's why you will too."*

_____

_____

_____

_____

_____

_____

_____

_____

_____

_____

_____

Step 8: Why Kickstarter? (What Makes it Special) – Explain what makes this campaign or edition unique. Why should someone back now instead of waiting for a retail release (if any)? Common angles: limited edition content or swag, the chance to support the creative process, early access (backers get it first), or simply that without Kickstarter you couldn't make the project happen.

Example: "I'm launching on Kickstarter to create a deluxe hardcover with premium art that wouldn't be possible otherwise. By backing, you're essentially pre-ordering a collector's item that won't be available in stores." If you have any special **Kickstarter-exclusive** perks (like their name in the book, exclusive cover, etc.), highlight them here. Convey that this is a unique experience or product only available through this campaign.

_____

_____

_____

_____

_____

_____

_____

_____

_____

_____

Step 9: Technical Specs & Status – Backers want to know the nuts and bolts too. Provide details such as:

- Book specifics: e.g., *"Approx 300 pages, 5.5x8.5" paperback, professionally edited. Genre: YA sci-fi. Book is written and currently in final proofreading."*

_____

_____

_____

_____

_____

- Production status: *"Manuscript is 100% complete and proofread. Cover art is done. If funded, the book can go to print within a month."* (If you're still writing, be transparent and give a timeline for completion.)

_____

_____

_____

- Delivery timeline: *"Estimated delivery for rewards: Ebooks in June 2025, Physical books by August 2025."*

_____

_____

_____

- If relevant, mention any collaborators (illustrators, editor, etc.) to show you have a team.

_____

_____

_____

Basically, reassure backers that you have a plan to complete and deliver. This can be a short bullet list or a paragraph. Also, clarify if the book is part of a series and if backers need prior knowledge (if Book 2 of series, for instance, tell them if Book 1 is included or available as an add-on).

Sample or Excerpt (Optional) – If you want, you can offer a sample chapter or excerpt to read. This often isn't on the campaign page due to length, but you can provide a link (e.g., *"Read the first chapter here"* as a PDF/Google Docs or your website). In the worksheet, note if you will have a sample and where it's accessible. On the Kickstarter page, you might just have a line with a link. Some authors skip this, but it can help convince those on the fence by showing your writing quality.

At this stage, your page content flow might look like: **Intro hooks -> Cover & blurb -> Author's passionate intro -> Project specialness & specs.** This covers *what* the book is and *why* it's exciting. Next, we need to explain *how the Kickstarter works* for your book – essentially, lay out the rewards and ask for support.

PRESENT THE REWARDS AND CALL TO ACTION

Now you'll detail what backers get at each level and encourage them to pledge. Even though the sidebar on Kickstarter lists tiers, it's wise to summarize or highlight them in the story section too, especially if you have visuals.

Reward Tier Breakdown – List your pledge tiers and what's included in each (you developed these in Module 2).

This section can be a simple list or a chart. Make it easy to read:

- *$10 – Ebook Edition:* Ebook (all formats) + Name in thank-you section.

- *$25 – Paperback:* Print paperback + Ebook + Thank-you in book.

- *$50 – Hardcover:* **Exclusive hardcover** + Ebook + Name in book.

- *$75 – Hardcover + Art:* Hardcover + Ebook + 3 Art Prints + Name in book.

- *$100 – Mega Bundle:* Hardcover + Paperback + Ebook + Merch Pack (prints, bookmark) + Name in book.

- *$250 – Be a Character:* All Mega Bundle rewards + name a character in the next book.

(This is just an example; use your actual tiers.) **Bold or highlight** particularly good deals or exclusive items so they stand out (like I did with "Exclusive hardcover" above). You can also include small images of the items if available (for instance, a little icon of a book or merch). Ensure that what you write here matches exactly what you set up in the Kickstarter reward tiers, to avoid confusion.

If you have many tiers, you might not list absolutely all here – perhaps focus on the main ones and the best-value ones. But transparency is good, so many creators do list all. It's up to you.

You've already done this above, but if you'd like more practice, or have made changes, write your rewards below.

Russell Nohelty

_____

_____

_____

_____

_____

_____

_____

_____

Special Perks – If you decided on early-bird rewards, weekly perks, or stretch goals, mention them clearly.

_____

_____

_____

_____

Call to Action – End your page with a heartfelt appeal and next steps:

- Thank readers for checking out your campaign.

- Invite them to become a backer: *"I would love your support to bring Book Title to life. Choose a reward tier that suits you and join us on this adventure!"*

- You can also encourage sharing: *"Even if you can't pledge, sharing this campaign with friends or on social media makes a huge difference."*

- Reassure them of your commitment: *"With your help, I'm confident we can make this book a reality. I'm grateful for every supporter and excited to deliver a fantastic story and rewards to you."*

- Some creators add a personal sign-off, like a signature image or just "Sincerely, [Your Name]".

_____

_____

_____

_____

_____

_____

_____

_____

_____

_____

CHAPTER 12

VISUAL POWER

A Kickstarter page is a multimedia experience. A visitor will skim and scroll, their eyes catching on images, video, and headings just as much as on paragraphs. Great visuals can significantly boost a potential backer's confidence and excitement. They make your project feel *real* and professional.

Kickstarter's own statistics have shown that projects with a video tend to have higher success rates. The project video is your chance to **personally connect** with potential backers in a way text can't. So, do you need a video? *Yes.* If at all possible, include one. But don't panic – it doesn't need to be a Hollywood production. Many authors have succeeded with simple, heartfelt videos. Here's how to make yours effective:

1. **Keep it short – 2-3 minutes max.** Attention spans online are short. Aim for the sweet spot of introducing your project without rambling. Around 2 minutes is ideal.
2. **Outline a clear structure:** A simple five-part flow works well:

- o **The Sting:** Because Kickstarter now autoplays videos, you should have a quick graphic and audio sting, just like TikTok, to get people excited and tuned in. This doesn't have to be long, and you can use it in multiple campaigns if you want, but it has been proven to stop scrolls effectively so people pay attention.
- o **Introduction:** Appear on camera (if you're comfortable) and greet viewers. *"Hi, I'm [Name], the author of **The Sunken Kingdom**."* Let them see the face or hear the voice behind the project – this builds trust.
- o **The Story Pitch:** In a sentence or two, describe what the book is about (similar to your tagline/blurb). *"It's an epic fantasy about two sisters on a quest to save their kingdom from a cursed fate."* It's a really good idea to add imagery as you talk about this bit.
- o **The Project Goal:** Explain why you're on Kickstarter. *"I'm launching this Kickstarter to fund a gorgeous, illustrated hardcover edition of the book..."* Tell them what their money will help create.
- o **Excitement & Why Backers Should Care:** Share why you're excited and what backers get. *"I've always dreamed of holding this story in a beautiful hardcover, and with your help, it can happen. Backers will get the book before anyone else, plus exclusive art rewards – it's going to be an amazing journey to share!"* Let your

passion come through; enthusiasm is
contagious.

o **Call-to-Action & Thank You:** End with a
direct appeal. *"Please check out the rewards
and consider backing today. Thank you so much
for your support – I can't wait to send you this
book!"*

You can adjust this structure, but hitting these points in
order ensures you cover the essentials succinctly.

1. **Be yourself and be authentic.** You might not be used
to talking on camera, and that's okay. You don't need
fancy effects or a memorized script. In fact, avoid
reading a script word-for-word on camera – it can
sound stilted. Instead, jot bullet points for each of the
above sections and practice a few times so you can
speak naturally. It's absolutely fine if it isn't perfect – a
little bit of "ums" or a nervous laugh just shows you're
human. Smile and imagine you're explaining the
project to a friend who loves books.

2. **Quality basics:** You don't need professional equipment
but do ensure good lighting and clear sound. Film in a
quiet environment (turn off fans/AC for the recording if
they create background noise). Face a light source (like
a window) so your face is well-lit. Your phone camera
or webcam can do the job if used correctly. Pro tip:
check your background – a tidy, book-filled shelf or
some artwork might be nicer than, say, a pile of
laundry.

3. **Add visuals if possible:** While it's great to see you
speaking, you can edit in a few images to illustrate what

you're talking about. For example, when you mention the beautiful artwork, you could cut to a slide of your cover art or a sample illustration. If you're not techy, you can keep it simple and just hold up a printout of your cover when you talk about it. The point is to give some visual variety. There are free or low-cost video editing tools that are fairly user-friendly if you want to get fancy (iMovie, Windows Video Editor, etc.). But again, authenticity beats flashy production. A straightforward, earnest video can outperform a slick but soulless one.

4. **Don't forget the ask:** It might feel awkward to "ask for money," but remember, you're inviting people to be part of something cool. So clearly ask viewers to support the project. Many creators have found that literally saying "I'd be honored to have your backing" or "Please pledge today and help make this happen" increases conversion. People sometimes need that nudge.

Videos aren't necessary for a campaign, but they are really helpful. However, the biggest thing you need is enthusiasm. I have seen hundreds of videos where the people are bored and listless. This will actually hurt your campaign. If you can't do "excitement," find somebody who can, but you have to be amped if you want anyone else to get amped.

You don't need to have a fancy setup, or anything like that, but you do need to have excitement.

IMAGES THAT IMPRESS

Beyond the video, your campaign page should be sprinkled with images that **inform and engage**. Think of images as anchor points that catch the eye during scrolling and convey important information at a glance. Here are the must-haves and some nice-to-haves:

- **Book Cover:** This is non-negotiable. A large, high-resolution image of your cover should appear near the top (likely it's already in the header/above-the-fold). You can also show it again in context with other rewards. The cover gives an instant feel of the genre and quality of your book. If you don't have final cover art yet, consider using concept art or even a placeholder title image, but do indicate it's a placeholder to manage expectations.
- **Interior art or sample pages:** If your book has illustrations, include a couple of examples on the page. Even if it's a novel with no art, you could show a snapshot of the interior layout or a particularly beautiful chapter header design if you have it. For comics or graphic novels, sample pages are key. For a prose book, an image of a nicely formatted page or an excerpt can subtly prove that the project is well along. It's proof of concept – *"look, this book is real and it's gorgeous inside."*
- **Author photo (optional on page):** At minimum, ensure your Kickstarter profile has a photo, because people do check the creator bio. On the page itself, you might include a small picture of yourself in the "About

the Author" section. It's not required, but seeing the face behind the project can further humanize the campaign. If you're camera shy, don't worry, the video likely already showed you. But a smiling photo with a short bio caption ("About [Your Name]") on the page can be nice.

- **Rewards graphic:** As discussed before, a visual showing the contents of your main pledge levels can hugely help backers understand what they get. This could be a composite image (book + merch laid out). For example, for a deluxe box set, you might have an image with the book, prints, bookmark, and whatever else, all in one frame with labels like "Exclusive Art Print (8x10)" pointing to the print, etc. If you have multiple interesting tiers, you can do a small image for each (but don't overload the page with too many separate graphics – you could combine them into one image with different sections).

- **Timeline graphic:** Many campaigns include a timeline to show key dates (writing done, editing, printing, fulfillment). A simple graphic with a timeline arrow or a series of icons (Writing -> Editing -> Printing -> Shipping, with months/years labeled) can reassure backers you have a schedule. It's not mandatory, especially if you've described the timeline in text, but visuals help people absorb info quickly.

- **Budget pie chart or breakdown (if you want transparency visually):** Some creators show a pie chart of how funds will be allocated (e.g., 50% printing, 20% shipping, 15% art, 15% Kickstarter fees). It's a quick way to demonstrate that you've done your homework on costs. If you choose to include a graphic, keep it very clear and simple.

- **Stretch goal progress:** If you have multiple stretch goals, a fun graphic listing them (with locked/unlocked indicators) motivates backers. For instance, a thermometer or progress bar, or just a list with checkmarks as goals unlock. You might not have this at launch, but if your campaign hits the goal quickly, you can add it in updates or edit the page to include it mid-campaign.
- **Any other imagery that adds flavor:** This could include character art, concept sketches, maps of your story world, or even photos of a prototype (if you already printed a proof copy or have merchandise samples). For example, if you already have a proof of the hardcover, a photo of you holding it can be powerful *proof* of concept. Or if your story involves a real location, a nice photo of that locale might set the mood.

Each image should serve a purpose: either to *inform* (show what something looks like, explain a concept) or to *excite* (beautiful art, cool visuals from the story). Avoid generic or filler images that don't add value—everything should tie back to your project.

Technical tips: Make sure your images are clear and appropriately sized. Kickstarter allows you to insert images in the story, but they may get resized for various screens. Use a readable font on any infographics (nothing too small; remember many people view Kickstarter on mobile). Stick to a consistent style: if your book cover has a certain color scheme or font, you can echo that in headers or graphics for a cohesive look. Consistency in design gives a professional vibe, like you have a "brand" for this project. I coordinate my campaign graphics with my book's aesthetic. I call this "vibes." It creates an immersive experience aligned with the project's tone.

LAYOUT AND PAGE DESIGN

How you format your page text can greatly affect readability. A well-laid-out page will keep people engaged longer, whereas a giant wall of unbroken text can send them running. Follow these layout best practices:

- **Use headings and subheadings:** Break your content into clear sections (like we have in this book!). On a Kickstarter page, you might not have formal "HTML" headings, but you can simulate them with bolded all-caps lines or creative typography. For instance, label sections like *ABOUT THE BOOK, REWARDS, THE STORY, STRETCH GOALS*, etc., in a way that stands out (Kickstarter's editor allows header styles or at least bold large text). This helps scanners find the info they want. I like to break each section with graphics.
- **Keep paragraphs short:** Aim for 2-4 sentences per paragraph in your page content. Long blocks of text feel heavy on a screen. White space is your friend; it makes the page feel accessible. If you find a paragraph getting too beefy, find a spot to break it into two.
- **Bullet points and lists:** Whenever you're enumerating things (features, rewards, steps, whatever), use a list format. Bullets or numbers add visual structure and

make it easier to absorb multiple points. We've encouraged lists for rewards or stretch goals for exactly this reason.

- **Emphasize key phrases:** You can use bold or italics to highlight the really important points (sparingly). For example, in a long paragraph about your background, you might bold **"19 successful campaigns"** when mentioning your track record, so even skimmers catch that impressive fact. Or italicize a book title for emphasis. But don't overdo it. If everything is bold, nothing stands out.

- **Images as section breakers:** You can use images not just as content but as natural dividers. After a few paragraphs of text, an image provides a visual break and resets the reader's attention span. People will naturally pause at the image, maybe read its caption, then continue. This rhythm of text-image-text keeps things flowing.

- **Check on mobile:** Kickstarter pages will be viewed on phones, tablets, laptops, you name it. Use the Kickstarter preview to see how your layout adapts. Make sure images resize correctly (nothing is cut off or too tiny to see). Ensure that any text on images is still readable on a small screen. If not, you may need to simplify those graphics.

- **Consistency:** Use a consistent tone and formatting style throughout. Decide on a format for headers, stick to one or two fonts at most (Kickstarter has default fonts, but if you embed text in images, keep that consistent). If you start each section with a certain style (like an emoji or an icon), do it for all sections as appropriate. This kind of attention to detail subliminally tells backers, "this creator is organized and professional."

Remember, a well-designed page not only looks good but also enhances comprehension. The easier it is for someone to quickly get all the info (due to good structure and visuals), the more likely they are to say *yes*. We're in an age of skim-readers; design your page to cater to both the in-depth reader and the skimmer.

CHAPTER 13

TRANSPARENCY, FAQS, AND PROOF

At this point, your page should already hook interest and explain the project well. The final step is to eliminate lingering doubts. A visitor might love your idea and want the book, but still hesitate with questions like, "Will this creator deliver? Where exactly is my money going? What if something goes wrong?" This chapter is all about answering those questions before they're even asked, turning a hesitant visitor into a confident backer.

Transparency is *paramount* on Kickstarter. Backers appreciate creators who are open about the process and the use of funds. Here's how you can be transparent on your campaign page:

- **Break down the budget (in plain terms):** You don't necessarily need a detailed spreadsheet on the page but do give backers a sense of how the money will be used. For example: *"Our $5,000 funding goal covers: printing 200 hardcover books ($2,000), shipping materials & postage ($1,000), artwork and design costs ($1,200), and Kickstarter fees/taxes ($800)."* This rough breakdown shows you've done the math and aren't just pulling a random number for the goal. If any chunk is especially large or important, you can note it (e.g. "High-quality printing is about 40% of the budget – worth it for a book that lasts."). Being transparent about costs also educates backers that your goal isn't pure profit – it's to create something awesome.

- **State the project status and timeline clearly:** Reiterate (perhaps in a dedicated section or in the FAQ) where you are in the process and what comes after the campaign. *"Manuscript is complete and edited. Cover art is finished. Once funded, I will immediately send the book to print, which takes about 6-8 weeks. I expect to ship rewards by [Month, Year]."* You might have mentioned some of this earlier, but it's worth consolidating in one place. This assures backers you know what you're doing and sets realistic expectations. If your timeline has some wiggle room, be upfront: *"I've built in a buffer for potential delays (like printing queue backups), so even in a worst-case scenario, rewards should ship by [later date]."*

- **Address any potential hiccups openly:** If there are any aspects of the project that could raise eyebrows, better to address them yourself. For example, if this is your first book, you might say, "This is my debut novel, so I've consulted with mentors and fellow authors who have successfully crowdfunded to ensure I'm following best practices in printing and fulfillment." Or if you're writing in a second language or doing something experimental, acknowledge it and explain why you're confident in success (perhaps you have an expert on board, etc.). Transparency defuses uncertainty. Backers don't expect perfection or zero risk; they appreciate honesty and preparation.

When you lay out these details, do so in a **positive, confidence-inspiring tone**. It's not an apology, it's a plan. Show that you're excited and ready to deliver. For instance, I often say things like *"As soon as the campaign ends, our team leaps into action – we've done this 18 times before, and we can't wait to do it again!"* Backers read that and feel reassured that, okay, this person has a system.

FAQS

Including an **FAQ (Frequently Asked Questions)** section on your campaign page can preempt common queries and save everyone time. Think about what a skeptical or detail-oriented backer might wonder, and address it upfront:

Common questions for publishing projects include:

- **"When will I get my book?"** – You can answer with the expected delivery date and any factors that might affect it. *"Books are slated to ship by August 2025. You'll get updates if anything changes."*
- **"Is the book content complete?"** – Answer if the writing is done, if editing is done, etc. *"Yes, the novel is fully written. It's currently being proofread, so it will be polished and ready for print by the time we fund."*
- **"Can I get previous books/add-ons?"** – If you have previous work or extra goodies, people will ask if they can grab those through the campaign. *"Yes! You can add on my earlier novel or additional copies in the pledge manager after the campaign – see the Add-Ons*

section above for details." (If you didn't mention add-ons earlier, you can briefly explain here how they'll work.)

- **"Do you ship internationally?"** – If applicable, state which countries you can ship to and any extra shipping fees that were set up. *"We ship worldwide. Note: Due to high postage costs, international backers have an added shipping fee which will be shown at pledge time. Books will be shipped via USPS International."* If you cannot ship to certain regions (maybe due to COVID or other issues), be clear about that too.
- **"What if the book is delayed or something changes?"** – Reassure them you will keep backers updated. *"If any delays happen (e.g., printer backups or shipping slowdowns), I will communicate openly via Kickstarter updates. Backers will never be left in the dark – you're part of the team."*
- **"Is my pledge money refundable if the project doesn't fund?"** – Some newcomers to Kickstarter might not know: if a project doesn't hit its goal, no one is charged. You can clarify: *"Kickstarter is all-or-nothing. If we don't reach the goal, you won't be charged. But we fully intend to hit it and make this book real!"* (This last part is a bit of a rallying cry too.)

You don't need to overload the FAQ with every tiny detail – too much can actually create doubt by raising obscure issues. Stick to the top 5-7 questions you honestly expect. You can format the FAQ as a simple Q&A list on the page. Kickstarter also has a dedicated FAQ feature where backers can see questions separately; you could use that as well, but having key ones in the page content ensures they're seen.

By answering questions proactively, you remove reasons for someone to hesitate. It shows you've put yourself in the backer's shoes.

RISKS AND CHALLENGES

Kickstarter requires a "Risks and Challenges" section (usually at the bottom of the campaign page in a dedicated field) where creators must talk about potential risks. Don't treat this as just a requirement to gloss over. Use it as another opportunity to build trust through honesty.

- **Acknowledge the risks:** Every project has some risk. Maybe printing could be delayed, or maybe a collaborator could back out. Briefly mention the realistic things that could happen. *"There is always a chance of production delays. The printer might experience a backlog, or international shipping could face customs delays."* By saying this, you're showing you're not naive – you're aware of real-world issues.
- **Explain how you'll handle them:** Importantly, follow up each risk with your mitigation plan. *"However, I've padded the timeline to account for possible printer delays, and I've chosen a reputable printing company I've worked with before. If any issues arise, I will keep backers updated with transparency and work to resolve them quickly."* This turns a potential negative into a demonstration of your problem-solving approach.
- **Highlight your preparedness:** If you have done things to reduce risk, mention them. *"The book content is complete, which significantly lowers the risk of not delivering. We're essentially funding production, not*

writing time." Or *"I have quotes from multiple printers, so if one falls through, I have a backup ready."* These specifics show that you've thought ahead.

- **Mention past reliability if applicable:** This overlaps with credibility, but the risk section is a fine place to say, *"This is my third Kickstarter project. My previous two campaigns delivered all rewards as promised, and I learned a lot about logistics from them."* Even if it's your first, you could say, *"I've consulted with several experienced Kickstarter creators to make sure my plan is solid."* It shows you're not doing this in a vacuum.

The tone of your Risks and Challenges should be reassuring but realistic. You're basically telling backers, "Look, I know what could go wrong, and here's why you shouldn't lose sleep about it." Many creators fear that talking about risks will scare backers. On the contrary, pretending there are no risks is what scares savvy backers. So, confront it head on with professionalism.

My campaigns typically have a candid risks section. I might say something like, "Challenges: Things can always go wrong – printers mess up, freight gets delayed. I've built in extra time and will be upfront with you if the timeline shifts. This isn't my first rodeo, and I'm confident in getting the job done." Reading that, a backer feels, *"Alright, this guy is experienced and honest. I trust him with my money."*

PROOF OF QUALITY

Finally, "Proof" in this context means providing evidence or validation that what you're offering is worthwhile. We've touched on some elements of this (like testimonials and track record), but here are a few ways to reinforce that a backer's faith in you will be rewarded:

- **Testimonials & quotes:** Do you have any advance readers, reviewers, or fellow authors who have said great things about your book? A short quote or two can be powerful. For example: *"'A breathtaking adventure of magic and sisterhood' – Early reader review."* If a known name in your genre has endorsed your book, definitely include that: *"Jane Bestseller, author of XYZ, called this book 'thrilling and original'."* These are like mini-reviews that add credibility. Even testimonials from regular readers (without big names) can help, because they show *someone* has read and enjoyed the story.
- **Awards or recognition:** If your manuscript or you as an author have won any awards or distinctions (even small ones), you can mention that briefly. *"Winner of the 2023 Imaginative Fiction Award (Manuscript Category)"* or *"Author was a Pitch Wars 2021 finalist."* Industry recognition, however small, signals quality to backers who don't know you.
- **Previous Kickstarter success (proof of deliverability):** We've mentioned this, but it bears repeating. Citing that you've delivered previous campaigns on time is huge proof. It tackles both quality

and trust. I always note on my sales page not just the number of campaigns but also how much was raised or how many backers, as proof of both community trust and my ability to handle scale. For instance, *"I've fulfilled orders to over 2,000 backers across my campaigns, so you can pledge with confidence that I know how to get these books into your hands."* If you have any similar stat, flaunt it. If you don't, maybe mention a smaller proof like a successful beta run: *"I did a small print run for local readers last year and successfully delivered 50 signed books – now I'm taking it to the next level with Kickstarter."*

- **Work samples:** Some creators include a link to a sample chapter or a preview. For example, a link to a PDF of the first chapter or a short story in the same world. This is a "proof" of your writing quality. Not everyone will click and read it, but its mere presence says, *"I have nothing to hide – check out my writing for yourself."* If you have an existing following, maybe you don't need this. But if you're newer, offering a taste can convert a curious onlooker into a fan. (Make sure if you link externally, you're allowed to under Kickstarter rules and that it's a safe link; or alternatively, mention that a sample is available upon request, etc.)
- **Prototype or physical proof (if available):** If you already have a prototype of the book (like an advance copy, or a previous edition), show it. A photo of the author holding a book and smiling is literal proof that this can exist. Some authors do a short video clip flipping through a proof copy to show printing quality. It makes it tangible. If you don't have that, even

showing printed concept art or paper samples can be something. But don't worry if you can't; it's not expected unless you happen to have done early prints.

All these forms of "proof" build a case that backing your project is a sound decision. It appeals to the rational side of the brain ("This looks legit, and others vouch for it") to complement the emotional excitement you've hopefully stirred already.

When you incorporate transparency, FAQs, risk management, and proof into your page, you're essentially removing the last reasons not to pledge. A well-informed backer is a confident backer. The difference between a curious visitor and a backer often comes down to trust. They might love your concept but think, *"Eh, I'm not sure this person can actually do it,"* or *"I have a question, I'll decide later."* We don't want "decide later" – later often never comes. By building trust directly into your page content, you urge them to decide **now** and feel good about it.

Don't be afraid to be a little vulnerable in this part of the page too. It's okay to say, *"I'm a one-person operation and this is my dream. I might hit a snag or two, but I promise I will do everything to get this book to you and make you glad you supported it."* That kind of genuine pledge from the creator to the backer can be very compelling. You're essentially making a pact: if you trust me with your support, I'll honor that trust with my actions.

CHAPTER 14
AUDIENCE ACTIVATION

A Kickstarter campaign isn't about shouting, "Buy my book." It's about having a conversation with your readers to show them why your book is worth their attention. Everything you share is another chance to explain what makes your story special. Every day of your campaign is another opportunity to highlight something new and meaningful about your book, gradually building a case that resonates with your audience.

When you first announce your campaign, the case is simple: *The book is live, and you can be one of the first to get it.* That's your starting point. But as the days go on, you have to keep building on that message. It's exhausting, but it's also supposed to be fun. If it's not fun *for you,* then it won't be fun *for them.*

One day you might talk about what inspired the story. Another, you could share an early review or a behind-the-scenes look at the writing process. Maybe you dive into a character's backstory or offer a sneak peek of the first chapter. Each piece adds depth, helping readers connect with your book in a new way.

The middle of a pre-order campaign is often where things slow down, and that's where your creativity matters most. ***Think about what excites you about the book and share that with your readers.*** If you're writing a series, remind them why they love this world and what makes this installment special. If it's a standalone, lean into the unique themes or emotional core of the story.

Over time, you build a language with your readers by giving them reasons to love your book. No single interaction will likely push them over the edge, but creating a campaign allows you to find the story that will connect with them.

Your readers aren't all the same. Some will pre-order the moment you announce, while others will need a little more time and nudging. Maybe they're on the fence and need to see a glowing review. Maybe they just need to be reminded a few times because life is busy, and your book hasn't made it to the top of their to-do list. That's why variety matters. Each day of your campaign gives you a chance to catch someone's attention in a new way.

Kickstarter campaigns are about more than just selling a book. They're about sharing your enthusiasm, creating anticipation, and showing readers why this story matters, not just to you, but to them. When you approach each day with a fresh perspective and a new piece of your book's heart, you're not just building a case. You're creating an experience that readers will remember.

As a newer author, it's easy to feel like you'll never get anywhere and that you'll always be overshadowed by superstar authors with massive followings, endless resources, and access to the biggest promotional platforms, but *you have something they don't.* You can show up for your readers in a way they can't. Your presence is your superpower.

When a superstar author releases a book, their reach might be enormous, but their connection with individual readers is often diluted. They can't respond to every comment, answer every email, or personally thank every reader who supports them.

But you can. Your ability to connect directly with your fans, to make each one feel seen and valued, is a secret weapon that superstar authors can't replicate.

This doesn't just make a difference in your pre-order campaign. It builds a foundation for lasting loyalty. Readers don't just want to buy books. They want to feel connected to the authors who create them. By showing up authentically and consistently, you create relationships that turn casual readers into passionate advocates.

Here's how to use your presence to its fullest potential:

- Respond to comments and emails with genuine enthusiasm. A quick thank-you or thoughtful reply can make a reader's day.
- Engage directly with your audience through live streams, Q&A sessions, or private community spaces. Let them see the person behind the book.
- Share personal insights, behind-the-scenes moments, or even the struggles of the creative process. These glimpses of authenticity resonate deeply with readers.

Your availability and willingness to connect are what make you stand out. Readers might admire superstar authors, but they'll champion *you* because they feel like they know you. Lean into that, and you'll create a reader base that grows not just in numbers but in loyalty and passion.

CULTIVATE YOUR EMAIL LIST

If you take one thing away from this chapter, let it be that your email list is your most powerful asset for a launch. Social media algorithms come and go, but email remains a direct line to your true fans. Here's how to leverage it:

- **Start now (seriously, now):** If you already have an author newsletter, fantastic. You're ahead of the game. If not, set up a simple mailing list immediately. Even if your launch is months away, every single email sign-up between now and then counts. Don't think "I'll wait until I have big news"; by then it's too late. It's okay if the list is small – 50 engaged people can create a snowball effect on day one.
- **Offer a sign-up incentive (lead magnet):** People are more likely to join your list if there's something in it for them. Offer a freebie related to your project: a free short story, a sample chapter, a cool printable, etc. For example, *"Sign up for Kickstarter launch updates and get a free exclusive prequel story."* This not only grows your list but also gets readers invested in your world.
- **Tease the project in your emails:** In the weeks before launch, send periodic emails to build excitement. Share progress: *"Just got the first proof of the cover – look at this beauty!"* or *"I'm finalizing the bonus content for*

backers; here's a sneak peek at one of the art prints." Make your subscribers feel like insiders. Countdowns work too: *"Only 2 weeks until launch day!"* (and remind them of the date). By the time you launch, they should be eagerly anticipating it.

- **Prime them for Day One:** A few days before launch, send an email with the exact launch date and time. *"We go live on Kickstarter this Tuesday at 9am EST!"* Encourage them to back early: *"The first 48 hours are crucial; if you're in, I'd love your pledge on day one to build momentum."* Many fans want to help you succeed – sometimes they just need to be told how.

- **Segment and personalize:** As your list grows, recognize that some people are superfans (they open every email, click every link) while others are lukewarm. It can be worth segmenting your list. For example, a segment for your most engaged 10%. You might send that core group a more personal note like, *"Hey, you've been such a big supporter, I wanted to reach out personally. It'd mean the world to have you as a Day-1 backer on Kickstarter."* These folks are your street team; treat them like VIPs. Conversely, for the less engaged, keep messages upbeat and maybe less frequent, so you don't annoy them. Some mailing services let you target by engagement level easily.

In summary, build that list and love on that list. Even a small but dedicated email list can be a launchpad for a big campaign.

ENGAGE YOUR COMMUNITIES

Not everyone will join an email list, so social media and online communities are your next best way to gather and warm up an audience. But the key word is "engage." Shouting into the void "I have a Kickstarter coming" isn't enough. You want people talking back, sharing, and feeling connected. Here's how:

- **Choose your platforms wisely:** You don't have to be everywhere. Be where your readers hang out. If you write YA fantasy, maybe BookTok (TikTok) or Instagram's book community is big. If you're a sci-fi author, perhaps Twitter (BookTwitter) or specialized forums. Are there Facebook groups relevant to your genre? Identify 1-2 places where you can reasonably show up consistently and where potential backers spend time.

- **Share progress and involve the audience:** Similar to email, share your journey on social media. Show a snippet of the artwork, post a video of you unboxing a sample, or even share your word count milestone if you're still writing. People love behind-the-scenes content; it makes them feel part of the process. You can do fun polls or questions: *"Which character should I feature on the next art print? A or B?"* or *"If we hit a stretch goal, would you rather get a bookmark or a sticker?"* These little interactions serve two purposes: market research and investment. When someone votes in your poll, they've psychologically invested a bit in your project's outcome.

- **Don't oversell. Provide value or entertainment:** The last thing you want is to sound like an endless ad. Mix in genuinely interesting or useful content. For example, write a blog or post about a topic related to your book (if your book is about mythology, maybe a short thread on a cool myth you researched). Or be entertaining – share a funny behind-the-scenes anecdote. The rule of thumb often given is 80/20: 80% content that's not directly "buy my thing," 20% promotional. As the launch nears, that ratio can tilt more towards the promotional scale, but always strive to make posts engaging, not just "Coming soon: my book."

- **Use visuals and video on social:** social media is a visual medium. A post with an image or short video will grab more attention. As you prepare your campaign images and video, repurpose them. Teaser graphics, a short 10-second clip of your project video, cover reveals – these are social gold. Leading up to launch, you could do a countdown series: e.g., "5 Days to Kickstarter: Meet the Protagonist" with character art or "3 Days to Go: What's in the Deluxe Box?" with a photo of all the goodies.

- **Leverage Kickstarter's pre-launch page:** Kickstarter allows you to create a pre-launch landing page where people can click "Notify me on launch." The moment your campaign goes live, all those who clicked get an email. Use this! Share that link on your socials as soon as it's available. *"Want an email when we launch? Hit 'Notify' here!"* It's easier to get someone to click a notify button than to commit money on the spot – so gather those followers. It's not public how many you have, but when you launch, you'll see that number convert to early backers.

- **Consistency over intensity:** It's better to post a couple times a week steadily than to spam every hour for a day and then go silent for a week. People need multiple reminders, but they also tune out spam. So find a sustainable cadence. In the final week or days before launch, you can ramp up with daily posts, because now it's crunch time and you want as many eyeballs as possible aware of the imminent launch.

Remember, social media can be fickle (algorithms might show your post to only a fraction of followers), so don't rely on it alone – that's why email is first above. But it's still a crucial channel to drum up excitement and reach new folks via shares.

RALLY YOUR PERSONAL NETWORK

When thinking of "audience," we often focus on fans and followers. But don't neglect the personal network of friends, family, colleagues, and even acquaintances. These people might not be your target readers, but they often want to support *you*, the person. Early in the campaign, that personal circle can provide a vital boost:

- **Make a list of your people:** List out those who you think would be happy to hear from you personally about your project. This could be close friends, supportive family members, old college buddies who always liked your creative streak, work colleagues who have shown interest, etc. You might be surprised –

some people in your life will back it just because they think it's cool you're doing this, even if they may never read the book. Every pledge counts for momentum.

- **Reach out individually, sincerely:** A mass Facebook post like "Hey everyone, my Kickstarter is live, please support!" is fine, but a one-on-one touch is far more effective. Send a personal message or email to each person on your list a day or two before launch (or right when live). Something like: *"Hi [Name], hope you're doing well! I wanted to personally let you know I'm launching a Kickstarter for my new book next week. It's been a long journey and I'm super excited (and a bit nervous). It would mean a lot if you could check it out when it goes live on [Date]. Even a small pledge or just sharing the link would help a ton in the early days. Thanks for always being in my corner!"* Make it heartfelt and *do not* make it feel like a copy-paste to 50 people (even if it mostly is, personalize each a bit). People respond to genuine appeals.

- **Emphasize participation over amount:** Some friends might feel they can't help because they're not into your book or they're tight on money. Let them know even $1 or a share is helpful. *"Even if the book's not your genre, just having your name as a backer (you can pledge $1) boosts our momentum, and that would be amazing."* Often, those $1-$5 "friend pledges" are given just to show love, and they absolutely help by making your backer count higher and fueling the algorithm. Also, some may end up pledging more than you expect when they see how excited you are.

- **Launch day cheerleading:** Get a few of your closest allies to essentially act as your launch team. They should pledge as early as possible and perhaps comment on the project page with encouragement ("This is awesome, can't wait!"). And they can share your announcements on their socials to extend reach. Having 10-15 personal contacts lined up to pledge Day 1 can sometimes get you 10-20% of your goal right out of the gate, which is huge for your public perception. Strangers are more likely to back a campaign that looks like it's already catching fire.

- **The ripple effect:** Personal network support often has a ripple. A coworker backs your project out of solidarity. Then they mention it to someone else who's into that genre, who then checks it out. Or your proud mom backs and then posts on her Facebook "I just supported my child's book project!" and one of her friends goes "Oh, I love fantasy books, I'll take a look." Don't underestimate these indirect pathways. The key is to not be shy in letting your circle know what you're doing. You aren't begging. You're sharing something exciting in your life and inviting them to be part of it.

Many creators feel hesitant to ask friends/family for money. Remember, crowdfunding is *voluntary*. You're not arm-twisting anyone; you're giving those who care about you a chance to support your dream. Most people are thrilled to see someone they know create a book or a game or art. Often the issue is they simply don't know about it until after the fact when they can't help. So, give them the chance!

WARM-UP CONTENT

We touched on this in earlier sections, but let's explicitly talk about warming up your audience with teaser content and building anticipation:

- **Exclusive previews:** Offer your followers little exclusive looks leading up to the campaign. This could be an excerpt from the book, concept art reveals, character bios, or a short video series. For example, each week leading to launch you might introduce one character from your novel with a fun graphic or quote. By the time you launch, your audience is acquainted with the world and characters. They're invested and want to see this project succeed so they can read the whole story.
- **Countdown events:** As the launch draws very near (like final week), treat it like an event. "One week until launch" post, "3 days until launch" live stream, "Tomorrow we go live!" reminder. This creates a sense of occasion. Some creators even do a countdown party – e.g., a live stream the night before launch, chatting with fans, doing a Q&A, maybe reading a chapter aloud. It builds community and hype.
- **Community challenges or goals:** You can gamify the pre-launch a bit. For instance, "If we get 100 people on the notify list before launch, I'll reveal a secret chapter title/artwork/character." Or, "When this post gets 50 shares, I'll drop a new piece of concept art." These can encourage your core followers to spread the word in

exchange for goodies. Just make sure to follow through on the reward.

- **The personal touch:** Amidst all the teasers, make sure to occasionally speak from the heart. Express your excitement and even your nerves. *"I've been working on this book for 3 years, and in 5 days I finally get to share it with you on Kickstarter. I'm not going to lie; it's equal parts exhilarating and terrifying. But knowing you're out there rooting for me gives me courage. I really hope you'll join me on launch day and help make this dream real."* Posts/messages like this galvanize your true fans—they *want* to rally behind you. People support Kickstarter projects not just for the product but often for the person. Let them feel your humanity; it's powerful.

By doing all of the above, you are essentially simulating a mini campaign *before* the campaign. It primes the pump. When launch day arrives, instead of announcing something cold to an unprepared audience, you'll be more like *"Alright, you've been waiting, here we go!"* and they'll respond, *"Heck yes, we've been waiting, let's go!"*

TRACK PRE-LAUNCH METRICS

It's a good practice to give yourself some **pre-launch targets**. This makes you proactive and also gives you a sense of progress:

- **Email sign-up goal:** e.g., "I want 200 people on my email list by launch." Even if it's arbitrary, it motivates you to push those sign-ups. Track your count each week and adjust tactics if it's not growing (maybe offer a better incentive or promote the sign-up more prominently).

- **Notify-me count goal:** "Aim for 100 followers on the Kickstarter pre-launch page." You won't know who they are (Kickstarter doesn't show you until they convert at launch), but the number is a good indicator of interest. Share that milestone with your audience too: *"We have 80 people ready to go on launch day – can we hit 100?"* It builds excitement.
- **Social engagement or reach goals:** For instance, "Get 50 shares on the cover reveal post," or "Grow my Facebook group by 30 new members before launch." If you have a goal, you'll be more driven to do the actions that achieve it (like actually asking people to share or actively inviting folks to your group).
- **Segments warm-up goals:** You might set a goal like, "Personally reach out to my top 20 superfans pre-launch" or "Have 10 confirmed day-one pledgers from my inner circle." These are qualitative but important. Actually write down the names and check them off as you contact them.
- **Remember the 4 media channels:**
  - **Owned:** Your own channels (email list, your blog/website). Goal: maximize these since you control them.
  - **Borrowed:** Other people's audiences through collaborations
  - **Bought:** Paid ads or promotions
  - **Earned:** Word-of-mouth and press

Pre-launch, you mostly focus on the first three: your channels, your socials, and borrowing audiences via maybe a cover reveal on someone else's blog or a small cross-promo mention (more on that soon). Setting goals in each category ensures you're not leaning on just one thing. For example, if your entire plan is only emailing your list, that might limit you. But if you also aim to get on a fellow author's newsletter (borrow) and hype on Twitter (build), you have more shots.

Monitor and adapt: As you approach launch, gauge the temperature. Are people reacting and signing up like you hoped? If you're falling short on a goal, step up your efforts or try a new tactic. If email sign-ups slowed, maybe do a last-minute push with a bigger incentive (e.g., "All new subscribers this week get entered to win a free copy"). If social engagement is tepid, consider focusing on the one channel that's doing best and doubling down there.

THE VELOCITY OF YOUR CAMPAIGN

Collecting "Notify Me" clicks and email sign-ups is only half the job. The other half is reading the velocity of your campaign, how fast those numbers grow week over week. A healthy pre-launch isn't just a big pile of names; it's a *moving* pile that keeps adding fresh fuel every seven days.

I recommend giving yourself a full month between opening the Kickstarter pre-launch page and pressing Launch. This gives you data points across multiple weeks, and lets you see trends instead of a fluke. Work the same playbook each week (one newsletter, two social pushes, a personal-network nudge) and watch the deltas:

To see why velocity matters, imagine two four-week pre-launch campaigns that end with roughly the same follower total—but reach that total in very different ways.

In the **first scenario**, Week 1 opens with a respectable twenty-five people clicking "Notify me on launch." Unfortunately, the energy collapses after the initial push. **Week 2** brings in only four new followers, **Week 3** trickles in three to five, and **Week 4** adds just another handful. The trajectory is trending downward, a clear warning sign that your messaging isn't landing or your warm-up content has gone stale. If you launch on that curve, expect a sluggish Day 1. The audience isn't cooling, they're already cold.

Now contrast that with a **steady-build scenario**. Here, fifty readers follow in **Week 1**, forty-eight more arrive in **Week 2**, fifty-three jump aboard in **Week 3**, and another fifty-one in **Week 4.** The weekly deltas hover around the same healthy range, proving that people are still discovering, sharing, and talking about the project. When you see that kind of flat, consistent growth line, no sharp drop-offs, no stagnation, you can launch with confidence, knowing momentum is primed to convert into a strong opening surge.

The totals might even seem similar on paper, but the slope of the line tells the real story. A tapering curve predicts a soft launch; a steady, level climb predicts backers pouring in the moment you go live. This allows you to judge how long the campaign should be, what you should offer, what you should change, and even if you should launch at all. Nobody is forcing you to launch, and if you have to redesign something, you should.

HOW TO REACT TO A VELOCITY DROP

- **Change the bait.** If your teaser graphic stalled, release a new cover mock-up or a spicy excerpt.
- **Rewrite the page.** If you're sending out copy, and it's not working, change the copy.
- **Change the "basics".** Mainly what people see on the pre-launch page are the headline, the tagline, and the image. If people are not clicking to get notified, then you should change them around and try again.
- **Educate people.** You can only click the notify button if you have a Kickstarter campaign, so it might be that people on your list don't have an account, and you need to do some education.
- **Add an incentive.** "Hit 200 followers by Friday and I'll drop the prologue for free."
- **Increase personal outreach.** DM superfans, ask them to share, or host a live reading to reignite buzz.
- **Delay if necessary.** If velocity never recovers, push launch back a week and run a bigger warm-up sequence. A one-week delay costs nothing; a dead-on-arrival Day 1 costs the campaign.

Depending on your rewards, you should expect somewhere between $5k-$15k per 100 followers. This is a big range, but if you're selling a $150 special edition then you'll be making way more than a $25 paperback. I generally tell people not to launch until they have 100 backers, and that gives a good base of support. There is no maximum time to have a pre-launch page live.

Track the numbers, read the slope, and tune your outreach until the graph points up. Launch only when momentum— *not just tally*—tells you the crowd is truly activated.

The bottom line is, treat pre-launch audience building with the same seriousness as the campaign itself. It's a project with deliverables (content to post, emails to send, people to reach) and with metrics to hit if possible. This not only leads to a better launch, it also calms your nerves because you can see tangible progress. Instead of just biting your nails waiting for launch day, you have mini-wins: "Yes! 10 more people on the list today!" That confidence will carry into your campaign.

CHAPTER 15

OUTREACH STRATEGIES

Once your campaign is live and your pre-built audience has hopefully given you a strong start, the work isn't over. Now it's about **casting a wider net** and keeping the energy up for the duration of the campaign. Let's look at how to do that.

CROSS-PROMOTE WITH FELLOW CREATORS

One of the most powerful (and free) ways to reach new supporters is through **cross-promotion** with other creators. The indie author (and artist, and comic) community can be incredibly supportive. Many creators are open to helping each other.

The key is to find the right partners and make it mutually beneficial. Since literally every campaign is available to spy on, you can look through every live campaign, or campaign in pre-launch, and reach out to the creators.

- **Identify complementary creators:** Look for authors who have campaigns around the same time as yours or who have an upcoming launch to coordinate with.

Ideally, their work should appeal to the same audience. For example, if you wrote a sci-fi novel, find other sci-fi authors. I often coordinate with other authors in the fantasy and sci-fi space because he knows their backers might enjoy his work and vice versa.

- **Build a relationship (if you haven't):** It's easier to cross-promote if you've had some prior interaction. If there's an author you admire, maybe engage with them on social media or comment on their campaign if it's live (genuinely!). Then, you can slide into a message like, *"Hey, I see you have a Kickstarter running too – your project looks great. I think our books appeal to a similar crowd. Want to do a quick cross-promo? I can mention your campaign in an update to my backers if you'll consider doing the same."* Keep it friendly and low-pressure.

- **Update swaps:** A very common technique on Kickstarter is the backer update swap. You and another live campaign agree to shout each other out in an update to your respective backers. It usually goes like: *"Hey everyone, quick note: our friend [Name] has an awesome campaign for [Project] that I think you'd enjoy. Check it out [link]!"* Because backers of one campaign are predisposed to liking that genre, they're quite likely to click and possibly back the other. Do this with a few campaigns and you can steadily pick up extra backers throughout your campaign.

- **Newsletter swaps:** Similar concept, but via email. Even if you're not overlapping with another Kickstarter, you could arrange with an author friend to mention your campaign in their newsletter while you mention their book or site in yours. The goodwill you've built in your email list can rub off as a warm recommendation for you in someone else's list.

- **Bundle or group promotions:** Sometimes creators team up to offer something special. E.g., "Back both our campaigns and get a bonus art print" (careful with Kickstarter rules – such collaborations are allowed but structure it clearly and manage fulfillment). Or simply a group of authors does a collective shout-out post: "Check out these 5 author Kickstarters blowing up this month!" which you all share. United signals boost credibility.
- **Reciprocate and schedule wisely:** If you agree to cross-promote, do follow through. And timing matters: you might arrange one cross-promo for week 1, another for mid-campaign, and another during the final week. That way you have little boosts when you need them. Also, choose partners who will likely hold up their end and have a decent audience size. Ten swaps with tiny campaigns might not move the needle; a few swaps with moderately successful ones will.

Don't be an island. Other creators are allies, not competitors, when it comes to Kickstarter. By helping each other, everyone's boat rises.

LEVERAGE INFLUENCERS AND PRESS

Beyond fellow creators, consider reaching out to influencers, bloggers, or media outlets that cater to your target audience or the creative community:

- **Book bloggers and YouTubers (BookTube):** There are many reviewers and content creators who love highlighting new books, especially unique projects. A Kickstarter can be a cool story for them ("Crowdfunded fantasy novel reimagines African folklore"). Research a few who cover your genre. Send a polite, concise pitch email or DM: *"Hi [Name], I love your blog/channel. I'm an indie author launching a [genre] novel via Kickstarter – it's [one intriguing line about your book]. Because it's a bit different (limited edition, etc.), I thought it might interest your followers. I can provide an ARC or images if you'd like to feature or review it. Thanks for considering!"* They might not all respond, but even one or two saying yes can bring in new eyes.
- **Podcasts:** Are there writing or genre-related podcasts you could be a guest on? Many podcasts look for interesting stories. *"Author funds novel on Kickstarter"* is an angle. Reach out to ones you know or have connections to. But keep timing in mind—podcasts often schedule weeks out, so this works best if you plan ahead or if they can release an episode during your campaign.
- **Local media:** Don't underestimate local newspapers, radio, or community blogs. They often love human interest pieces like "Local teacher turns fantasy author, launches book via Kickstarter." Craft a simple press release or personal email for local media. Even a short article or mention can get random supporters or at least make you look more legit.
- **Social media influencers:** Maybe there's a TikToker who does sci-fi book recommendations, or an

Instagrammer who features fantasy art. A gentle approach works: engage with their content genuinely first, then mention your project. Some might have advertising rates – be cautious spending money (more on that below) – but some might just share because they think it's cool. For example, if your book has a strong theme (say, a diverse cast or addressing mental health), there might be influencers passionate about that who'd amplify it.

- **Niche communities and forums:** Consider Reddit (subreddits related to your genre), Discord communities, or specialty forums. Each has its own rules about self-promo, so respect that. Often, being a genuine participant before promoting yields better results. If you've been active on r/Fantasy or a Mystery readers Facebook group, members will be more receptive when you say, "Hey, I hope this is okay to share – I've been working on something special: [brief plug]." And because you're one of them, many will gladly check it out.

- **Make it an interesting story:** When reaching any media or influencer, frame your project not just as "buy my book" but as a story or benefit to their audience. For example, I might pitch myself to an entrepreneurship podcast as "I've raised over $300k on Kickstarter with publishing projects – I can talk about creative crowdfunding." That's offering value (insight) to the podcast, while also letting me mention my current campaign. Likewise, a fantasy blogger might be more intrigued that your book's world is inspired by a rare folklore, or that you're a single mom writing at 4am to make this book happen – whatever is compelling beyond the book itself. They call this "being newsy."

Influencer and press outreach can be a long shot, but landing even one good mention can cause a nice bump. On top of that, press builds over time. You unlock bigger press opportunities by getting smaller ones.

And sometimes, these things snowball (one site covers you, another sees that and also features you, etc.). Allocate some effort here, appropriate to your scale. If you're trying to raise $2k, you probably don't need a full press tour. But if you're aiming big or just want to maximize reach, give it a shot.

A quick reality-check. Many influencers get tons of requests, so don't take non-responses personally. Focus on those who are the right fit and personalize your approach to each. And remember, micro-influencers (with smaller but devoted followings) can have a surprisingly strong impact – sometimes more than a big name with a disengaged audience. A bookstagrammer with 2,000 die-hard follower-readers might net you more backers than a general news outlet.

CONSIDER PAID ADVERTISING – CAUTIOUSLY

Paid ads (Facebook, Instagram, etc.) are a tempting way to get the word out, but they can also be a **money sink** if not done carefully. In general, don't even consider ads unless your campaign has a $60+ average pledge value and at least 100 organic backers. Here are some pointers if you're thinking about ads:

- **Only spend what you can afford to lose:** Treat any ad spend as extra, not as a cornerstone of your strategy. Many successful campaigns spend $0 on ads. If you do have a budget, set a hard limit like "I'll spend $500 on Facebook ads, and only if I see results will I consider more." Just know, lots of campaigns that use advertising don't even know if their ads are working until they spend at least $500-$1,000.
- **Timing of ads:** Running ads to a Kickstarter can be tricky because of the limited time window. Some creators run a small ad campaign a week before launch to build the email list or notify-me clicks (so they have a warmed audience). Others wait until mid-campaign lulls to try to get new eyes. Generally, I think you should start ads at the beginning.
- **Targeting is key:** If you do Facebook/Instagram ads, target fans of authors or genres similar to yours. For example, target people who like George R.R. Martin if you have a grimdark fantasy, or people who like specific comic franchises if you're doing a graphic novel. Broad targeting like "all book lovers" will waste money. Think in niches.
- **Ad content:** Show your best stuff – likely your book cover or a beautiful graphic with a clear headline like "Special Edition Novel on Kickstarter" and a call-to-action to check it out. If you already have some credibility (like "150% funded in 48 hours!"), that can be great to include as social proof in the ad, later in the campaign.
- **Track results:** Use tracking links or at least monitor if you see pledge spikes when ads are running. If you

burn $20 and see nothing, probably stop or change your approach. If you see pledges coming, ensure the cost per acquisition makes sense (e.g., spending $5 per $25 backer might be okay; spending $5 per $1 backer is not).

- **Alternatives to traditional ads:** There are also niche opportunities like sponsoring a genre-specific newsletter or a project discovery site. For instance, there are newsletters that highlight cool Kickstarter projects (sometimes for a fee). If one is reputable, it might be worth the $30 to reach a bunch of known backers. Again, research and reviews are your friends here – see if others had success.

STAGGER YOUR OUTREACH

Campaigns often have a strong start and finish, with a dip in the middle. To combat that "mid-campaign slump," plan your outreach in waves:

- **Early campaign (Launch + first few days):** This is when your core fans and personal network hit the campaign. Also, any press you arrange to drop at launch will bring people. It's a frenzy – enjoy it! Share publicly any big milestones ("50% funded in 2 days!"). Those early wins themselves become marketing material (people love backing something that looks like it's doing well).
- **Mid-campaign boosts:** Schedule some special events or promotions around the middle. Perhaps a cross-promo update in week 2, an influencer's review going live in week 3, or a themed social media event (like an

AMA – Ask Me Anything – on Reddit or a live reading on Instagram). These give you something new to talk about instead of "still funding, please back." For example, "We just unlocked our second stretch goal!" or "Check out this awesome artist who just endorsed our project" can reignite interest.

- **Update your backers and encourage sharing:** As the campaign goes on, keep communicating with your current backers through updates. Share progress ("manuscript is off to the printer!") or excitement ("new character art reveal!"). In those updates, it's okay to occasionally ask backers to spread the word: *"If you're enjoying the campaign, please share it with a friend who'd love this book. The more the merrier!"* You can even create a specific social media post for them to share. Often backers want to help; they just need a nudge.

- **Approach stretch run (final week):** Have a game plan for the final 48-72 hours. Many creators save one cross-promo or big ad push for the last days to maximize the ending rush. Also, Kickstarter sends a "48 hours left" email to anyone who clicked "Notify me" but hasn't backed yet – expect a flurry from that. Use it: update your page or campaign updates with any last-minute news ("Only 2 days left to join 300 other backers!"). Build that FOMO (fear of missing out) in a friendly way: *"Last chance to get this exclusive edition – don't miss out!"*

- **Staggered content:** If you have a lot of media assets (like multiple art pieces or bonus reveals), don't show them all at once. Drip them out, one per week or so.

This keeps giving you "news" to share. For instance, unlock a new stretch goal reward at 150% funded, and announce it when you hit that. Or reveal a new cover variant at 200 backers. Each reveal is an excuse to post an update and shout externally, *"Look what we just added!"* People love campaigns that evolve.

- **Monitor and adapt again:** Throughout, watch what outreach is working. If a certain tweet went semi-viral, maybe put some ad money to boost it further. If a cross-promo brought 20 backers, consider doing another of that style. If you hear crickets mid-campaign, perhaps double down on personal messages or another email to your list with a new hook ("We're funded, now let's hit that stretch goal – here's why it's exciting…").

The idea is to avoid a long stagnant period where nothing is happening. You don't want *you* to lose momentum or motivation either. Having scheduled outreach keeps you busy and proactive, rather than just refreshing the Kickstarter page hoping for backers.

COMMUNITY SNOWBALL

We touched on social proof earlier, but during the campaign, it becomes a powerful marketing tool in itself:

- **Celebrate milestones publicly:** Whenever you hit something noteworthy – 50% funded, 100 backers, fully funded, $10k raised, whatever – broadcast it. *"Wow, we just crossed 100 backers! Thank you all!"* People who haven't backed yet see those messages. Success breeds success: many will jump on when they see a bandwagon forming. It's not bragging if you frame it as gratitude.

- **Encourage backer engagement:** A lively comment section or active backer community can itself attract more backers. New people often check the comments to gauge how engaged the community is. So spark that engagement. Ask backers a fun question in an update ("Which character are you most excited to read about?") or do a small contest ("Post a photo of your current bookshelf, and one random backer will get an extra bookmark in their package"). When backers talk, it signals to onlookers that this is more than a transaction – it's a community.

- **Share backer excitement:** If a backer tweets "Just backed this awesome project!", retweet it or share it. Testimonials from actual supporters are gold. You can even compile a few quotes from comments (ask permission if it was a private message) and share something like, *"Backers are loving what they see: 'This project is a dream come true!' – a new backer."* That's social proof in real time.

- **Create a sense of team:** Use inclusive language with your backers. *"We're in this together and look what we've achieved!"* When people feel part of your success, they're more likely to bring others in, almost like recruiting to a cause. I've seen backers proudly say, "I've gotten 3 friends to join this campaign because I want that next stretch goal unlocked." They feel ownership and that's wonderful.

- **Community beyond the campaign:** Mention any community spaces you have (or plan to have) beyond

Kickstarter. For example, a Facebook group for fans, a Discord server, etc. Some backers will join there and bring friends. Or they'll just appreciate knowing the fun continues after funding. It also makes newcomers think, "This isn't just a one-off, it's an ongoing community – maybe I want in on that." Even something like, *"All backers will be invited to a backer-only livestream party after the campaign"* can galvanize people to join now so they don't miss the after-party.

People like to be where other people are, it's human nature. It often takes 14+ times before they make a decision. So, the more you can showcase that *people are backing and loving this project*, the easier it is to get new people to back and love the project, continuing the cycle.

CHAPTER 16

HOW TO BUILD AN EMAIL SEQUENCE

When I tell authors I send daily emails during a Kickstarter launch, they look at me horrified. They tell me things like, *"I don't have anything to say,"* and *"My readers will hate that."* I can only say, *"Yes, you do,"* and *"No, they won't,"* so many times before it gets tedious. That amount of times is significantly fewer than the thousands of times I've had that conversation over the years. Today, I'm going to explain how you can send emails daily during a book launch without pissing off your audience and give you the exact sequence I used along the way.

Authors believe readers will tune out if you email them daily, even if for a short time. **This is bunk.** Assuming people signed up for your list ethically, then they are there to hear about your work.

Period.

Subscribers want to hear about your work. *That's why they signed up for your email list.*

Yes, some contingent prefers to hear from you rarely, which is why you should always give them a choice of how often to hear from you. At the end of my automation sequence for new readers, I ask them to tell me how often they want to hear from me: weekly, monthly, or just at launches. If they don't choose one, they agree to let me email them as often as I want, and I say that explicitly in the email.

In my own data, 96% of people are perfectly cool hearing from me more often than weekly, as long as it's interesting. *The absolute worst thing you can be to a reader is boring, ever.*

Of course, that is a colloquial example, but there is a whole industry of daily emails like 1440 and Morning Brew with millions of people excited to hear from them every day.

The difference is they send new and interesting information with every email, and that's what we're going to help you fix about your launch sequence today. I'm going to show you how to send unique emails to your list they (should) love if they like your books.

I have raised $500,000+ on Kickstarter alone, and I use this strategy in almost every campaign.

Since I have 5+ launches a year it's a little harder, but if you're like most authors who launch 1-2 books a year, then there's no reason you shouldn't get some value out of this.

I'll be giving you my exact emails from multiple campaigns pulled together into what I think is an effective email sequence. These are only examples. Please don't flat out crib them. *Use them as guidance and make your own.*

These emails are built upon the principle of buying triggers.

4 WEEKS FROM LAUNCH

When you're a month out from launch, you should already have your book on pre-order or your pre-launch Kickstarter page live. Therefore, ***your first email should be a simple announcement.*** You need your book on pre-order or your pre-launch page live so you can start collecting sales/interest.

Even if the book isn't 100% done, you should be able to use Book Brush or a similar service to generate a cover mockup, which is what I use to make mine. However, you can also just use the front cover to make your announcement.

The end is coming...

Hi,

The end of The Obsidian Spindle Saga is coming in January.

Pre-launch link

This is my favorite series I've ever written. It contains several of my favorite books that I've ever written. If you have not read this series, and you love my work, then you will absolutely ADORE this series. If you have known of my work and been waiting to try something, then this is my best work.

Portal fantasy is my absolutely FAVORITE genre of fiction, whether it's The Wizard of Oz, Alice In Wonderland, The Magicians, His Dark Materials, The Lion, the Witch, and the Wardrobe, The Hazel Wood, Caraval, Ten Thousand Doors of January, Peter Pan, Neverwhere, or literally any other book about characters traveling to different places, worlds, realities, they are my jam. I poured all that love into this series.

Each book of The Obsidian Spindle Saga is told from multiple different perspectives from all across the world of Urgu, weaving together a narrative between them. This was the most complex project I've ever worked on, getting each character right, and telling different but cohesive stories between them.

One of the things I appreciate about Game of Thrones is that each character is not only rich and unique, but they also have their own type of fantasy story. Sansa is having a story about political intrigue while John Snow is having a classic fantasy adventure story, all while Arya is having a coming-of-age fantasy story.

It's like 30-40 stories in one book.

These stories are quite pared down in comparison to Game of Thrones. Each book comes in around 275 pages compared to 500+, but I loved the idea that each story can be its own thing and bring different elements of fantasy into it.

THREE WEEKS FROM LAUNCH

If you're using Kickstarter for the first time, then I recommend an email explaining what Kickstarter is and why you're using it. Otherwise, this can be substituted for a "why I love this series" or "history of this series" post.

OPTION 1

What is Kickstarter?

Hey,

Even though this is my 17th campaign, it is always the first campaign for many people on my list, so I wanted to reach out and share with you how Kickstarter works in case you don't know.

KICKSTARTER LINK

How Does Pre-Ordering on Kickstarter Work

If you're new to Kickstarter, don't worry... it's a very easy, fun platform, one that's helped me bring tons of our awesome products to life over the years.

A few things to know if you choose to back:

*1. You can pledge today, and you will not be charged until the campaign is complete on **June 17th, 2021.***

*2. Kickstarter is an all-or-nothing funding platform, meaning we needed to raise our **$2,000 goal** (which we did in the first three hours) in order for the project to move forward.*

Your support means EVERYTHING, and we could not do this without you.

*3. This campaign has a hard end of **Thursday, June 17th, 2021 at 8:00 PM**. You will need to pledge before then in order to secure your rewards for this campaign.*

4. You can back today at any pledge level, and you have until the end of the campaign to up-or-downgrade your pledge.

5. The earlier you back, the more access you'll have to surprise campaign goodies and extras like our early bird perks, which go to backers ONLY.

So, if you don't want to miss out on any of the fun, join us on Kickstarter today!

Speaking of early bird perks, I put together an awesome bundle of EARLY BIRD perks.

Everybody who backs the campaign by Saturday night gets some amazing digital books, absolutely free, and included in your pledge.

All backers who pledge by Saturday (even for $1) get Lady Serra and the Draconian by Cat Banks, School for Dragons by Amy Wolf, Seeking the Salamander by Matt Harry and Stranger: Academy for Peculiars by Isadora Brown, absolutely free!

I am so super excited for this series. I spent the last three years building up the universe and writing these books. I can't wait to share it with you.

So, head over and check out the campaign right now to lock in these awesome rewards.

OPTION 2

Why would you even do this to a beloved classic, you monster?

Hi,

Alice is my favorite literary character of all time. I love her so much that I have read both of her books at least 100 times. Every time I read it, I think it must have been written in a fever dream. The way Wonderland acts always makes me feel like she's on a strange, ethereal drug trip.

Then, I had this very weird idea that maybe it was a drug trip, and maybe the Red Queen had drugged everyone, which led me to the idea that maybe, just maybe, the people of Wonderland revolted against the Red Queen and the drugs were removed from the water supply.

Would that be a good thing for Wonderland? Certainly, it would seem that way, but what if the real world was too much to handle? What if reality kind of sucked? What would people do in order to get back to Wonderland? What would they give up? What would they risk?

Some would likely risk everything, and that led to building the whole world, full of characters you'll recognize, from Dormouse to Caterpillar to the White Queen, and locations you'll love like The Looking Glass Lounge.

*This is NOT a fantasy book. It's a straight thriller with nods to the original fairy tale. **I won't lie, this is VERY polarizing to Alice fans.** People who read the original* *story are split right down the middle on whether they love it or hate it.*

2 WEEKS BEFORE LAUNCH

Assuming you are launching a Kickstarter, the next email that should be sent is something previewing the actual page and asking your fans for feedback. This is a critical piece because your best fans will tell you what's wrong (or right) with your campaign. It also acts to get people excited about what they are going to get when your campaign goes live.

If you don't have a "page" then you can replace this with a "Read the first chapter" email, which you'll see later.

Can you help me?

Hi,

We're two weeks from the release of The Obsidian Spindle Saga and I need your help. You are always so helpful when I ask you to check out the build of the page and give me your input, so I'm asking you to do it again, if you have a minute.

Preview link

On top of giving me your thoughts, hopefully you'll get a better sense of the project, the world, and the characters. I love Kickstarter because it allows me to dive in deeper than a simple blurb and give you all the juicy details about the world.

While you're on the page, don't forget to click the top left to be notified when the books launch on June 1st.

Thanks so much!

ONE WEEK FROM LAUNCH

One week from launch is a great time to highlight a bonus people get for buying early. If you have direct access to your readers, it's easy to see who bought when, but you can also ask readers to submit their receipts to get their bonus.

Publishers do this all the time with new releases, and I think it's very smart. If you have a longer pre-order you can start this even earlier as a way to get people to buy the book before it launches.

Early bird perks announced…

Hey,

We're just one week out from the start of the Dragon Strife trilogy Kickstarter, and I'm just so so so excited. Maybe part of that is the insane amount of sugar I've had in the past week since being home, but I like to think it's because I love this story so much.

Notification link

Today, I am announcing some other books I love a whole lot, namely the early bird perks for this campaign.

*Everyone who backs in the first week of the campaign will receive digital copies of **Born of Magic** by Jack Holder, **Of Dreams and Dragons** by Karpov Kincade, **The Herebey Dragons** by Simon Birks, Eda Çağıl Çağlarırmak, and Lyndon White, and **Wildskies** book 1 by Melissa Hudson.*

Russell Nohelty

I am so thrilled to include these books in this bundle, some of which are old friends and others are brand new that I just found in the past couple of months.

Whether you already love my work or haven't tried it yet, I think The Dragon Strife trilogy is the perfect series for you. Why? Let me tell you.

If you love my work, then you'll love this series because:

1. *It deals with a lot of the religious, political and socio-economic themes of my previous work in a very interesting way while still being filled with action and pathos.*

2. *There are plenty of interesting characters and plot twists that will keep you turning the page.*

3. *It's a first person POV story from the perspective of a powerless woman who grows to become one of the most important people in the history of this world.*

4. *It is an empowering theme that will make you feel like you have agency in a world where there is mercilessly little of it.*

5. *Dragons!!!*

If you haven't tried my work before, then this is the perfect series for you because:

1. *It's a self-contained trilogy. There is a second trilogy that is planned, but there is no more of this particular story planned.*

2. *There is very little (if any) cursing.*

3. *Most of the violence happens off the page, so if you think my previous work is too gory, this series is for you.*

4. *There is a very serious and heavy romance theme through the books.*

5. *The character is a pacifist who abhors violence.*

6. *Most of the main conflict of these books are political and things don't get resolved with punchy punching like much of my most popular work. That's not to say there's no battles or violence, just that the plot hinges mostly on diplomacy and gathering allies together.*

7. *You won't have to remember a hundred different timelines and a thousand characters that hop around between books, or have a very long time commitment.*

I hope you'll join us next Tuesday to kick this year off right, and I hope you have a very happy and prosperous new year.

So those are the emails I would send before a launch. This cadence is only weekly, which should be doable for any author's audience. If you send less frequently than that, I highly recommend emailing earlier and giving people a chance to opt out of this launch or choose to remain at their current cadence.

I would send this email a few months early to give people a chance to take action. This can be as simple as adding something like this to your emails.

In a couple of months, I will be launching my next book and will be experimenting with a much more aggressive email strategy for two weeks. I think it will help you learn more about the world and history of this series, but if you'd like to opt out of it, please do x and I will make sure you are removed from those emails before they are sent.

As an author you should be able to test new things, and it might make sense to even say something about it being a test.

LAUNCH DAY

Regardless of your feelings about email, I don't think anyone will object to sending an email on launch day announcing your book is live.

THE OBSIDIAN SPINDLE SAGA KICKSTARTER IS LIVE

Hey,

The Obsidian Spindle Saga is live on Kickstarter!!!

KICKSTARTER LINK

I am absolutely floored with how excited you all are for this book series, and I can't wait to share it with you!

Fairy tales are real.

Rose Briar is a diabetic, college student without insurance.

She's been scraping by through a combination of maxing out credit cards and relying upon the kindness of strangers.

Unfortunately, she's spent every dollar at her disposal. There's no money left to buy her life-saving insulin.

Without her medication, Rose falls into a diabetic coma. She tumbles into a deep slumber and wakes up in a fantastical place called the Dream Realm, where fairy tales and legends of old are still very much alive.

She has one chance to wake up.

She must trek across the world, visit the most powerful object in the land, the Obsidian Spindle, and entreat with the fates; the only beings powerful enough to send her soul back to Earth.

But evil forces don't want her to leave.

They will stop at nothing to capture her and make sure she never goes home again.

Now, with the help of her half-gorgon girlfriend and a mysterious red rider, Rose must race across the land fighting dragons, monsters, and the forces of the Wicked Witch, Nimue, in order to reach the Obsidian Spindle before her body dies on Earth and she's trapped in the Dream Realm forever.

Will she be able to wake up? Can she survive? That is the genesis of the Obsidian Spindle Saga (TOSS), and the first book The Sleeping Beauty.

For backing this series early, everybody who backs the campaign by Saturday night gets some amazing digital books, absolutely free, and included in your pledge.

*All backers who pledge by Saturday (even for $1) get **Lady Serra and the Draconian** by Cat Banks, **School for Dragons** by Amy Wolf, **Seeking the Salamander** by Matt Harry and **Stranger: Academy for Peculiars** by Isadora Brown, absolutely free!*

I am so super excited for this series. I spent the last three years building up the universe and writing these books. I can't wait to share it with you.

See you behind the backer wall.

DAY 2

I often send my "read the first chapter" email before the launch (as I talked about above), and only on books where it's not a spoiler. This is always one of my best-performing emails and yes, I add the whole first chapter right into the email.

Read the first chapter of The Dragon Scourge right in your browser

Hey,

Happy New Year!

*The Kickstarter for **The Dragon Strife** trilogy is live on Kickstarter, and I wanted to share the first chapter with you so we can start the new year off right with some cool dragon books.*

Notification link

Today, I will die.

This wasn't a surprise to me. I had been preparing for it my whole life, but I never thought it would come until it crashed upon me this morning like a suffocating wave. Fifteen years on this Earth seemed like so much time, but now I realized how little of my life as a ceremonial sacrifice afforded me.

I was always an early bird. I woke with the sun, ready for the start of a new day. However, when the tender kiss of light touched my eyes on my final morning alive, I shut them tighter and pulled my sheets over my head. If I didn't face the day, then perhaps my death would never come.

I trained for this since I was a small child, but there is no amount of preparation that readied you for being swallowed by a dragon; its horrible, jagged teeth ripping through the white dress Sister Milka sewed special for the occasion and tearing your flesh as it gnashed against your virgin body.

Somebody softly knocked on the door to my room. "Gilda, we need to get started. Today is a big day."

Sacrifices were given every privilege. We wanted for nothing in our short lives, and after our deaths, those we loved were taken care of for the rest of their days. It was what the villagers bestowed upon us to assuage their guilt, and it was a small price to pay compared to the one we paid.

We were the salvation of the village, after all. It was only because of our noble sacrifice that the great dragon lord Ewig stayed satiated in his cave inside the volcano that loomed above us and didn't sweep down to destroy us.

Russell Nohelty

That was the pact, cemented in blood a hundred years ago. Every five years, one of us must willingly walk to our deaths, and in return, the great dragon would watch over our village and prevent the great volcano that loomed over us from erupting, burying our village under its magma.

It was a great honor to be chosen as the sacrificial lamb. That was what the line they told me at least, but today it certainly didn't seem like an honor. It seemed like I was raised like a lamb for slaughter, provided every luxury to die at the right moment.

"Coming!" I said after a long pause. Sister Milka was a harsh and unforgiving mistress, and would not accept anything but perfection today, on my last day of life. Every day of my life she watched over me, training me to die well. Even now, at the end, she would not take her foot off my neck. Especially now, with so much on the line, with the prosperity of our town riding on the spillage of my blood before the clock struck midnight tonight.

I slipped my sandals on my feet and rose to stand. Before I answered the door, I spun and made my bed, as I was trained to do; the first sign of an uncluttered mind was a perfectly made bed. It was the least we could do to show how much we appreciated all we were given.

As I pulled the corner of the bed taut, I thought about not tucking in the final edge as a little sign of rebellion. However, when I tried to leave it mussed, pangs of guilt washed over me, until they were so overwhelming that, with shaking hands, I forced the last edge of my blanket in tightly.

Once I was dead, my house would become a museum, and my room a shrine, preserved exactly how I left it, and I didn't want my mother to have to explain that her perfect daughter died a slob. Why do I care what people think of me after my death?

With the bed made, I walked to the door and placed my hand on the knob. The minute I opened it, the machinations of my last hours, those that I trained for my whole life, would wash over me one after another.

"It's time to open this door, missy."

I closed my eyes and felt my breath against my chest, rising and lowering in slow, rhythmic time with the beating of my heart. They were small gestures, in the grand scheme, but right now, they were everything, and soon, much too soon, they would fall fallow and motionless forever.

What would happen after I took my final breath? According to the church, I would rise up into the sky and take my place among the stars, but what did they know? The gods were long dead, and the dragons that remained had none of their love of humanity.

Banging came from the other side of the door, and Sister Milka's shrill voice cut through the air. "That's quite enough of this dawdling, Gilda! Open the door this instant."

Her shouting pulled me out of my calm, and I turned the doorknob. She exploded into the room, her trim frame and long face cutting an imposing image against the harsh light that fell into the room. She was not a big woman, but her presence filled my small room like none other.

"Good morning, mistress," I said, bowing my head to avoid her gaze. You never looked the nuns in the eyes.

She didn't answer for a long moment, busying herself with checking my room, inspecting my bed, and running her fingers across the top of my dresser, looking for dust. She rubbed her fingers together and gave a small nod. "I see your mother took this cleaning seriously."

I nodded to her, keeping my eyes turned to the ground. "Of course, mistress. She scrubbed all day and into the evening."

Sister Milka not only ran the monastery and school in town but personally looked over all of us chosen for sacrifice, of which there were three at any time. It was a job she took seriously and had since taking her vows fifty years ago.

"Well, let me get a look at you," she said. "Stand up straight."

It was crucial that I not have a flaw or imperfection on my naked body, and for fifteen years I can't remember a time when I lifted a finger in manual labor. My mother made all my meals, or a member of the community would deliver it, and everything else was taken care of so I could keep myself flawless for my date with Ewig.

I dropped my nightgown to the floor and endured the intense gaze of Sister Milka as she examined every inch of me. Two years ago, I judged a livestock competition, and she looked at me like the other judges looked at the cattle on display, trying to decide which one would give the best meat.

"You need to shave every inch of you, except your hair," she said. "We do not want the great dragon lord to get a hairball now, do we?"

I shook my head. "No, mistress."

"Good, good." She placed her hands under my breasts and then pinched the sides of my waist. "You have put on decent weight in the past year, my dear. Yes, I think the dragon lord will be most impressed with you." Then she moved her hand to my face and brushed her hand along my cheek. "You are truly one of my greatest girls. I am so proud of what you have become."

A compliment? She never gave me a compliment before. She had nothing but bitter, terse words for me, that stuck into my gut with pain and tore at my mind.

"T-thank you, mistress."

She moved her hand to my chin and pulled it up to meet her eyes, a great honor she afforded very few. "No, thank you, my dear. The sacrifice you make tonight is a greater burden than any child should bear."

Tears filled my eyes as I stared into Sister Milka's face. Her eyes were a cold, dark brown, and even though her words were kind, her face was sharp, and her voice terse, taking much of the tenderness from them.

"No need for that." Sister Milka pulled her hand from my face and slid a white handkerchief from her pocket. "This

is a happy occasion, after all. Your sacrifice will save us all. There is no greater gift. Now, clean yourself up, and I will draw your bath."

That's just the beginning of the story. I hope you'll join us behind the backer wall, and you can read a few more chapters by clicking here.

Plus, if you back, you'll get a ton of awesome extra books.

*Everyone who backs in the first week of the campaign will receive digital copies of **Born of Magic** by Jack Holder, **Of Dreams and Dragons** by Karpov Kincade, **The Herebey Dragons** by Simon Birks, Eda Çağıl Çağlarırmak, and Lyndon White, and **Wildskies** book 1 by Melissa Hudson.*

And and and and and you can pick up the below 5" x 7" postcard print by backing @ the $22 or $75+ physical pledge levels.

Let's kick this year off right and fill it with magic and dragons.

DAY 3

On day three I like to talk about why I love this series and why I think they will love it, too. We've passed the nadir point of excitement, and so I try to bring it back to the heart of the book.

The best series I've ever written?

Hi,

I am prone to hyperbole and tend to downplay it when other people say that one book or another is the best book I've ever written.

*However, across the board everybody who has read The Obsidian Spindle Saga has said that it's not only **MY** best series, but it's one of their favorite series of all time…*

…and the first four books are coming to Kickstarter on June 1st. You can sign up to get notified at launch <u>by clicking here.</u>

I've been developing this series since 2018, and I'm soooo excited to finally be able to talk about it. My small team of readers has been sworn to secrecy for YEARS and the cat is finally out of the bag, as they say.

The Obsidian Spindle Saga started with a simple premise. Knowing everything I knew about writing after finishing over a dozen novels, if I could go back and design my perfect series, the one that would stand the test of time and encapsulate everything I loved in the world, what would it be?

I gathered the pieces very quickly: a dash of fairy tales, a scoop of mythology, a spoonful of portal fantasy, a sprinkle of romance, a bit of social commentary, and a whole heap of worldbuilding, and when I sat back I realized…I wasn't a good enough writer to take on this series yet.

That doesn't mean my other books weren't good, but The Obsidian Spindle was more complicated than anything I had ever done.

I didn't know enough about writing romance, or YA, and I had never had a story written from multiple perspectives, so I set out on a very ambitious project, and wrote non-stop for the next eighteen months, in order to learn everything I thought I needed to know in order to take on this series.

Some of those books you might have seen before. The Marked Ones, Invasion, The Void Calls Us Home all came from that process. Our Wannabe+ exclusive serial Anna and The Dark Place was the final book I wrote during that time span, the capstone that proved to me I was ready to write The Obsidian Spindle Saga.

This is the series I was talking about last year when I released all those books in my summer slate. All of those books were leading to this series.

And so, in June 2018 I wrote the first book in the series, The Sleeping Beauty, pouring everything I ever wanted to say into it, and spilling everything I loved onto the page.

I absolutely adored the book. I'm not the type of writer where things fall out of me easily. It's always a struggle to get a book on the page, and then I have to manhandle it to cooperate. I love all my book babies, but they are stubborn as a mule and twice as ornery most times.

That's not the case with this series. The Sleeping Beauty slid out quickly and without much struggle, almost exactly as I imagined it in my mind.

Then, over and over the people who read it said it was my best work ever, and even now, several dozen books later, they still mention The Sleeping Beauty, and the whole Obsidian Spindle Saga, as among their favorite series.

Here is the set-up for the whole book, and the whole universe.

Rose Briar is a diabetic, college student without insurance. She's been scraping by through a combination of maxing out credit cards and relying upon the kindness of strangers.

Unfortunately, she's spent every dollar at her disposal. There's no money left to buy her life-saving insulin.

Without her medication, Rose falls into a diabetic coma. She tumbles into a deep slumber and wakes up in a fantastical place called the Dream Realm, where fairy tales and legends of old are still very much alive.

She has one chance to wake up.

She must trek across the world, visit the most powerful object in the land, the Obsidian Spindle, and entreat with the fates; the only beings powerful enough to send her soul back to Earth.

But evil forces don't want her to leave. They will stop at nothing to capture her and make sure she never goes home again.

Now, with the help of her half-gorgon girlfriend and a mysterious red rider, Rose must race across the land fighting dragons, monsters, and the forces of the Wicked Witch, Nimue, in order to reach the Obsidian Spindle before her body dies on Earth and she's trapped in the Dream Realm forever.

Will she be able to wake up? Can she survive? That is the genesis of the Obsidian Spindle Saga, and the first book The Sleeping Beauty.

I invite you not to take my word for it, though. Try the first ten chapters for yourself by clicking here.

I hope you love it as much as me. I've currently written eight novels in this series, and the first four launch on June 1st.

These first four books act as one complete thought and make up what I'm calling The Dream Realm arc of this series.

If you want to be notified when it goes live, click the button below. This is going to **be a Kickstarter EXCLUSIVE book series**, *which means it won't be anywhere, including the Wannabe+ app, until the series is concluded in either 2023 or 2024.*

DAY 4

In most launches, I'll have an exclusive item people can only get during the initial launch period, and I want to highlight that during the first week of the campaign. I've probably hinted at it before, but I want to make sure to focus on it for one day.

The special postcard print

Hey,

We're still running through our first campaign of the year, but I wanted to talk for a second about the awesome 5" x 7" postcard print you can get for backing the campaign at either the $24 or $75+ physical book level.

Kickstarter link

My awesome cover designer, Paramita Bhattacharjee from The Complete Paramita has allowed me to print off a one-time reward of the virgin cover from The Dragon Scourge as a very special print.

I love it sooo much and we're NEVER going to reprint it. I'm only printing 100 of these and when they are gone, they are gone forever.

*Plus, everyone who backs in the first week of the campaign will receive digital copies of **Born of Magic** by Jack Holder, **Of Dreams and Dragons** by Karpov Kincade, **The Herebey Dragons** by Simon Birks, Çağıl Çağlarırmak, and Lyndon White, and **Wildskies** book 1 by Melissa Hudson.*

Gilda will die today. She has lived her whole life for one purpose—to be sacrificed to the great dragon lord, Ewig. And now, when the sun falls over the horizon, the time will come to fulfill her duty and walk to her death.

It was a fine life, but a lonely one. As payment for her service, the City Council lauded her with riches, allowed her to live in the lap of luxury, and fed her the finest food. She never knew hunger, or strife, even when others worked themselves to the bone and suffered starvation.

The others always resented her for that, but they never knew her pain. Theirs was a hard life, but at least they got to live it. Gilda never had that choice. She would not live to see adulthood. She would never be married or have children.

All that remained of her brief existence was to walk up the lonely volcano to the dragon's keep with honor, even though nobody treated her with any during her life.

Join her as she lives the last hours of her life, and find out what happens once she enters the dragon's cavern and everything changes; for her life, for her town, and for the world.

DAY 5

I usually launch on a Tuesday, and my early bird perks end on Sunday. Whether you have them for three days or ten days, make sure to make a big deal about them closing down. The urgency and FOMO associated with that will get some number of people off the fence.

Last chance for early bird perks...

Hey,

*This is your last chance to lock in the early bird perks for the **Dragon Strife** trilogy.*

Kickstarter link

*Everyone who backs in the first week of the campaign will receive digital copies of **Born of Magic** by Jack Holder, **Of Dreams and Dragons** by Karpov Kincade, **The Herebey Dragons** by Simon Birks, Eda Çağıl Çağlarırmak, and Lyndon White, and **Wildskies** book 1 by Melissa Hudson.*

Gilda will die today. She has lived her whole life for one purpose—to be sacrificed to the great dragon lord, Ewig. And now, when the sun falls over the horizon, the time will come to fulfill her duty and walk to her death.

It was a fine life, but a lonely one. As payment for her service, the City Council lauded her with riches, allowed her to live in the lap of luxury, and fed her the finest food. She never knew hunger, or strife, even when others worked themselves to the bone and suffered starvation.

The others always resented her for that, but they never knew her pain. Theirs was a hard life, but at least they got to live it. Gilda never had that choice. She would not live to see adulthood. She would never be married or have children.

All that remained of her brief existence was to walk up the lonely volcano to the dragon's keep with honor, even though nobody treated her with any during her life.

Join her as she lives the last hours of her life, and find out what happens once she enters the dragon's cavern and everything changes; for her life, for her town, and for the world.

Plus, you can get an awesome 5" x 7" postcard print for backing the campaign at either the $22 or $75+ physical book level.

Hope to see you behind the backer wall to start the new year.

END WEEK 1

Now, we've finished the first week. Hopefully, you can see that every email sent so far highlights a different aspect of the launch and gives readers a different angle to get excited about in a way that even people who already bought would be happy to get them, too.

For week 2, I'm focused on what's called the sideways sales letter, a classic marketing technique that works like gangbusters.

With every email, you break through one of the objections holding people back from buying and help them build a deeper connection with you. Ideally, you would use them to deliver something akin to a sideways sales letter for each of your major series.

"You are basically showing off your series over several different emails that rely on different psychological triggers to get people excited to read it.

"Psychological triggers are powerful tools that copywriters can use to create compelling messages that resonate with their audience. These triggers appeal to the deep-seated needs and desires of people, and when used effectively, can persuade them to take the desired action." -Maria Espo

The goal here is to break apart all the knowledge a reader needs to get excited to read the series and spoon-feed it to them over several days. This is because nobody ever reads every part of a page, and most people discount things they don't understand. If you build a narrative, then you'll have a better chance of getting people to pay attention.

WEEK 2

DAY 8 – OPTION 1

I already shared a post about "the best series I've ever written," which kind of does the part about why you love the series, but I think you need to share how much you love your work multiple times throughout your launch in different ways. If you've already launched books in this series, you could also send a collection of testimonials about your other books. Social proof is very important to get people off the fence.

Why do I love the Dragon Strife trilogy?

Hey,

*The Kickstarter for **The Dragon Strife** trilogy is in its second week and I wanna tell you more about why I love it so so much.*

Kickstarter link

So, why do I love this story?

Because I'm obsessed with writing stories where people with no power end up changing the world, and Dragon Strife may be the best encapsulation of that in all my books.

Russell Nohelty

Gilda is literally a sacrifice. Her entire town, including her mother, have agreed to allow her to die in the most brutal way possible; by being eaten alive by a dragon.

Nobody cares about her, except for the other people who have been forced to die, and yet...

...those same people become the key to saving everything.

It's the overriding thesis to all my works; those people who you look over and pass by are just as important as anyone else, and if you raise them up, they might just change the world.

Gilda starts as a sacrifice, but she becomes so much more, and it's empowering as fuck to read. People have always told me the thing they like about my work is that people have agency in a world where they feel like they have none.

I love that about my work, and I definitely lean into it hardcore with this book. I can't wait to share it with you.

Plus, if you back, you'll get a ton of awesome extra books. Usually, I throw the most perks to early bird backers, but this campaign I'm trying something different, and unlocking a huge slew of new perks for people who back by the end of the campaign.

*Everyone who backs by the end of this week will receive digital copies of **Mythic Creature Trainer #1** by Rene Pfitzer, **Luminous Ages #1***

*by Antonios Christou, **Dragonwar** by Mirren Hogan, **School of Dragons***

by Amy Wolf, **Gods of Aazurn** *by Gary Scott Beatty
and* **Gage and the Dragon's Tear #1** *by Patrick Kellner,
Donny Hadiwidjaja, Bryan Valenza, Ed Dukeshire, Marta
Tanrikulu, and Randy Michaels.*

*And and and and and you can pick up the below 5" x 7"
postcard print by backing @ the $22 or $75+ physical
pledge levels.*

*I hope you'll join us behind the backer wall to kick this year
off right, filled with magic and dragons.*

DAY 8 – OPTION 2

The reviews are in…

Hey,

*We crested over $6,000 last night, which is amazing. I'm
absolutely blown away by how much love you all have
shown The Godsverse Chronicles.*

<u>KICKSTARTER LINK</u>

*Today I didn't want you to hear from me. I wanted to show
you some of the reviews from the Godsverse throughout the
years. One of the awesome parts of adding to a series that's
already out is that people have read it already!*

*These are readers, just like you, who have read and
reviewed the books on Goodreads and Amazon.*

*This campaign features THREE NEW never before seen
novels, including:*

Russell Nohelty

- *And Conquest Followed Behind Them, an Avengers-style team-up book between Katrina, Kimberly, Akta, and Julia as they fight to prevent Ragnarok.*

- *And Chaos Followed Behind Them, an Avengers-style team book between Katrina, Kimberly, Akta, Julia, and Rebecca where the women of the Godsverse fight to stop the end of the universe.*

- *And Darkness Followed Behind Her, three story collection starring fan-favorite Kimberly before, during, and after the events of And Conquest Followed Behind Them, including a story set during the first days of the Apocalypse.*

The Godsverse takes my two most popular graphic novels, Katrina Hates the Dead/Katrina Hates Dead Shit and Pixie Dust, novelizes them, and adds FIFTEEN additional stories set across 13,000 years!

These books are exciting, action-adventure mythological fantasy novels steeped in mythology, then filled with humor, action, and fun.

If you've travelled through the Godsverse before, these new adventures will fill in gaps in the universe you have asked me about for years, and if you're new to the Godsverse, there has never been a better time to get started.

*Plus, everyone who backs by Saturday will get digital copies of **The Twelve Labors of Nick** by Amy Wolf, **A Tribe of Kassia** by Tom Leveen, **Harsh Line** by Ann Gimpel, and **Snowed** by Maria Alexander!*

So, head over and check out the campaign right now to lock in these awesome rewards.

DAY 9 – OPTION 1

For this series specifically, I was using the heroine's journey, which operates much differently than the hero's journey, and I wanted to highlight that for people who might not have wanted to read another typical adventure series. If you have anything like that, this is a perfect time to write that email. If you don't have that, consider taking an unfair objection you hear about your series or genre and talking about how your book is different.

The heroine's journey…

Hey,

*The Kickstarter for **The Dragon Strife** trilogy is in its second week and I wanna tell you more about why I love it so so much.*

Kickstarter link

So, most of us know the hero's journey, where a person goes out into the world and finds their destiny.

What we don't talk about enough is the heroine's journey, which is a thing, and one of the driving forces in a lot of my work.

In the heroine's journey, the main character doesn't go out and get imbued with power from their journey. Instead, they learn to use the power that was inside themselves the whole time.

It's one of the things I love most about Captain Marvel. She does not find power, she learns to use the power that was inside of her the whole time.

The Dragon Strife trilogy is very much about Gilda finding a power that was inside herself the whole time; a power that not only didn't she know was there, but that people told her didn't exist.

Yes, there are many elements of the hero's journey in the story, but at the end it's a trilogy about Gilda's inward journey from sacrifice to hero by using the unique things about her that people always told her weren't important.

People have always told me that my stories made them feel empowered, like they had agency in a world that tried to convince them they didn't.

I believe the true journey of our lives isn't going out and finding glory, but learning to live with the unique, wonderful humans that we are, and that using what makes us unique is what makes us a hero.

The Dragon Strife trilogy is very much about that, and I hope it's something you latch on to, and something that you can share with everyone in your life that has felt powerless or weak because they don't see the wonderful person they are, and how that makes them uniquely special.

I hope you'll join us on this journey.

Plus, if you back, you'll get a ton of awesome extra books. Usually, I throw the most perks to early bird backers, but this campaign I'm trying something different, and unlocking a huge slew of new perks for people who back by the end of the campaign.

*Everyone who backs by the end of this week will receive digital copies of **Mythic Creature Trainer #1** by Rene Pfitzer, **Luminous Ages #1** by Antonios Christou, **Dragonwar** by Mirren Hogan, **School of Dragons** by Amy Wolf, **Gods of Aazurn** by Gary Scott Beatty and **Gage and the Dragon's Tear #1** by Patrick Kellner, Donny Hadiwidjaja, Bryan Valenza, Ed Dukeshire, Marta Tanrikulu, and Randy Michaels.*

And and and and and you can pick up the below 5" x 7" postcard print by backing @ the $22 or $75+ physical pledge levels.

I hope you'll join us behind the backer wall to kick this year off right, filled with magic and dragons.

DAY 9 – OPTION 2

"Why would I read anything but romance?"

Hi,

Some years ago, I was at a conference talking to attendees, as I often do, and I got into a conversation with a woman.

I asked her what she read, to which she said romance, and then told her I wrote fantasy. I asked her if she read anything but romance, and she said something along the order of:

Russell Nohelty

"Why would I read anything but romance? It's the only genre where women are treated well and can expect to have a happy ending."

I went to respond, but the words didn't come out, because she's kind of right. Romance is the one genre where women can reasonably be expected to have rich inner lives and have their needs centered in a narrative.

In pretty much any other genre, they are generally used as side characters, emotional baggage, and "fridged" to give the protagonist a reason to go on their quest.

This is a gross generalization, but it made complete sense to me. I went back to my own work with this lens, and it made me realize why a lot of women probably really like my work...

...because like romance, the women of the Godsverse lead both rich inner and outer lives. They have agency in the story and can actively work for a happy ending.

Are their lives perfect? No. Do they struggle? All the time. Am I sometimes sadistic with what they have to go through? Yes.

But the women are all fully developed with their own inner and outer lives. People don't talk down to them (and those that do eventually get their teeth knocked out), and they aren't placed into the narrative just so the main character has a reason to go on their quest.

There is little romance in The Godsverse Chronicles, but I've thought of that woman often when I write books, and it gave me a guiding direction in my writing.

If that is why you mostly read romance, or you're looking for a series where the main characters have agency and lead rich lives, then I hope you'll try The Godsverse Chronicles.

As I mentioned before, I write noblebright fantasy, which means that the good guys are trying to improve the universe, and even though they face struggles, they do the right thing when the pressure is on them.

Plus, they're pretty funny, and really fun books, even though there's often dark themes that run through them.

Are you ready to dive into The Godsverse, whether for the 1st, 8th, or 11th time? Then, make sure to check out our Kickstarter.

Kickstarter link

*Plus, backers this week get some really cool early bird perks. Everyone who backs by 5/29 (including people who've already backed), get digital copies of **The Mantle** by WT Meadows and Chrishaun Keller-Hanna, **A Curse, A Key, & a Corkscrew** by Anna McCluskey, **Merlin's Secret** by Jamie Davis, and **The Shadow Reader** by Sandy Williams.*

Hope to see you behind the backer wall.

DAY 10

On this day, it's good to talk about the world your book is set in (even if it's the real-world talk about why you chose that city/time/setting).

The world of Dragon Strife

Hey,

It's been a week since I launched the Obsidian Spindle Saga, and I'm so so so so so excited for how far we've come, and how supportive you are of my...well, it would not be untrue to call it my obsession over the past three years.

<u>*KICKSTARTER LINK*</u>

So, what is the Obsidian Spindle?

The Obsidian Spindle is one of the most powerful objects in the universe. There is one in every dimension and every inhabited planet in the known galaxy. It is a transport hub between planets for gods and magical creatures, but it is also a focus for magical energy, as it takes an incredible amount of power to make it work.

Think of it like The Wheel of Time, or the Dark Tower. It is a powerful magical object that much of the story relies on and many of the character's destinies depend.

In the Dream Realm, the Fates live inside the locked tower of the Obsidian Spindle, and Rose must find a way to open it if she ever hopes to return back to Earth before her body dies and she's stuck in the Dream Realm forever.

Every "arc" of this series will feature different realms and characters. These first four books are what I am calling The Dream Realm arc.

Each book tells a good chunk of the story with a satisfying conclusion, but there are cliffhangers between books that are only resolved at the end of each arc, and each arc also has a beginning, middle, and end.

This week, you get SIX digital books for backing the Obsidian Spindle Saga (including if you already backed).

*All backers who pledge by Saturday (even for $1) get **Secret of Moldara** by Brianne Earhart, **The Farshore Chronicles** box set (that's THREE books) by Justin Fike, **Sanyare** by Megan Haskell, and **Crimson Fire** by Mirren Hogan!*

DAY 11

Aside from the world, the characters are the other biggest reasons a person buys a book. Depending on the genre, people might buy for a character or a world more, so we should talk today about the main characters.

Who are the main characters?

Hey,

There's only one week left to back the Obsidian Spindle Saga, and we haven't even talked about any of the characters yet.

<u>*KICKSTARTER LINK*</u>

So, who are the main characters of The Obsidian Spindle Saga (TOSS)?

Each book of The Obsidian Spindle Saga is told from multiple different perspectives from all across the world of Urgu, weaving together a narrative between them.

This was the most complex project I've ever worked on, getting each character right, and telling different but cohesive stories between them.

One of the things I appreciate about Game of Thrones is that each character is not only rich and unique, but they also are having their own type of fantasy story. Sansa is having a story about political intrigue while John Snow is having a classic fantasy adventure story, all while Arya is having a coming-of-age fantasy story.

It's like 30-40 stories in one book.

These stories are quite pared down in comparison to Game of Thrones. Each book comes in around 275 pages compared to 500+, but I loved the idea that each story can be its own thing and bring different elements of fantasy into it.

Rose *- The narrative of The Obsidian Spindle Saga rotates quite heavily around Rose. She plays the role of the Sleeping Beauty in our narrative, but also Alice, and Dorothy, as she is the character we see the first moments of the Dream Realm through, and the one filled with the most wonder about what she's seeing. Rose is a college student with no magical powers, who is so poor she lives in a van in the school parking lot with her half-gorgon girlfriend, Chelle. She is also a diabetic, who often has to choose between medication and eating, which is what sets her on her path.*

Chelle *- Chelle is Rose's half-gorgon girlfriend. As a "monster," she has been chased and hunted for her whole life by monster hunters trying to make a name for* *themselves. Her mother was slaughtered and her parts sold on the black market. She has some of her mother's gorgon powers, and also other magical powers. She has learned to defend herself and protect the ones she loves.*

Nimue - *The Wicked Witch of our universe is the ruler of the Land of Oz. She deposed the previous ruler, Ozma, and has ruled for the last hundred years, since the time Hypnos vanished without a trace. She is the most powerful witch in Urgu, as she was blessed by Hera, and is working in consort with her to open the locked door to the Obsidian Spindle and return to Earth by any means necessary.*

Red - *Red is the titular Red Riding Hood in our universe. She is one of Ozma's royal guards and has searched for a way to depose the Wicked Witch and return Hypnos to the world for the last century. She believes that Rose is the key to bringing back Hypnos and restoring order in Urgu and will do anything to protect her.*

Queen Aine - *The ruler of the Forbidden Forest, Queen Aine is a powerful Unseelie fairy that led a brutal war, wiping out the Seelie and consolidating power. She is ruthless about obtaining and maintaining power. However, she is very adept at diplomacy, and molding wills to her own ends.*

Each book in this arc follows these characters along their journey. As you can see above, there are many different paths these characters will walk over the course of this first arc, as they try to keep and maintain power, while attempting to mold fate to their will.

This week, you get SIX digital books for backing the Obsidian Spindle Saga (including if you already backed).

*All backers who pledge by Saturday (even for $1) get **Secret of Moldara** by Brianne Earhart, **The Farshore Chronicles** box set (that's THREE books) by Justin Fike, **Sanyare** by Megan Haskell, and **Crimson Fire** by Mirren Hogan!*

DAY 12

We've talked about objections to your work, but I also love including things I've heard about my work and how it makes them feel. This is a bit different from reviews, but it hits the same feelings of "Other people have read these books and like them so maybe I should, too."

"your books make me feel like I have agency in a chaotic world..."

Hi,

There was a book released last year called "7 Figure Fiction" which talked about the "universal fantasy" your books offered readers.

It set the author world on fire as writers asked themselves what special thing they offer readers with their books.

I did not get worked up into a tizzy about it, because for years readers have told me exactly what my books gave them; agency.

Throughout my career, readers have consistently told me that my books "made them feel like they had agency in a world where they often felt like they had none."

This is especially true in The Godsverse Chronicles, which is about strong-willed women who fight against the fates the gods have given them. They take their destiny into their own hands to influence the direction of the universe on a cosmic level.

These women are rarely endowed with powers, or godhood. They are usually just ordinary women, or fairies, who are sick of their plight and have had too much foisted onto their shoulders.

Who hasn't felt that in the past two years especially?

I know I have, and I also know that writing these books made me feel powerful; they made me feel like I had some control over my destiny, just like the women I wrote about.

Yes, they face trials, but they never give up.

I write what is generally referred to as noblebright fantasy, which is the opposite of grimdark. It's about good, or nebulously good, characters who do the right thing for the right reasons.

These women are not Pollyannas, and sometimes they're not even very good at being good, but they strive to make the world a better place.

The world could use more of that, frankly, and I'm very proud to bring that energy into my worlds, and hopefully, into yours.

Because who doesn't want to feel like they have agency in a world that often seems intent to take it away from you.

What do you think? Have you read the Godsverse Chronicles? Is that how the books made you feel?

Are you ready to dive into The Godsverse, whether for the 1st, 8th, or 11th time? Then, make sure to check out our Kickstarter.

Kickstarter link

*Plus, backers this week get some really cool early bird perks. Everyone who backs by 5/29 (including people who've already backed), get digital copies of **The Mantle** by WT Meadows and Chrishaun Keller-Hanna, **A Curse, A Key, & a Corkscrew** by Anna McCluskey, **Merlin's Secret** by Jamie Davis, and **The Shadow Reader** by Sandy Williams.*

Hope to see you behind the backer wall.

DAY 13

We're nearing the end, so now we switch to talking about how there's only one day left either of the launch, or the special offer, or whatever you're doing.

One day left...

Hey,

There's just one day left to back the Dragon Strife trilogy on Kickstarter and get all the amazing perks we unlocked this week.

Kickstarter link

Usually, I throw the most perks to early bird backers, but this campaign I'm trying something different and unlocking a huge slew of new perks for people who back by the end of the campaign on Saturday.

I am so excited for these books.

*Everyone who backs in the first week of the campaign will receive digital copies of **Mythic Creature Trainer #1** by Rene Pfitzer, **Luminous Ages #1** by Antonios Christou, **Dragonwar** by Mirren Hogan, **School of Dragons** by Amy Wolf, **Gods of Aazurn** by Gary Scott Beatty and **Gage and the Dragon's Tear #1** by Patrick Kellner, Donny Hadiwidjaja, Bryan Valenza, Ed Dukeshire, Marta Tanrikulu, and Randy Michaels.*

And and and and and you can pick up the below 5" x 7" postcard print by backing @ the $22 or $75+ physical pledge levels. I hope you'll join us behind the backer wall to kick this year off right, filled with magic and dragons.

I hope you'll join us behind the backer wall to kick this year off right, filled with magic and dragons.

DAY 14

This is it, the last day. You'd be surprised how many people wait until the last minute to make a decision, so you should absolutely send an email on the last day to give people one last nudge.

Just hours left...

Hey,

There are only a few hours left to back the Dragon Strife trilogy on Kickstarter and get all the amazing perks we unlocked this week.

Kickstarter link

Usually, I throw the most perks to early bird backers, but this campaign I'm trying something different and unlocking a huge slew of new perks for people who back by the end of the campaign on Saturday.

I am so excited for these books.

*Everyone who backs in the first week of the campaign will receive digital copies of **Mythic Creature Trainer #1** by Rene Pfitzer, **Luminous Ages #1** by Antonios Christou, **Dragonwar** by Mirren Hogan, **School of Dragons** by Amy Wolf, **Gods of Aazurn** by Gary Scott Beatty and **Gage and the Dragon's Tear #1** by Patrick Kellner, Donny Hadiwidjaja, Bryan Valenza, Ed Dukeshire, Marta Tanrikulu, and Randy Michaels.*

And and and and and you can pick up the below 5" x 7" postcard print by backing @ the $22 or $75+ physical pledge levels. I hope you'll join us behind the backer wall to kick this year off right, filled with magic and dragons.

FINAL THOUGHTS

This is only one example, but I hope you have an idea about how you can send more emails without burning out your audience. Even if you only send a couple emails about your launch, please try to vary them up and keep them interesting.

The cardinal sin of email is being boring.

Sending the same email is boring. Nobody wants to be spammed with the same information, but if you can remain interesting people will eat that up all day. You can send more emails than you think and you're more interesting than you believe.

The natural fear to have in all of this is that everyone will unsubscribe. So, I will tell you a story. A few days before writing this, I sent an offer to 5,000 leads I've gotten through Sparkloop. It was a bloodbath with 2% of people unsubscribing. To give you some context, .5% is the top threshold for most providers, so this was 4x higher than that.

I would consider that a slaughter, and yet, still 98% of people did not unsubscribe and it still had a 46% open rate. Even if that carried on for all 14 days of this sequence, I would still only lose 1,400 subscribers, far from everyone unsubscribing.

Think about it. I basically email people every day, but as far as I know, the majority haven't unsubscribed. I would guess it's because either:

- They like me so they put up with my nonsense
- They know it's coming from a good place
- They are entertained by it or
- They gain something from every email enough to put up with the nonsense of sending so much.

No, you can't email every day, ***unless you are entertaining about it and send new information.*** Then, you can do just about whatever you want.

Assuming you are using a program like Convertkit, you can also add a bit to your emails that says, "If you want to stay on my list, but you don't want to hear about this launch, click here" and then make something like "NO X LAUNCH" tag, and then make sure to exclude those people, and then they won't get those emails.

Here's the thing: BookBub sends me daily emails, so does Chirp, and so do many, many people, but I enjoy getting them, so it's okay. Once you start believing that YOU are somebody's favorite email, the rest kind of falls into place. If somebody doesn't feel that way, then I don't want them there anyway.

CHAPTER 17

LAUNCH DAY TACTICS

A campaign is a marathon, but you need to start with a bang. The goal is to build immediate momentum, ideally reaching 20-30% of your funding goal in the first day or two. If you can hit 30%, you have over an 80% chance of funding, and the quicker you hit that number, the more Kickstarter's algorithm in specific and momentum in general can help you.

So let's talk about what to do from the moment you click "Launch" through the next 24-48 hours: timing your launch, mobilizing your audience, leveraging Kickstarter's early traffic boost, and setting the tone for the entire campaign.

TIME YOUR LAUNCH FOR MAXIMUM IMPACT

Don't just launch at a random time, strategize your launch moment. Pick a launch day and hour when your core supporters are awake, online, and ready to act. Many creators choose a weekday morning (e.g. Tuesday 9am in your target time zone) so that people see the announcement during an active time. Avoid odd hours like 3am; you want a critical mass of supporters to jump in immediately. Before you press that Launch button, everything should be prepped: an email draft ready to send, social media posts composed, and a list of personal contacts to message. The minute your campaign goes live, you'll unleash a coordinated promotional blitz.

Also, consider your internal mindset. Launch day is high energy and yes, a bit stressful. Plan to clear your schedule if possible so you can focus on campaigning. Treat it like an event kickoff. Some creators even gather a few friends or team members for a "launch party" (even if virtual) to help share posts and celebrate the moment. Do whatever gets you energized and organized for a strong start.

ANNOUNCE EVERYWHERE – ALL AT ONCE

The moment you go live, shout it from the rooftops. Send out that launch email to your mailing list within minutes of launching. Make the email celebratory and action-oriented: *"We're LIVE! [Project Name] is now on Kickstarter – be among the first backers!"* If you've promised any early-bird rewards or limited quantities, mention them loudly: *"Pledge in the first 48 hours to get the exclusive early-bird bonus!"* This creates urgency from the get-go. At the same time, post on all your social media accounts with the Kickstarter link and a compelling image or the campaign video. The message should be clear: *Now is the time to back.* Don't be shy or apologetic about promoting – you've been building up to this, now is when you cash in on that attention.

Hit every channel you have:

- **Email newsletter:** often your highest conversion, so send that first.
- **Facebook/Twitter/Instagram:** announce on your author pages, personal profile if appropriate, and any groups you manage (if rules allow). Include a striking image of your book or reward.
- **Personal messages:** For those close contacts who *promised* to back early, drop them a quick direct message with the link and a thank-you in advance. Example: *"Hey! We just launched on Kickstarter! Here's the link – thank you so much for jumping in early like you said you would."* Many people appreciate the personal reminder.
- **Other Platforms:** Wherever your readers hang out (Discord, forums, TikTok, etc.), share the news in a way fitting to that platform.

Do this near-simultaneously. The idea is to create a big splash of initial traffic. Kickstarter's algorithm notices early momentum, and public perception does too. A campaign that looks busy out of the gate attracts even more backers (social proof is powerful). It's far better to have a concentrated surge on Day 1 than to trickle out your announcements over several days. You only get one "launch day" – make it count.

Insider Tip: If you've cultivated relationships with any bloggers, influencers, or groups, let them know your exact launch time in advance. Some might be willing to share your project on Day 1 if you ask nicely. A coordinated press or community push on launch day can amplify that first-day burst.

ENGAGE IN REAL TIME WITH EARLY BACKERS

As the first pledges roll in, be present and engaged. Keep your Kickstarter dashboard open (you'll be hitting refresh a lot, let's be honest). When you see backers coming in, consider posting a public Update on your project by the end of Day 1 thanking all the "Day One backers" for getting you off to a great start. This not only shows gratitude, it signals to newcomers that people are already supporting you. If your campaign has comments enabled, monitor them and reply promptly to any questions or cheers. Early engagement sets a tone of you being an accessible, responsive creator.

On social media, you can also share mini-milestones throughout Day 1: *"20 backers in the first 3 hours – you all rock!"* or *"We just hit 50% of our goal on Day One!"* (if that happens). These posts excite your existing backers (they love to see the campaign succeeding) and can entice fence-sitters to jump in ("wow, lots of people are backing this, I better not miss out"). Ride the energy. Launch day is not the day to be shy or silent. It's perfectly fine to make multiple posts on each platform on Day 1 – e.g., morning announcement, afternoon progress update, evening "last chance for Day 1" reminder – especially if you vary the content (one might be a short video thank-you, another a photo of you with the prototype book, etc.). People expect a flurry of activity around a launch. Enthusiasm is infectious, so share yours widely.

One more real-time tactic: thank individuals behind the scenes. You don't have to publicly list every backer, especially if hundreds, but you can privately message or email notable supporters as they pledge. Kickstarter shows you the usernames of backers and allows you to message them. A quick thank-you note to early big backers or to friends/family who pledged can really make their day. It's that personal touch that turns backers into superfans. Just keep it short, grateful, and avoid any hint of "and please give more" – launch day thank-yous are purely about appreciation and excitement.

LEVERAGE EARLY MOMENTUM

Kickstarter loves campaigns that start strong. The first 48 hours are critical for getting on Kickstarter's radar for things like "Projects We Love" badges or category spotlight sections. While you can't control Kickstarter's internal curation, you *can* maximize the factors that influence it: a rush of backers, lots of page activity (video plays, comments, likes). Encourage backers to click the little heart on your campaign page to "Follow" the project – that can help popularity metrics. Also, if you hit certain benchmarks (like 30% funded quickly), your project is statistically far more likely to succeed and thus appears less risky to Kickstarter's staff and algorithms. Momentum breeds momentum.

If you set a lower initial goal, it's possible you might even fully fund on Day 1. That's the ultimate momentum-generator. Backers who come on Day 2 or 3 will see you have already succeeded, which often motivates them to join the party (no one wants to miss a winner). Even if you don't fully fund Day 1, hitting 20-30% early is immensely valuable. Kickstarter's own stats show that about 79% of projects that reach 20% of their goal end up successfully funded. And crossing that threshold quickly sends a message to everyone watching: *this project is happening.*

So, aim high in those first days. Rally your true fans to pledge early and maybe even a little higher if they can. Don't be afraid to explicitly say, "We have a big goal of reaching 25% in the first day or two – help us blast past it!" Backers love being part of a winning team and giving them a common goal like that can galvanize action. Early success creates a snowball effect.

EARLY-BIRD REWARDS

If you have early-bird rewards (special pricing or bonus items for early backers), highlight them everywhere on launch day. Nothing motivates action like a ticking clock or limited quantity. For example: "First 50 backers get a signed bookmark included for free – don't miss out!" or "48-hour special: upgrade to hardcover for free if you back within the first two days." These kinds of perks reward your most eager supporters and create FOMO for others to jump in now rather than later. If you chose not to do any early birds (which is fine), you can still simulate urgency by framing Day 1 as *the* chance to "be an original backer" or to "help us hit the ground running." Psychological triggers matter. People love to be part of a big Day 1 push.

Another launch tactic some use: live streaming during launch. For instance, go live on Facebook or Instagram an hour after launch to talk about the project, celebrate hitting 100% (hopefully), and personally invite viewers to back. Seeing you live, excited and hustling, can convince onlookers to stop by the campaign page. It adds a human face to the launch. You could even count down to launch time on a short livestream ("3…2…1… we're live!") which is a fun way to include your audience in the moment. This depends on your comfort on camera and if your audience is active on platforms with live video, but it's worth considering creating an event-like atmosphere on Day 1.

STAY ORGANIZED AMID THE CHAOS

Launch day can feel chaotic with the surge of notifications, messages, and posts. Prepare a **checklist** ahead of time (even hour by hour) so you don't forget important tasks in the excitement. For example:

- **T-minus 0:** Click "Launch" on Kickstarter.
- **+5 minutes:** Publish social media posts (Twitter, FB page, IG, etc.).
- **Within the first hour:** Personally message key supporters and close contacts.
- **+2 hours:** Send email announcement to subscribers.
- **Throughout Day:** Monitor comments and messages; post 1-2 updates on Kickstarter (perhaps a "We're 20% there!" update).

- **Afternoon:** Thank and tag a few early backers on social media (if they're public supporters and you have their okay).
- **Evening:** Final push post, e.g. "Last chance to grab the Day-1 bonus – ends at midnight!" if applicable.
- **End of Day 1:** Write a short Kickstarter update thanking everyone for an amazing first day and perhaps sharing the plan for Day 2.

Having a schedule ensures you hit all the right notes. Use whatever tools help you: set alarms, have your posts pre-written, enlist a friend to double-check you didn't miss anything. This structured approach will keep you productive rather than just anxiously refreshing the funding total (though you'll do that too, it's unavoidable!).

THANK EVERYONE AND SET THE TONE

Finally, end your launch day by thanking your backers and reinforcing the excitement for what's to come. Post a Day 1 recap update on Kickstarter that evening or the next morning: express your heartfelt gratitude, share how much was raised in 24 hours, and maybe preview a bit of what's next ("Tomorrow we'll reveal our first stretch goal!" or "Can't wait to show you some behind-the-scenes art in upcoming updates."). This not only makes backers feel appreciated, it also lets latecomers scrolling your page see that you are active and communicative from the start.

If any individuals went above and beyond on Day 1 (like someone who pledged at a high level or rallied others), you might mention them by first name in the update or privately message them a special thanks. Building that positive relationship early pays off; these people will cheerlead your campaign to others.

Also, thank your broader community on social media. For example: *"Wow, what a launch! We're already 40% funded on Day 1. Huge thank you to every backer who believed in this project immediately. You all are amazing!"* People love being acknowledged. Those who haven't backed yet will see that and might think, "I want in on this excitement." Gratitude is attractive; it shows you're the kind of creator who values your supporters, which in turn encourages more support.

Importantly, carry that tone of enthusiasm and confidence forward. Even if you didn't hit some internal target on Day 1, focus on the positive — any progress is good progress. Publicly celebrate what you did achieve (10 new readers? $500 in funding? It all matters). No whining about what didn't happen. There's plenty of time to keep pushing, and a positive mindset will inspire others to jump on board. As a leader of your campaign, your attitude is contagious. Choose optimism.

CHAPTER 18

HOW TO THINK ABOUT YOUR CAMPAIGN

People think Kickstarter success is about having the best product or the prettiest video or the most polished rewards.

It's not.

Success lives or dies in your strategy. And strategy is just a fancy way of saying: how do you keep momentum moving from Day One to Day Thirty without burning out or making your audience hate you?

It's the stuff you don't see on the campaign page. It's the prep, the pacing, the structure behind the show. And it's the reason some campaigns raise $20,000 and others sputter out at $1,500 even with similar products. Let's talk about how we build a strategy that performs.

KICKSTARTER'S RECOMMENDATION ENGINE

Most creators picture Kickstarter as a passive storefront—people click your link, decide to pledge, and that's it. What they overlook is the **network of internal recommendation**

loops quietly pushing projects to curious readers even when you're asleep. Knowing how those loops work lets you design a pre-launch and live-campaign strategy that maximizes "free" discovery.

HOW KICKSTARTER SURFACES CAMPAIGNS

1. **Search Results and Category Sorts**
    When someone types "witchy romance" or browses the Publishing › Fiction shelf, Kickstarter ranks projects by a blend of relevance, recent traction, and campaign health. Keywords in your project title, headline, and first paragraph feed the relevance side; early-day pledges and steady comment activity feed the traction side.
2. **Inline "You Might Also Like" Tiles**
    Scroll to the bottom of almost any campaign page and you'll see a horizontal strip of projects with similar tags, funding velocity, or overlapping backer graphs. If your campaign is active and healthy, you'll be slotted under bigger projects in your niche—essentially riding their traffic for free.
3. **After-Backing Recommendations**
    The second a backer confirms a pledge, Kickstarter flashes a "Discover more" screen that recommends 3-6 additional campaigns. Those suggestions rely heavily on shared backer behavior: if readers who love gothic fantasy keep backing your project *and* mine, the algorithm pairs us. Translation: cross-pollination happens automatically once you attract the right early audience. They also include other campaigns in the

backer confirmation page, and after you fill out your survey.

4. **Daily and Weekly Email Blasts**
Kickstarter sends automated digests, "Fresh Publishing Picks" and "Projects We Love", to millions of users. They also push niche emails such as "New Fantasy Campaigns" if that's what someone backed before. Tag your campaign properly (Fantasy, Supernatural, LGBTQ, etc.) and you become eligible to appear. Hit early funding milestones and maintain update momentum, and the staff algorithm is more likely to grant you the coveted **Projects We Love** badge— practically a golden ticket into these emails.

5. **Back-in-the-Day Backer Emails**
If you've run previous campaigns, Kickstarter will often email your past backers automatically once the new one goes live. That means fulfilling past projects on time, posting periodic updates, and keeping cancellation rates low directly increase the size of the free mailing list Kickstarter activates for you next time.

HOW TO LEAN INTO THOSE LOOPS

Every pledge you win through your own marketing is a seed. The healthier and more numerous those seeds, the more often Kickstarter's own garden will self-propagate in your favor—placing your project in newsletter spotlights, post-checkout banners, and "More Like This" carousels you never paid for.

- **Keyword Discipline:** Nail the genre and subgenre in your project title and first paragraph so search relevance is undeniable. "Dragon-Rider Epic Fantasy Hardcover" beats "Chronicles: A Novel" every single time.

- **Early-Day Momentum:** The recommendation engine loves velocity. Hitting 20–30 percent funding within 48 hours raises your "trending" score, which in turn drops you into more bottom-of-page tiles and after-back screens.

- **Frequent Updates & Comment Sparks:** Every time you post an update or answer a question, Kickstarter logs "creator engagement." High-engagement campaigns surface higher in automated digests. Ask questions in updates to encourage backer replies and watch the algorithm nod approvingly.

- **Healthy Backer Graphs:** Backer cancellations and failed cards are normal, but high percentages cripple your health score. Communicate clearly, set realistic shipping fees, and chase failed payments quickly so your graph stays clean.

- **Staff Picks Mindset:** While nobody can guarantee a Projects We Love tag, you improve odds by presenting tight graphics, a clear budget, transparent risks, and an interesting hook. Staff members are readers too; give them a reason to click "Love" and you'll catch an instant recommendation boost.

Your job is to hand the algorithm the strongest signals possible: sharp keywords, early traction, steady engagement, and stellar backer trust metrics. Do that, and the platform itself becomes an unpaid member of your launch team, quietly funneling new readers into your campaign day after day.

LAUNCH STRONG OR PLAY CATCH-UP LATER

Day One sets the pace for your entire campaign. A strong launch builds confidence for both you *and* your potential backers; a slow start can create an uphill battle. Remember that Kickstarter is an all-or-nothing platform, which means urgency isn't reserved only for the final deadline, it begins the moment you launch. People are more inclined to back when they see others already backing. Hitting 20-30% of your goal quickly provides powerful social proof and momentum. In contrast, if someone visits your page in the first couple days and sees 2% funded with only a handful of backers, they may hesitate and say, "I'll check back later" (and sometimes never do). First impressions count.

By mobilizing every channel and contact at launch, you create a virtuous cycle: backers attract more backers. Kickstarter might even give you a promotional boost if it sees lots of activity. The effort and hustle of launch day are intense, but it's for a short period and the payoff is huge. As the saying goes, *you don't get a second chance at a first impression.* So, leave it all on the field at launch.

Also, expect an emotional rollercoaster on Day 1. Adrenaline will be high; you'll likely obsessively refresh your funding total and email. You might experience ecstatic highs ("We're 25% funded already!") and dips of anxiety ("It's been an hour with no new pledges, are we hitting a wall?"). This is normal. Stick to your plan, continue executing your outreach throughout the day, and *breathe.* Once Day 1 is over, you'll have a clearer picture of how the campaign is trending and can adjust strategies if needed. But no matter what, keep showing up. A creator who is visibly present and passionate from the start gives backers confidence that you'll be equally dedicated to delivering the project.

WEEKLY PERKS

One of the biggest misconceptions I see is this idea that weekly perks—those stretch goals, bonuses, reveals, new tiers—are just fun little surprises for your backers.

They're not. They're **pacing mechanisms**.

They're how you break up a 30-day campaign into something that feels active instead of exhausting. Something that has a pulse instead of a flatline.

Every week, you need a beat. A reason to post. A reason to update. A reason to re-engage people who already backed and give the fence-sitters something new to say yes to.

This is how you build **campaign rhythm**:

- Week 1: Early bird bonus ends Friday
- Week 2: Backer goal unlocks new reward
- Week 3: Surprise add-on or new merch tier
- Week 4: Final push bonus, countdown bundle, all-in tier

Each move is a **marketing event**, not a giveaway.

You're not handing out perks because you're generous. You're pacing your story. And your campaign is the story you're telling.

CAMPAIGN LENGTH = MARKETING LOAD

So, how long should your Kickstarter run?

The answer isn't about audience size. It's about **marketing stamina**.

If you're launching with five days of pre-written emails, two updates, and one graphic, then **a 30-day campaign will destroy you**. You'll run out of things to say by Week Two, and your energy will die before your deadline even shows up.

But if you've got:

- Weekly bonus content planned
- Mid-campaign perks queued up
- A warm list ready to back
- A visibility strategy across channels

Then a 30-day campaign gives you room to breathe, and room to scale.

Short campaigns are like sprints. Great when you've got high momentum and a hot list.

Long campaigns are marathons. Worth it if you've got enough water stations (aka content) along the way.

You can't just pick a date and hope it works out. You have to plan how you'll keep the engine running at every turn.

The perk isn't the point. The **engagement** is.

THE FIRST 48 HOURS ARE EVERYTHING

If you don't walk into launch day already 30% funded, you're fighting an uphill battle.

The algorithm isn't going to save you. "Kickstarter magic" isn't real. What is real? **Intent**.

I want a couple hundred people ready to click "Back this project" the second it goes live. That means I've been warming them up for 2–3 weeks with behind-the-scenes posts, early looks at rewards, teaser videos, polls, maybe even preview pages.

I don't hope for momentum, I build it. If you can get that momentum going, the Kickstarter discovery engine starts working, and more people start sharing about it, creating a positive feedback loop.

STRETCH GOALS ARE STORY BEATS

A good stretch goal plan isn't just a list of rewards. It's a pacing strategy.

You're giving people **a reason to care after they've already backed**.

Think of them like episodic milestones. When we hit $5k, everyone gets a foil upgrade. At $7,500, you unlock a digital wallpaper set. At $10k, you get a brand-new bonus story.

And we don't dump them all at once. We reveal them as we go. That way, there's always a reason to check in again, to share the campaign, to bump up your pledge.

And don't forget **backer goals**. "When we hit 300 backers, everyone gets a bonus bookmark." That gets your community to spread the word for you. Because now it's not just about money, it's about momentum.

But stretch goals only work if you've priced your base campaign correctly. If you're counting on stretch goals to survive, you're already screwed.

You don't use them to save your campaign. You use them to scale it.

EARLY-BIRD AND WEEKLY PERKS

In a well-run campaign, stretch goals act like the **major plot twists**—the fork in the road where the story surges forward in big, cinematic jumps. But novels aren't only turning points; they're built on smaller moments of tension and release that keep readers flipping pages between the tent-poles. In Kickstarter terms, those smaller moments are your **early-bird perks** and **weekly bonuses.** They're what I call the *short beats*—micro spikes of interest that bridge the quiet chapters and keep momentum alive.

Early-Bird Perks light the fuse: An early-bird reward is the very first spark in the narrative. It's a time-boxed or quantity-capped offer—usually 24 to 48 hours or the first 50 backers—that answers the subconscious question every browser asks: *"Why shouldn't I just come back later?"* By dangling a fleeting upgrade (edge-sprayed hardcover at the paperback price, a signed bookplate, an exclusive pin), you transform curiosity into instant action. The purpose isn't raw revenue; it's to pile up social proof so the wider audience wakes up on Day 2 to a project that already looks inevitable. **Velocity feeds visibility.** And because the perk expires quickly, you regain margin for the rest of the campaign.

Weekly Perks: Weekly perks are your serialized chapter endings. Scheduled, weightier bonuses—say a five-page side story, a live Q&A, or a behind-the-scenes video—arrive on the same day each week, creating anticipation cycles. I like Friday drops; weekend browsers open to a fresh update and a burst of comments that drive algorithmic love. If stretch goals are the novel's acts, weekly perks are its mini-cliff hangers: satisfying enough to reward loyalty, open-ended enough to make readers wonder what next Friday will bring.

Viewed together, early-bird, daily, and weekly perks form a pulse of micro-urgencies that plug the silent gaps between stretch-goal reveals. They also buy you data: if a daily perk post gets crickets, you know engagement is cooling and can pivot messaging before the lull becomes a free-fall. Conversely, a spike of comments on a Wednesday wallpaper tells you that art assets resonate; maybe the next stretch goal should be an art print set.

Most importantly, these beats reassure backers. Activity equals confidence. When strangers land on a campaign with daily movement, they see a living, breathing community—not a static storefront. And the more story beats you provide, the longer readers stick around to witness the ending.

DAILY/FLASH PERKS

What we've set up so far will get you a long way to your goal, but sometimes you need an emergency ripcord for when things aren't going well. That's where Daily, or Flash Perks, come in. They are the arsenal you fire *only when the graph demands it.* Think of them as adrenaline shots. You deploy one when momentum slumps, or when a funding rocket needs an extra boost to punch through the next altitude band.

WHEN TO PULL THE TRIGGER

1. **The Plateau Alert:** Your pledge chart has been flat for forty-eight hours and social shares are cooling. A quick, surprise unlock—say a printable bookmark set or a time-lapse cover video—jolts the comment thread awake and gives backers something fresh to broadcast.
2. **The Break-the-Barrier Push:** You're inches from a headline milestone (100 backers, $10 K, 200 percent funded). Announce that if the community tips you over the line by midnight, *everyone* gets a tiny upgrade: edge-design mock-ups revealed, a bonus scene PDF, a name-in-the-hat giveaway. The perk accelerates an already rising curve instead of letting it stall one dollar short.
3. **The Final-Hours Frenzy:** In the last forty-eight hours, urgency is already high, but a flash-perk can convert lurkers. Offer a back-end treat like an exclusive AMA

replay or a backers-only Discord channel—cheap for you, irresistible for fence-sitters who suddenly fear missing out.

GUIDELINES FOR EFFECTIVE FLASH-PERKS

- **Keep cost near zero.** Digital art, audio snippets, or behind-the-scenes PDFs work best. The perk's power is psychological, not monetary.
- **Limit frequency.** Two to four well-timed flashes in a thirty-day campaign are plenty. If every lull triggers a perk, backers learn to wait you out instead of pledging.
- **Tie it to community action, not just dollars.** "50 new shares unlock a surprise" builds social proof and stretches reach well beyond your existing list.

Handled this way, flash-perks become tactical accelerants, not a daily chore. They nudge a drifting campaign back on course or slap a turbocharger onto one that's already screaming toward the finish line, exactly the job small bonuses are meant to do.

WELCOME TO THE DEAD ZONE

Every campaign hits it. Eventually, the excitement fades and the middle days are just… slower. The launch rush fades, the final countdown hasn't started yet, and you're sitting there staring at a stalled graph wondering if it's over.

It's not over, but this is where you earn your paycheck.

Dead zones are where you inject **new energy** into the campaign. That could mean:

- Introducing a new bundle
- Dropping a mid-campaign bonus
- Adding a time-limited add-on
- Doing a stretch goal reveal
- Posting a creator update or backer Q&A

And you don't have to do it all at once. Drip it out. One move every few days keeps the wheel spinning.

Dead zones aren't death sentences. They're just strategy gaps waiting to be filled.

On a normal campaign, 1/3 of your raise will come in the first week, 1/3 in the dead zone, and 1/3 in the last week. If you don't have a strategy for the dead zone, you're missing 1/3 of the money you could raise.

CLOSE WITH CONFIDENCE

Most campaigns end the way they started, fast and chaotic. You want that. You want the final 72 hours to feel like a launch all over again.

Here's how we do it:

- Schedule reminder emails for anyone who's followed but not pledged.
- Hit your list again: "Last chance for the exclusive bundle."
- Add a final-day-only offer. Something clean and exciting.
- Post a heartfelt update thanking backers and setting up the final goal.

Make the last few days feel **personal and exciting**. Don't guilt people. Don't panic. Just lead like a pro and trust your momentum.

Because here's the truth: backers remember how your campaign made them *feel*. And a strong finish leaves a better impression than a flashy start.

You can't see a great strategy from the outside. But you can feel it.

A good strategy makes your campaign feel inevitable. Like it was always going to win. Like the creator knew what they were doing and had their shit together.

That's what we're building.

This isn't a magic trick. It's just work. Smart, premeditated, paced work.

CHAPTER 19

MANAGING BACKER FLOW

The golden rule of a live campaign is, don't disappear. A common mistake creators make is to go hard on launch, then assume they can relax and let Kickstarter do the work. Wrong! You need to put in consistent effort throughout the campaign. This doesn't necessarily mean exhausting yourself with frantic tasks every hour, but it does mean maintaining a *daily presence* and responsiveness.

Plan to touch your campaign every day in some way, whether that's to post an update, respond to comments, send a social media post, or just check your stats. Backers, and potential backers watching silently, will notice if the creator goes AWOL. Imagine you're considering backing a project and see they haven't posted any updates or social posts in a week. It raises doubts about how involved or reliable the creator is. Conversely, if you see regular updates and the creator actively answering questions, you feel confident this project is being handled professionally.

Don't forget, your true fans want to hear from you. You are not spamming them by sharing your enthusiasm and progress; you are including them in the journey. So, err on the side of more communication rather than less (provided it's valuable or at least authentically excited, not just noise).

One practical way to ensure you're consistent is to establish a routine. For example, decide that every morning you'll spend 30 minutes on campaign tasks (checking overnight pledges, responding to comments, posting a quick social update), and every evening you'll spend another 30 minutes (writing the day's summary, planning tomorrow's post). Put these times on your calendar like appointments. Treat the campaign like a part-time job for its duration – because it is! Consistency breeds momentum. Even on slow days when no new pledges come in, stick to your habit of engaging and promoting. Activity creates opportunity.

KEEP THE CONVERSATION GOING

Project Updates on Kickstarter are one of your most powerful tools for daily engagement. Aim to post updates regularly, at least 1-2 times per week in the middle stretch and more frequently during major moments (launch, hitting goals, final countdown). Updates are broadcast to all backers via email, so it's a direct line to the folks who already believe in you. Use them to keep excitement high and make backers feel involved in the process.

What makes a good update? It could be:

- **Progress reports:** e.g. *"Week 1 update: 60% funded thanks to 150 amazing backers!"* Celebrate milestones.
- **Behind-the-scenes content:** Show a sneak peek of artwork, a snippet of a new chapter, a day-in-the-life of

you working on the project. This rewards backers with insider content and keeps them interested.

- **Backer spotlights or shout-outs:** Thank your community, maybe highlight a few enthusiastic comments (with permission) or say "welcome" to new backers from different countries. Make people feel seen.
- **Interactive questions:** Ask backers their opinions on something. For instance, *"Help us choose a quote to put on the back of the bookmark – which do you like better?"* or *"What character are you most excited to meet in the book?"* Getting comments on updates not only boosts engagement metrics, but it creates a sense of community. Engaged backers are *happy* backers, and happy backers tell their friends.
- **Mini-goals and stretch goals:** Use updates to announce when you've added a stretch goal or when you're close to a target. *"Just $200 away from unlocking the next art print – almost there!"* This can spur backers to increase pledges or spread the word to hit the goal.

By consistently posting upbeat, content-rich updates, you signal to backers (and observers) that this campaign is alive and well. It also provides fresh material for you to share externally – you can take snippets from an update and post on social media, driving more people to check out the campaign.

Plan out a rough update schedule ahead of time. For example, commit to an update every Tuesday and Friday during the campaign. Having a schedule prevents the "what do I post?" paralysis. Of course, you can post more if something exciting happens spontaneously (like a sudden surge of pledges or a cool media feature), but having a baseline plan ensures you won't neglect updates on those less eventful days.

If you have weekly perks, then you can always tell your backers what they got that week just for backing. A campaign is as much about retention as getting new backers. Additionally, every update is a chance to unveil a new upgrade to the campaign.

ENGAGE BACKERS AND BUILD COMMUNITY

Remember, Kickstarter isn't just a store, it's a community experience. Treat your backers like team members helping to bring this project to life. Encourage them to spread the word and give them reasons to be proud of backing. For instance, in updates or backer-only communications, use language like *"we're in this together"* and *"you all are the driving force making this possible."* When backers feel like part of your inner circle, they're more likely to stay pledged (reducing cancellations) and to recruit others.

Consider creating fun little moments for backers:

- **Polls or votes:** Kickstarter updates allow polls. Maybe let backers vote on a minor aspect of the project (which cover design variant, or the name of a side character, or which bonus print to include). This involvement deepens their investment.
- **Backer milestones:** If you hit, say, 100 backers, celebrate it! *"100 backers – woohoo! You all get a*

special wallpaper download as a thank-you!" Small rewards or even just public recognition of milestones can motivate everyone to reach the next one.

- **Hashtags or social sharing:** Create a campaign hashtag and invite backers to post about the project. Example: *"Share why you're excited about #MyBookKickstarter on Twitter and tag me, and I'll enter you in a giveaway for an extra swag item!"* (Just be careful to follow Kickstarter's rules – you can encourage sharing, but you can't *require* it for a reward in a way that violates their rules. Generally, optional community contests are okay if no additional purchase is needed.)
- **Show appreciation:** Maybe mid-campaign, do a quick backer thank-you roll call in an update (first names or initials). Or share a photo of the "thank you" page in your book where all backer names will be listed and express how excited you are to add more names. These gestures reinforce that backing your project is joining a family, not just a transaction.

Engagement matters not just for morale, but for the algorithm, lively campaigns with comments and updates tend to get more visibility. Plus, engaged backers are less likely to drop or forget to fix failed payments. They feel connected to you and the project's success.

PACE YOURSELF

After the rush of the first week, it's easy to hit a bit of a wall. The adrenaline fades, and you might be looking at 20+ days still to go. This is where your daily strategy and mindset are crucial. **Anticipate** that the middle of the campaign will be slower; it's normal. You may have days with very few new pledges. Don't let that discourage you into inaction. Instead, use the slower pace as an opportunity to get creative and *work your plan.*

Stick to a **baseline routine** of daily promotion:

- **Daily social media post:** Even if it's something small like a favorite quote from your book or a progress graphic (e.g., "65% funded!"), keep the project in your followers' feeds regularly.
- **Regular outreach:** Continue any planned outreach to blogs, podcasts, or cross-promotions. Maybe each day, target a small task: Monday send a pitch to a blogger, Tuesday follow up with that local newspaper, Wednesday reach out to that Instagram book reviewer, etc. Little by little, you expand awareness.
- **Advertising tweaks:** If you decided to experiment with a small ad campaign (Facebook or others), monitor it daily. If it's yielding pledges, maybe scale it up; if not, tweak the targeting or pause it. Don't set and forget – daily adjustments can save you money and improve results.
- **Address any concerns quickly:** Check if backers have asked questions in comments or if anyone is confused about a reward. Answer within a day at most. Good customer service *during* the campaign sets the tone that you're a responsible creator.
- **Keep an eye on the goal line:** Remind yourself (and occasionally your audience) of how far you've come and how far is left. *"We're two weeks in and 70%*

funded – so close to the goal!" This frames the slow mid-period as still-progress, not stagnation.

Also, use this period to plan for the finale. As part of your daily tasks, start crafting the final 72-hour strategy (emails, graphics for "48 hours left!", etc.). Having those ready will make the last days much easier. More on the final push soon – but the point is, keeping busy with productive tasks can ward off the mid-campaign blues.

Most importantly, keep a positive attitude in public. Even if internally you're a bit worried because you haven't seen a pledge today, never broadcast panic or disappointment. If you absolutely must acknowledge a slowdown (like in an update), spin it constructively: *"It's been a quiet week, which is normal for Kickstarter, but that's why I'm so grateful for each and every one of you here! I'm using this time to line up some exciting things for next week – stay tuned."* Always focus on what's next and the progress being made, however small. Your confidence reassures backers and potential backers that the campaign is going to succeed.

MONITOR, MEASURE, AND MODIFY

Successful Kickstarter creators act like the pilot and air traffic controller at once: you're flying the plane *and* monitoring all the gauges. Take advantage of Kickstarter's dashboard analytics and any tracking links you set up. Every day or two, review where pledges are coming from. Are people finding you via Kickstarter's search, or mostly from your email link, or perhaps from a particular

Facebook post that got shared? If you see a source bringing in backers, double down on it. For example, if your Twitter posts are actually converting a lot of pledges, maybe you increase to two tweets a day during a hot streak. If a certain partnership or cross-promotion didn't yield anything, perhaps focus energy elsewhere.

Be ready to pivot your strategy based on data. Daily monitoring allows you to be nimble. Suppose you notice mid-campaign that a lot of traffic is coming from an unexpected mention on a forum or blog, hop on that, go leave a thank-you comment on that blog or engage with that forum thread (if appropriate) to further capitalize on the interest. Or imagine you planned to do a paid ad and after 3 days it has zero conversions. Don't keep throwing money at it hoping for a miracle. Change the ad creative or target, or reallocate that budget to printing some flyers for a local event, etc. This on-the-fly adjustment is the benefit of a live campaign. You're not locked into a single approach.

Another thing to monitor is your pledge activity trends: Kickstarter's graph will show you each day's pledge totals. It's common to have a big spike at the start, a valley in the middle, then a spike at the end. But if you see a multi-day flatline, that's a signal to *do something different* that day – like a new reveal, a bold update, an extra email push. When you see a day with an uptick, ask "What did I do yesterday that might have contributed?" and learn from it. Treat the campaign like a living organism you're tracking.

Through all this, maintain perspective on the *overall* goal. A day or two of slow pledges isn't catastrophic if you planned for it and are working to liven things up. It's the trend over a week or more that matters. Daily strategy means focusing on the immediate tasks while keeping the long game in view. You're effectively the project manager of your campaign. Each day's work is a step toward the ultimate deadline.

URGENCY THROUGHOUT THE CAMPAIGN

Urgency is easy to have on Day 1 and Day 30 (final day). But what about all those days in between? You have to manufacture micro-urgencies to keep people motivated. Humans are procrastinators; many will naturally say "I'll pledge later." Your job is to give them reasons to pledge *sooner* rather than later, repeatedly throughout the campaign.

Here are some tactics to inject urgency and excitement on a regular basis:

- **Mini-Deadlines:** For example, a mid-campaign challenge like, "If we hit 75% funded by the end of this week, I'll add a free sticker for all backers!" Now there's a reason to push toward a short-term goal. It gets current backers talking and nudging friends, and it gives fence-sitters a deadline to consider.
- **Limited Bonus Windows:** Perhaps introduce a weekend-only bonus – "Anyone who pledges between Friday and Sunday will get their name printed in gold in the book" (or some fun perk). Limited-time offers during the campaign create little urgency spikes.
- **New Content Reveals:** Stagger your reveals of cool stuff. For instance, plan to reveal a new piece of

concept art on Day 10 via an update. Tease it a day or two before: *"Coming soon: a new character illustration reveal when we cross $5,000!"* People love looking forward to something. It's a soft urgency, but it keeps them tuned in.

- **Stretch Goals:** As you approach your initial goal, announce stretch goals that have tangible rewards. *"At $8k, all backers get a bonus short story."* Now even after hitting 100%, there's urgency to keep funding rising to unlock the next reward. Each stretch goal essentially resets the urgency meter because there's a new objective to strive for.
- **Backer-Total Goals:** Aside from money, challenge your community with backer count goals. *"If we reach 200 backers, I'll host a live reading of Chapter 1 for everyone."* This encourages current backers to recruit one or two more people, focusing on outreach rather than dollars.
- **Personal Deadlines:** Sometimes you can leverage your personal schedule to create urgency. For example, *"I'm doing a live Q&A on YouTube tomorrow – let's see if we can hit 90% before I go live, so I have something huge to celebrate!"* or *"My birthday is next week – hitting the goal by then would be the best gift!"* Don't overdo personal appeals, but if done sparingly and sincerely, they can rally folks.

Whatever tactics you choose, map them out on your campaign calendar. You don't want all your "tricks" bunched together or too early leaving nothing for later. A well-run daily strategy often looks like a series of waves: launch wave, then a mid-campaign wave (maybe around the halfway mark you drop a new add-on or do a special event), then a late-campaign wave (final 48 hours push). Smaller ripples (updates, minor bonuses) fill in the gaps. The key is to avoid long stretches where nothing new is happening – that's when backers and prospects tune out.

PREPARE FOR THE FINAL COUNTDOWN

While we'll cover the final 48-hour tactics in detail, your daily strategy in the latter half of the campaign should gradually ramp up toward that finish. About a week out from the deadline, start building anticipation for the end. Remind people "Only 7 days left" in an update. If some backers pledged for a low tier early, this reminder might spur them to upgrade once they see the deadline approaching and maybe some stretch goals in reach. Also, a week out is a good time to send another dedicated email to your list (different from the launch one) saying time is running out, highlight any new developments (like "we unlocked two stretch goals so far, don't miss these exclusives"), and generally try to catch those who meant to back but forgot.

In your daily social posts, increase frequency again as you approach the end. If you were doing one post a day in the middle, maybe do two a day in the last week, and even more in the last 2-3 days (people forgive more posting when a big deadline looms – it's expected). Countdowns are inherently compelling: *"5 days left...", "3 days left..."*. Use graphics or countdown timers if you want. Hammer home that *now* is the time, because it's truly the last chance soon.

Also, a few days from the end, do another round of personal nudges. Over the campaign you'll have noticed some supporters who said they would pledge but haven't yet (maybe they liked a post or commented but didn't back). It's absolutely fine to politely reach out again as the deadline nears: *"Hey, just a heads up – we're down to the final 48 hours of my Kickstarter. I remember you were interested in the project; I'd love to have you on board if you're still thinking about it! If not, no worries at all and thank you for following along. "* These one-on-one reminders often convert well at the end, because you're catching them at a moment of "speak now or forever hold your peace." People often appreciate the reminder, and the courtesy of your tone (no guilt-tripping, just a friendly nudge).

Your daily discipline and persistence will pay off here. By continuously engaging and adjusting throughout the campaign, you've avoided the dreaded "dead zone" where nothing happens. You've kept backers excited and new pledges coming in at a modest but steady rate. Now, as the home stretch approaches, you're in a strong position to sprint to the finish line rather than having to resuscitate a flatlined campaign. This is the payoff for managing the middle days with care.

CONSISTENCY AND FLEXIBILITY

Managing a Kickstarter day-to-day is like tending a campfire. You can't walk away and leave it unattended for long, or it might die down. But if you poke it, add some fuel periodically, and shield it from the wind, it will keep burning and even flare up when stoked. Consistency is your friend. A campaign often follows a U-shape pattern, big start, quiet middle, big finish, but that "quiet middle" doesn't have to be lifeless. With regular attention, you can maintain a warm glow of activity in those middle days.

Don't be discouraged by slower days; use them as motivation to try something new. If Day 10 had zero new backers, then on Day 11 you post an engaging update or reveal to change that. Always ask, "What can I do today to move the needle, even a little?" Sometimes the answer might be external (reach out to a new audience) or internal (introduce a new reward). Sometimes it's simply continuing your consistent outreach because seeds you planted days ago will sprout later.

Also, listen and adapt. Pay attention to your backers' feedback or questions. If multiple people seem confused by a reward tier, clarify it in an update or FAQ. If someone suggests an idea (like a new add-on they'd pay for) and it's feasible, consider implementing it and announcing it. Being responsive to opportunities and issues on a daily basis can net you extra pledges and goodwill that you'd miss if you were checked out.

Mindset-wise, get comfortable with the fact that crowdfunding is not a set-and-forget proposition. It requires active management. Embrace the grind in a positive way – treat it as a fun challenge that you *get* to tackle, not a burden. Celebrate small wins. A $20 pledge coming in on an otherwise slow day is still a win (that could be a new lifelong fan!). Keep yourself motivated by remembering why you're doing this and picturing the end result: that funded project and all those readers you've gained.

Finally, maintain urgency without burning out your audience or yourself. Find that balance of steady communication and strategic pushes. It's a long game of maybe 30 days, but it's also a short period in the grand scheme – you can rest after. During the campaign, pour your energy into it each day, but also take care of yourself. If you burn out by week 2, the daily strategy falls apart. So eat, sleep, and schedule brief offline breaks to recharge your mental energy. Consistency doesn't mean 24/7 obsession; it means showing up reliably and intentionally.

By managing backer flow and engagement daily, you build a strong foundation that makes the final urgent days far more effective. Each update, each social post, each answered question is a brick in a wall of trust and excitement around your project. People see you working hard and passionately, and it makes them want to stick with you till the finish line. You're not coasting, you're actively *leading* your campaign every day, and that leadership will inspire more backers to join you.

CHAPTER 20
OVERCOMING LULLS

In a properly run campaign, 1/3 of your funding will come in the first week, 1/3 in the last week, and 1/3 in the middle. And yet, people rarely plan for the middle, which means they are missing out on a lot of money.

On a $10,000 campaign, that's $3,333 that's sitting up for grabs that people are just letting slip through their fingers, but not you. Not anymore. Let's show you how to capture that money.

First, understand that a mid-campaign slowdown is normal. Campaigns often follow a U-shaped funding curve – a spike at the start, a plateau in the middle, and a spike at the end. So, when you hit that flat middle, don't panic and think, "It's over." Realize it's part of the natural flow. Many creators feel a wave of anxiety in week 2 or 3. The initial excitement has faded, new backers aren't flooding in, and you're not yet in the final countdown to get urgency going. This *"dead zone"* can be emotionally tough. The key is to *prepare for it in advance* and then take action during it.

The worst thing to do in a slump is nothing. If you throw up your hands and say "well, guess I'll just wait for the last 48 hours," you risk losing valuable time and even losing backers (people can cancel pledges if they sense a project has stalled or the creator has lost interest). Instead, approach the mid-campaign like a challenge to your creativity and persistence. This is where you differentiate yourself as a savvy creator. You *knew* this slowdown was coming, and you have some tricks up your sleeve to combat it.

Also, **check your mindset:** a day with no new pledges is not failure; it's a signal to shake things up. Don't take it personally or let it sap your motivation. Use it as a prompt: *"Okay, time to execute a slump-busting tactic."* Remember, even during the plateau you might still be getting *views* on your page or people considering backing. They're just not convinced yet. Your job in this phase is to give fence-sitters a reason to jump in now, and to remind existing backers why this campaign is still exciting.

CHANGE YOUR MESSAGE/OFFER/ AUDIENCE

When the graph stalls you have **three** main levers to pull, and each one reframes the campaign without panicking or discounting.

CHANGE THE MESSAGE

If your updates have sounded like "still funding, please share," it's time to rotate the lens.

- Shift theme: move from *"Support my dream"* to *"Unlock this community goal."*
- Spotlight something new: a villain POV excerpt, a process video, reader artwork.
- Invoke urgency through narrative, not numbers: "The prophecy says we need 200 heroes before the next moonrise—are you in?"

Half the time a plateau is just backer fatigue with the same headline. A fresh angle re-sparks curiosity without altering your reward stack.

CHANGE THE OFFER

You don't have to mint a brand-new product, just **shift attention** to tiers that need love or bundle existing items in a fresh way.

- **Tier spotlight:** "Today we're featuring the $60 hardcover + art-print bundle—here's a video flip-through of the foil detail you may have missed."
- **Micro-bundle:** Combine two languishing add-ons at a slight discount; often the convenience, not the price, converts fence-sitters.
- **Limited upgrade:** "First 50 backers who jump from paperback to hardcover get their name on a dedication page."

Changing the offer is about *focus,* not flooding the page with new SKUs. Keep complexity flat while renewing perceived value.

CHANGE THE AUDIENCE

If the current list is tapped, widen the circle.

- **Backer-update swaps:** Trade a shout-out with a parallel campaign so your link lands in hundreds of new inboxes.
- **Genre-adjacent groups:** Post an AMA in a themed Facebook group or subreddit you haven't visited yet.
- **Influencer cameo:** Offer a free review copy or quick Zoom chat to a micro-booktoker in your niche; a 30-second reel can spike traffic for a day.

Think of it as opening a new sales channel, not "bothering strangers." A fresh pool of readers resets the top-of-funnel math and restarts momentum.

HOW THE THREE LEVERS WORK TOGETHER

Start with the **message**. It's the fastest to deploy. If that lifts pledges, stick with it. If not, layer in an **offer** tweak. Still flat? Pull the **audience** lever with cross-promos or paid bursts. Rotate through the trio until the chart tilts upward again. Momentum is nothing more than getting one of these levers to click.

REFRESH YOUR PITCH

One of the easiest ways to inject life into a slow campaign is to release **new content** that renews interest. People might have seen your initial campaign page and thought, "Cool, maybe later." By giving them something new to chew on, "later" can become "now."

Consider doing a mid-campaign update that has some news or reveal:

- Unveil a new piece of artwork (cover art variant, character illustration, map, etc.). Make it a mini-event: *"Surprise Reveal: Meet [Character Name]"* with an image. This not only gives you a reason to ping backers (via the update), but you can share this update publicly to attract new eyes.
- Share an excerpt or a sample chapter if it's a novel. Perhaps you were holding back the first chapter – drop it in an update for all to read. Sometimes reading a sample will push someone on the fence to become a backer.
- Announce a **stretch goal** (even if you haven't hit the main goal yet, you can tease a cool stretch goal to come). For example: *"At $10,000, I'll add a bonus short story for all backers. Help us get there!"* This can motivate current backers to drum up support.
- **Mid-campaign video or live Q&A:** Do an update inviting everyone to a live stream where you'll answer questions, talk about the book, etc. The act of scheduling an event gives you and your backers something to look forward to and promote during the lull.
- **Keep building your case:** Every single day you are live, people should be realizing that they really do want your campaign, but only if you keep showing different angles to your campaign. Maybe it's ancillary characters, or the magic system, or just your drive. Anything can be a new angle, but something has to be.

By providing fresh material, you give yourself a reason to talk about the campaign again in a new way. It's not just, "still funding, please back." Now it's, *"Check out this brand-new artwork we just revealed – isn't it awesome? By the way, the campaign has 2 weeks left!"* It changes the narrative from old news to *current* news.

When you publish these updates, make them **public** if the content is something that could lure new people. Public updates can be viewed by anyone, not just backers, so you can share the link around. If it's really juicy content, even some media outlets or blogs might mention it ("Author reveals new artwork for upcoming graphic novel Kickstarter"). Use the update as a press moment.

Also, engage your existing backers in the update. Ask a question, encourage comments. If you reveal art, ask backers what they think of the character. If you share a chapter, ask for their initial reactions (people love to give opinions). More comments in your updates not only help the algorithm but create an engaged atmosphere that outsiders can sense. A lively comment section in an update can signal to someone considering backing that "wow, there's a community here; people are into this."

INTRODUCE A NEW REWARD OR INCENTIVE

Nothing sparks a stagnant campaign like a shiny new toy. Mid-campaign is a great time to introduce a new reward tier or add-on, ideally something your audience has been asking for or something that adds novelty without derailing your plans.

Examples:

- **Limited Edition Mid-Campaign Tier:** Perhaps you didn't originally offer a **cameo character** reward (where a backer's name is used for a minor character), but a few people asked about it. Add a new tier at, say, $200 for a limited number of cameos. Announce it in an update: *"New Reward Tier Added: Become a Character in the Book – only 3 available!"* Scarcity plus novelty can get a burst of pledges, especially from existing backers upgrading.
- **Combo Packs or Bundles:** If you realize some backers want "one of everything," but your tiers didn't offer a clear bundle, introduce a new bundle tier. For instance, *"All-In Deluxe Bundle"* that includes all books, all prints, all swag at a premium price. This can entice collectors or higher-end backers to increase pledges.
- **Add-Ons:** Kickstarter now allows add-ons. Mid-campaign, you can add a new add-on item, like a pin, sticker pack, or digital bonus. Promote it: *"By popular demand, we've added a T-shirt as an add-on option! You can now edit your pledge to include it if you want one."* This can get existing backers to throw a few more dollars into the pot for the extra item.
- **Upgrade Incentives:** Announce that anyone who is at a lower tier might want to upgrade to a higher tier by a certain date because of X. For example, *"Upgrade to a hardcover tier by next week and you'll also get a signed bookplate!"* (This kind of retroactive bonus must be handled carefully – make sure it's fair and within budget – but it can motivate mid-campaign upsells.)

However, a **caution**: Don't go overboard adding a ton of new rewards that complicate your fulfillment or confuse your backers. Any new item you introduce mid-campaign should be something you can realistically deliver and afford. It should also be strategic. Ideally, it's responding to backer feedback or an obvious gap. Randomly adding a new tier that no one asked for can fall flat and look desperate. Instead, pay attention to backer comments and suggestions. Often, they'll signal what else they might buy. If, say, multiple people ask "Is there an option to get two copies? I want one for a friend," and you didn't have a two-book tier – boom, mid-campaign you add a "Gift Pack: 2 hardcover copies" tier.

When you do add something, **make noise about it**. It's news! *"We're combating the mid-campaign blues by spicing things up – new reward just dropped!"* It gives you a fresh angle to promote and can bring previous visitors back to take a second look.

RUN A MID-CAMPAIGN EVENT

Sometimes, injecting a live or time-bound event can jolt people out of their complacency. Consider organizing a **mid-campaign event** around the halfway point or during a particularly slow week:

- **Live AMA (Ask Me Anything):** Host a Reddit AMA in a relevant subreddit (like r/Fantasy or r/IndieAuthors, if allowed) or a Facebook Live where you answer questions about your book or crowdfunding. Promote it to get people to come engage. Not only might you pick up a few backers from the event itself, it also gives you content to talk about: *"Join me live tomorrow and ask me anything!"* and afterward, *"Thanks for the great questions in the live chat today!"*.

- **Giveaway or Contest:** You have to be careful with Kickstarter's rules (you can't require a pledge for an outside contest), but you can do something like: *"Everyone who is a backer by Day 15 will be entered to win a special art print."* Technically no purchase necessary beyond being a backer at any level, which is okay. Or run a contest on social media such as *"Share this project with hashtag #X for a chance to win a free upgrade to hardcover."* Ensure you state it's not affiliated with KS and that anyone can enter (they can share even if not a backer) to keep it within rules. These little games can stir excitement. People love winning things, and it might encourage fence-sitters to back, so they're included in the backers-only draw.

- **Community Challenge:** Rally your current backers to help you fight the slump. For instance, *"If each of you recruits just 1 friend, we'd smash our next goal. So, here's a fun challenge: bring one friend to the campaign this week. If you do, have them leave a comment saying who referred them – I'll give both of you a shout-out in the next update!"* Even a small number of backers participating can bump your numbers and activity.

- **The Creator Does Something Cool (or Silly):** You've seen those campaigns where the creator says, "If we reach X by Friday, I'll record a video of me doing a happy dance / wearing a goofy costume / reading a chapter in a funny voice." It sounds silly, but that kind of personal, fun promise can engage people. It shows you're game to have fun and celebrate milestones. Some backers will increase pledges just to see you do the thing! Make sure it fits your personality and comfort level – the point is to entertain and motivate, not torture yourself. But a bit of creator shenanigans can humanize the campaign and endear backers to you even more.

Whatever event or challenge you do, promote it heavily for the days leading up and during. This breaks the monotony of "please back" messaging and gives people something to participate in. It also creates a mini-deadline *within* the campaign, which is key to overcoming slumps – you're manufacturing urgency and interest at a time when there naturally isn't any.

CROSS-PROMOTE AND COLLABORATE

The mid-campaign period is prime time to tap into external networks via cross-promotion. Early on, you focus on your own audience; late, on urgency. The middle is when you can say, "Who else can I collaborate with to swap audiences a bit?"

If you know other authors or creators running Kickstarters around the same time (especially in a complementary genre or niche), reach out to do an update swap. During the lull, this can bring a nice influx of new backers who trust the recommendation from a creator they already backed. Just ensure the other project is something you genuinely think your backers might like, and frame it as, "Hey, my friend X has a cool project Y, you might want to check it out." Don't overdo these (backers get annoyed if every update is pushing another project), but one or two well-chosen swaps can help both parties.

I would often do 30-50 during a campaign, roughly one every three days, and multiple in every update. It was a lot, but it helped so much. Every day I looked through every new campaign on the platform and reached out to the good fits. It wasn't a one-time thing. I did it all the time.

Another angle: reach out to any bloggers, podcasters, or media you contacted pre-launch who didn't respond or schedule something. Mid-campaign, follow up: *"Hi, just wanted to share that my Kickstarter is 60% funded and we've added some cool features. We still have two weeks to go – I'd love to chat about [interesting angle] if you're doing any crowdfunding coverage."* Sometimes, the media needs to see that a project is viable before covering it; now you have proof of momentum to show them. Even a small blog featuring you mid-campaign can net a few pledges (and at this stage, every pledge counts).

Leverage your **existing community** as well. If you have author friends, ask if you can do a guest post on their blog this week, or an Instagram Live together to talk about the project. These are low-effort collaborations that can bring attention during slow times. People often say yes if you approach politely and it's mutually beneficial or at least not a heavy lift for them.

Finally, don't forget your local community or personal networks you might have been saving. Midway, send a reminder to those friends or colleagues who didn't back yet: *"Hey, we're halfway through the Kickstarter and getting close to the goal. If you were planning to preorder the book, now would be an awesome time!"* Sometimes personal contacts procrastinate; a mid-campaign nudge can convert them without waiting until the final day rush (where they might forget altogether).

REIGNITE YOUR OWN PASSION

When the campaign excitement wanes, it can affect you as the creator. Maybe you're feeling a bit burned out by week 3, less peppy in your messaging, or worried about reaching the goal. Paradoxically, one of the best ways to overcome a slump is to **rekindle your own enthusiasm,** because it shines through in your communications.

Take a moment to remind yourself **why** you're doing this. Re-read some of the positive comments from backers so far. Look at that growing list of supporters. Those are people who believe in you! Even if growth has slowed, 100 backers (or whatever you have now) is significant. Get excited about delivering something awesome to them. Sometimes just shifting your mindset from "Ugh, we're stalled" to "Whoa, there are people here who can't wait for this book" will change the tone of everything you put out.

Share that excitement. Maybe do an update that's just a heartfelt, *"I want to share why this project means so much to me."* Stirring emotions can wake people up. Or tell a story you haven't told yet about the journey, something to remind everyone (and yourself) of the passion behind the project. During slumps, facts and figures might not move the needle, but *emotion* can. Rekindle the emotional connection with your audience.

It might also help to pivot your messaging a bit. If you've been very salesy, try a more personal touch in the middle: *"I so appreciate this community. Here's a bit about my creative journey... Thank you for being part of it."* Conversely, if you've been very low-key, maybe it's time to get a little bolder with, *"We really need your help to push through this plateau – here's how you can support (besides pledging, even just sharing helps!)."* Don't be afraid to directly enlist your backers as allies: *"Backers, assemble! Let's bust this mid-campaign slump together."* People love being part of a rally.

Now, you don't have to invest your own money like that (and you should only consider it if you were truly willing to fund the shortfall yourself), but the principle stands: do something that changes the story. The story was "campaign slows down," they turned it into "campaign climbing again." You can achieve similar narrative shifts with the strategies above – a new stretch goal, an exciting event, a big cross-promo. Anything that gives the impression (and reality) that *activity* is happening will help reverse the slump.

CHAPTER 21

FULFILLMENT PLANNING

The moment your campaign ends successfully, take a brief victory lap – you did it! But then, the work begins on the most important part of your campaign, delivering books to backers in a way that delights and excites them. If you do this right, then you'll build a fanbase ready to follow your next campaign the moment it goes live.

So how do we do this?

First, within 24 hours of funding, **communicate with your backers.** Post a campaign Update (and/or send a personal message to backers via Kickstarter) that accomplishes two things:

1. **Express heartfelt gratitude.** Let them know their support made your dream possible. A genuine thank-you goes a long way in setting a positive tone for fulfillment.
2. **Outline what happens next.** Backers shouldn't be left wondering. Tell them, for example: *"In about two weeks, you'll receive a backer survey to collect your shipping info and any choices (like which cover variant you want). I'm currently finalizing the print schedule*

and will keep you updated along the way. The estimated delivery is [month]. I'll post updates at least once a month to let you know how production is going."
Setting clear expectations upfront prevents anxiety and a flood of repetitive questions later.

By promptly thanking and informing everyone, you reassure backers that you haven't vanished now that you have their money. This builds trust and goodwill, which you'll need if any hiccups occur during fulfillment. It also helps *you* mentally shift into the fulfillment phase – the campaign might be over, but a new project (delivering the goods) has begun.

While you're on the campaign page, create a button on the page that sends people to your store, or somewhere to preorder your book. Of course, if you have set up late pledges this is less of an issue, but you should have a way for people to order the book.

COLLECT ESSENTIAL BACKER INFORMATION

To fulfill rewards, you need data: shipping addresses, and possibly other details like each backer's chosen book format, T-shirt size, name for acknowledgments, etc. Kickstarter itself does not automatically gather most of this during the campaign (except email and payment). So, it's your job to send out a **Backer Survey** after the campaign to collect what you need.

You have two main options for surveys:

- **Kickstarter's built-in survey:** Simpler and free. You create a questionnaire through Kickstarter, and it emails backers a link. Their answers get compiled on your backer report. Kickstarter has done some massive work upgrading their own platform, and I highly suggest you start there before you go to other platforms.
- **Pledge Manager service (e.g., BackerKit, Crowd Ox):** Third-party platforms that integrate with Kickstarter. They offer more robust features: backers can update their addresses themselves, you can offer add-on purchases post-campaign, etc. They cost money or a percentage of post-campaign sales, though some have free tiers for smaller projects.

For many author campaigns with a moderate number of backers and straightforward rewards, Kickstarter's own survey is sufficient. If you have thousands of backers, complicated multi-item orders, or you want to continue selling post-campaign upgrades/add-ons, a pledge manager can be worth it.

Whichever you choose, keep surveys concise. Ask only what you truly need to fulfill rewards. Typically:

- **Shipping address:** (Name, street, city, state, ZIP, country). Make sure to ask what country for international shipping.
- **Email address:** (if you need it to deliver digital rewards or e-books). Also make sure to ask if you can add them to your mailing list. Easily the most important question for future success. Roughly 80% of people should say yes.

- **Reward specifics:** e.g., "Which cover edition do you want?" or "What name should I print in the Special Thanks section?" (if that was a reward).
- **Sizes or variations:** if you offered T-shirts in different sizes, or patrons need to pick which poster from a set, etc.
- **Any personalization info:** e.g., "If your reward includes a character name in the story, write the name here."

Set a **reasonable deadline** for survey responses – typically 2-3 weeks. State in the survey or update: *"Please fill out by [Date] so we can begin fulfillment. If you submit late, your shipment might be delayed."* Expect that some stragglers won't fill it out on time; you'll have to chase them via email or Kickstarter message. That's normal. Just keep track and send polite nudges as needed.

Kickstarter now offers late pledges, too, so you can set up your campaign to keep getting orders through fulfillment. Even if it's only a couple of weeks until you deliver, it could mean hundreds, or even thousands, to your campaign. I am always super impressed by the amount of money you can make after the campaign is over.

MANAGE FUNDS AND FAILED PAYMENTS

About 2 weeks after the campaign ends, Kickstarter will transfer the funds to your bank (minus their fees). But in the interim, you need to watch for **failed payments.** Usually, a small percentage of backers' credit cards might decline (expired card, insufficient funds, etc.). Kickstarter gives those backers a 7-day window to fix their payment details. You can see on your Kickstarter admin panel who's in "errored" status.

It's a good practice to send a friendly note through Kickstarter to any backer with a failed charge around day 3-4 post-campaign: *"Hi [Name], just a heads up that your pledge didn't go through. Kickstarter will retry your card until [date]. I'd love for you to get your rewards, so please check that your payment info is up to date. Thanks!"* Many people resolve it. After 7 days, any unresolved pledges are dropped, and those backers don't get charged or included in your backer report.

Don't panic if you lose a few backers due to failed payments, it happens. Typically, it's maybe 1-5% of the total pledge amount. Make sure to account for that when looking at your final budget. For example, if you raised $10,000, after fees (approximately 8-10%) and 1-3% in failed pledges, you might actually receive around $8,800-$9,100 net. Always base your spending on the *net funds* in hand, not the big number on the Kickstarter front page.

Once funds hit your account, consider creating a separate spreadsheet or even a separate bank account to manage them. You want to use these funds explicitly for the expenses you planned – printing, shipping, packaging, etc. Keeping clean records will help in case you need to report for taxes (Kickstarter sends a 1099-K in the US if you raised over $20k, and yes, it's taxable income minus expenses). Organization now saves headaches later.

COORDINATE PRINT RUNS AND PRODUCTION

Now to the exciting part: turning those pledges into actual books and rewards. Hopefully, you researched your printing and production options *before* launching (as recommended in earlier chapters). Post-campaign, it's time to execute.

For Books:

- Contact your printer or printing service promptly. If you went with an offset printer for a large run, you'll need to finalize the quantity. Calculate that based on backer orders plus extra copies (always print more than you need – accidents and lost packages happen, and you'll want some stock for future events or sales). A rule of thumb might be 5-10% extra. If using print-on-demand for each backer (e.g., via IngramSpark), you'll be placing individual orders, but you should still ensure your files are uploaded and ready.
- **Finalize your files.** If you are still editing or tweaking the book up to campaign end, set a deadline to freeze it and export print-ready PDF files. Double-check specs from your printer (trim size, bleed, etc.). Perhaps order one last proof if time permits to ensure all is well.
- Once satisfied, **place the print order**. Earlier planning should mean you know the timeline (e.g., printer needs 4 weeks). Lock that in as soon as you have addresses and final counts.
- If you have multiple formats (hardcover, paperback), handle each accordingly. Maybe paperbacks are via POD, so you might not "order" them until you have

addresses (printing and shipping direct). Plan how you'll route that – many creators get a bulk shipment to themselves even for POD because shipping in bulk can be cheaper, then they do individual mail-outs. Others have POD do direct fulfillment for each backer. Choose what's cost-effective and manageable for you.

FOR OTHER MERCHANDISE/REWARDS:

- Identify each item you need to produce: bookmarks, art prints, pins, apparel, etc.
- Contact each supplier or use your pre-researched vendor. Place orders ASAP, as some swag can have surprisingly long turnaround (enamel pins often take 4-6 weeks production, for instance).
- If you have customizations to certain backer rewards (like a backer's name printed in the book), make sure you incorporate those into your files before printing. Often that's just one page listing special thanks names – gather those from survey responses and triple-check spelling.
- Order packing supplies too: boxes, padded envelopes, tape, labels. It's easy to forget until the books arrive and you think "Oh, I need to mail these…". Calculate roughly how many of each size envelope or box you need (based on reward combos). Always get a few extras. Shipping supply companies or Amazon can deliver these quickly but have them on hand in advance so you're not delayed when you're ready to ship.

Using tools can help: Many pledge manager services will give you a breakdown of exactly how many of each item is needed (like 250 signed hardcovers, 100 paperbacks, 50 mugs, etc.). If you used Kickstarter's survey, you may need to export the backer data to Excel/Sheets and do a bit of tallying. Do this the moment surveys are mostly in, so you can confidently order the right quantities.

One more thing: if anything in your project involves a **third-party contributor** (like an artist finishing a cover, or a printer for special edition boxes), now's the time to check in and schedule. Everyone should be aligned on timelines.

KEEP BACKERS IN THE LOOP DURING FULFILLMENT

Silence after a campaign is a killer of goodwill. Even if everything is going smoothly, update your backers periodically. Good points for updates include:

- **When surveys are sent** (and later, a reminder before the deadline for those who haven't filled it).
- **When funds are received**: maybe not necessary to announce, but you can tie it in with something like "The funds have arrived, and we've officially started printing!"
- **When orders are placed**: *"The books are at the printer! Here's a photo of the proof we approved."*
- **Production milestones**: *"All the art prints have come in, they look gorgeous (see pic below). Books are slated to arrive at my home next week."*
- **Any delays or issues**: If, say, the printer says the books will ship to you 2 weeks later than expected, be upfront

in an update. *"Our printer had a slight delay due to supply issues, so I will have the books in early May instead of April as initially planned. I'll keep you posted, but this might push shipping to backers into late May. Thank you for your patience!"* Most backers will be completely fine with this because you communicated it.

- **Fun shares**: The fulfillment period can feel long and uneventful to backers, so share little behind-the-scenes stuff to keep them excited: *"Check out these boxes of bookmarks that just arrived!"* or *"Here's a sneak peek at the art print you unlocked, fresh from the printer."* Photos are great – seeing the stacks of goodies builds anticipation that, yes, this is real and coming.

A rule of thumb is to update at least monthly post-campaign until everything is delivered. If your timeline is short (like you'll ship in one month), you might do just a couple updates in that span. If it's longer (several months for a complex project), do at least monthly even if nothing huge happened: *"Hey everyone, quick status: we're still on track. Editing is nearly done, and we're polishing the cover design. I plan to send files to the printer by X date. Just wanted to let you know it's moving along!"* Backers vastly prefer a quick "nothing major to report, but I'm here" update over radio silence. Silence makes them imagine worst-case scenarios.

LOCK ADDRESSES AND PREPARE FOR SHIPPING

In the weeks leading up to actually shipping rewards, you'll want backers to confirm their addresses. People move, things change, and an address from three months ago might be outdated. So, about a week or two before you ship:

- If using Kickstarter's survey, you cannot auto-update addresses, so send an update: *"We plan to start shipping on [Date]. If your mailing address has changed since you filled out the survey, please message me with the new address by [deadline]!"* Inevitably, a bunch of people will realize they need to update. Compile those and keep careful records.
- If using a pledge manager, typically they allow backers to update addresses themselves until you "lock" them. Announce the lock date so people have a heads-up to make any final changes. Then lock it and export your final shipping list.

Some creators even do an "Address Check" email to each backer individually, but that's usually only for very long gaps or super high tiers. For most, a general announcement suffices, plus individually chasing those handful who you suspect might have an issue (like international backers in countries known for addressing quirks – sometimes you might want to double-check formatting).

Now, **organize your fulfillment area**. When all your books and merch are in-hand, set up a workspace for packing. This could be your dining table or an entire garage, depending on scale. Pro tip: create an assembly line setup. Group items by reward tier. For example, Tier 1 backers get just the paperback, Tier 2 get paperback + bookmark, Tier 3 get hardcover + print + pin, etc. Make a stack for each item and perhaps even make stacks or bins per tier. Print out your backer list (or use a spreadsheet on a laptop in your workspace) that shows for each backer what they get.

Make sure to take a moment to inspect your products before shipping. Flip through a book to ensure no glaring print errors, check that merch isn't defective. It's rare, but catching a bad batch *before* you mail out 300 packages is important. If something's wrong, better to address it now (get reprints, etc.) than have lots of backers complaining later.

CHOOSE YOUR TOOLS

When it's time to actually send packages, you want this to be as efficient and error-free as possible. Invest in some tools:

- **Postal scale:** If you have varied package weights, a small digital scale lets you weigh and buy exact postage from home, avoiding post office lines and surprises.
- **Label printing:** Handwriting 300 addresses is not only slow, it's prone to errors. You can either print labels on regular paper and tape them, use Avery label sheets in a printer, or go big and get a thermal label printer (like a DYMO or Rollo, which online sellers often use). Even

a basic inkjet can do the job with half-sheet adhesive labels. Many shipping software solutions let you print addresses easily from your backer spreadsheet.

- **Shipping software or online postage:** Services like Pirate Ship, Stamps.com, USPS Click-N-Ship, or your country's postal service website allow you to buy and print postage at home. Often, they have discounts for commercial rates (Pirate Ship, for instance, gives US Commercial Base rates for free). You can upload a CSV of addresses or possibly integrate directly with BackerKit or other pledge managers. This saves money and time, and you can automatically get tracking numbers.
- **Customs forms for international:** If you're shipping internationally, any package over a certain weight needs a customs declaration. Online postage will prompt you for contents and values. A tip: mark items as "Gift" or "Documents" where truthfully applicable and keep declared value low (like the production cost of the book, say $5). Many authors do this to help backers avoid VAT/import fees. Ethically it's a gray area, yes – officially one should declare actual value – but practically, marking a $25 book as a $10 gift is common practice and rarely an issue. Use your judgment.
- **Organization:** As you pack, you might want to mark orders as shipped in a system. If you're not using a pledge manager to do it, maintain a spreadsheet column "shipped – yes/no" so you can check off each backer as you go. It's easy to lose track in the flurry of packages, so meticulous records ensure no one gets missed.

- **Batch your work:** Consider doing it in batches to stay sane. Maybe "Today: pack all international orders" (since those often need special forms), and "Tomorrow: pack all domestic". Or break by tier: "Day 1: all Tier 1 & 2, Day 2: Tier 3," etc. Breaking it down prevents fatigue and mistakes.

When you start shipping, it's a good idea to post an update letting backers know packages are going out and what to expect: *"Shipping has begun! I plan to ship roughly 50 orders per day, so it will take me about a week to send everything. You will receive an email with a tracking number once your package is on its way. (International backers: note that tracking may only work until it leaves my country.) If you don't get a tracking email within two weeks, let me know."* This heads off the "when will mine ship?!" questions. If you're using Kickstarter without a pledge manager, you may not have an automated way to send tracking to each backer unless you individually message or email them. It might be too laborious to do it one by one. In that case, tell them in the update: *"All packages will be shipped via USPS Media Mail in the next 10 days. US backers: I'll post another update when everything's shipped – if you don't have your package a week after that, contact me. International: times vary, but usually 2-4 weeks."* Manage expectations clearly.

HANDLE PROBLEMS QUICKLY

Despite your best efforts, things happen. A book might get lost in the mail, or arrive damaged, or a backer realizes they put the wrong address. Your approach to these issues can turn an upset backer into a loyal fan (or if handled poorly, turn minor issues into lingering resentment).

COMMON SCENARIOS AND HOW TO HANDLE:

- **Lost package:** If a backer says they never got it, first check tracking (if available). If it shows delivered, politely ask them to double-check with household members or neighbors (and verify the address they gave matches where they live). Sometimes packages are sitting at a post office waiting for pick-up due to customs fees or missed delivery. If truly lost, you as the creator should generally eat the cost and send a replacement. It's the cost of doing business. Budget a few extra books for this.
- **Damaged item:** A book arrives with a bent cover or soaking wet from rain. Apologize and replace it. Don't make the backer jump through hoops. You might ask for a photo if you need proof for your own supplier or just to gauge what went wrong in packing. But ultimately, send a new one. The goodwill you earn outweighs the cost of one book.
- **Wrong item received:** Maybe you mixed up packages and someone got two of one print and none of the other. Apologize, correct it by sending the missing item. If the mix-up resulted in them getting something extra they weren't supposed to, let them keep it as an apology unless it's very costly.
- **Address errors/returns:** If a package comes back to you because of a bad address or unclaimed, contact the backer. Confirm the address (maybe it was slightly

wrong, or they moved). Then resend. It's okay to kindly ask them to cover the additional postage if the error was on their end (e.g., they put the wrong address), but many creators just cover it once as a courtesy. Use judgment based on the cost and the backer's attitude. Often, they'll offer to pay; if it's a few bucks, you can be the hero and say no need. If it's a $50 international parcel, it's fair to discuss splitting cost or something.

- **Digital rewards issues:** Ensure your digital rewards (ebooks, PDFs, etc.) were delivered (usually via email or a download link). You might do this earlier, even immediately after the campaign for instant gratification. But if anyone can't access a file or link, remedy that quickly via a direct email.

Treat every backer with the same respect and care you'd give a friend. These are your early supporters, going the extra mile to make them happy is investing in your future fanbase. If that means spending a couple hundred from your own pocket to fix problems, so be it. Think long-term: a satisfied backer will back you again or tell others; a disgruntled one might disappear forever (or rant online).

It helps to keep a **cushion of funds** for these issues. Hopefully you budgeted a bit for "contingency" or extra shipping. If not, consider it a lesson for next time. But never let a small expense stop you from making a backer whole. It's just not worth the damage to your reputation or the backer's experience.

As packages start arriving, you'll hopefully get a flood of happy messages or social media posts from backers showing off their rewards. **Bask in that!** It's one of the most rewarding parts of running a Kickstarter, seeing your creation in readers' hands. Encourage backers (in an update or email) to share a photo of their reward on social and tag you. This not only pumps you up, it's marketing for the next release. Plus, positive backer experiences help overshadow any small bumps that occur.

Once you've shipped the last package and resolved the last issue, *congratulations*: you have fulfilled your Kickstarter! That's a big deal – many projects notoriously stumble here, but you delivered like a pro.

FULFILLMENT IS PART OF SUCCESS

Fulfilling a Kickstarter is not a pesky afterthought – it's the **critical final act** where you prove yourself as a creator and cement trust. The way you handle fulfillment will determine whether backers become repeat backers and evangelists for you. Do it well, and you turn one-time supporters into lifelong fans. Do it poorly (delays with no communication, shoddy packing, ignored issues), and you risk turning your victory into a PR headache.

So treat fulfillment with the same seriousness and professionalism as the launch. It's a project in itself that requires organization, communication, and care. But also, try to enjoy it – this is literally the moment your dream becomes a tangible reality in the world. Signing books, packing them with a thank-you note, seeing that big pile of outbound packages – it's hard work, but it's also a celebration of what you and your community achieved.

Many creators find a sense of closure and pride in the act of shipping their books out.

A few guiding principles:

- **Stay organized:** spreadsheets, checklists, labels – whatever it takes so nothing falls through the cracks.
- **Communicate:** when in doubt, update. Backers rarely complain about too much info, but they do complain about being left in the dark.
- **Be prompt but don't rush:** move quickly on ordering and shipping, but not at the expense of accuracy. It's better to ship one week later with correct items than to hurry and make mistakes. If you need a bit more time, tell backers; most are patient if you keep them in the loop.
- **Go above and beyond:** throw in a little extra sticker or bookmark for everyone? Sure, if you have spares – those unexpected bonuses delight people. Respond kindly even to backers who have complaints or endless questions. Your generosity and professionalism now will be remembered.
- **Learn and document:** as you fulfill, note what could be improved. Did you underestimate shipping to Canada? Did a particular vendor have issues? Capture those lessons for next time (we'll touch more on learning in the next chapter).

Think of fulfillment as not just delivering a product but delivering an **experience**. The unboxing, the feeling that "this creator cares about me" – that's what creates fans who stick around. You're not Amazon; you're an artisan hand-delivering a creation to supporters. That personal touch is your advantage.

Lastly, give yourself credit. Fulfillment is a grind, but you're doing it – you're making good on your promises. When the last package is out the door, take a moment to reflect on the journey from idea to funded project to delivered reality. It's pretty amazing. And in doing so, you've built a foundation of trust with an audience who will be eager for what you do next.

CHAPTER 22

PRINTING OPTIONS

I've always been fascinated with printing books. Even before I started printing them myself, back before I even considered myself a writer, I loved the feel and smell of books. So, when I made making books my profession, I dug in deep on the best ways to print books.

For years, I would try to talk to authors about how to print books in more economical, and more beautiful ways, but my enthusiasm fell flat. Nobody cared. Why would you print and store books if Amazon could just print and deliver books whenever somebody ordered one?

With the recent uptick in interest regarding direct sales, people are finally catching on to all the different ways that producing beautiful books can be a boon to your author business. Besides, it's fun to create something beautiful, especially when you have fans who appreciate the effort.

I've been printing books since before companies like BookVault and 48 Hour Books significantly expanded what you could do with print-on-demand books, back when the only economical way to create hardcover books was to print 1,000+ copies.

Back then, we basically had IngramSpark, CreateSpace (RIP), and Lulu, which was a beautiful but ungodly expensive option in those days. If you wanted anything special, or you wanted to print books in color, the only option was to produce an offset run of books.

I see a lot of authors asking questions about printing, and I see a lot of well-meaning authors giving god-awful advice, so I thought I would dump all the information about printing that I've acquired over the last 15 years of printing books. I've asked my friend Lily Wong from Alpaca Color Printing to help me with this task. She's been one of my printer reps since 2015 and helped me print almost all my offset runs.

POD (PRINT-ON-DEMAND) VS. OFFSET

POD is printed on smaller machines. If you want to print only a handful of books, or even just one copy, then POD is a fine choice. If you need to print thousands of copies, you should choose offset printing because the more you print the more you save. -Lily Wong

It used to be that the only choices you could make when printing books POD was whether you wanted gloss or matte laminate for our covers (*I always choose matte because the feel is delightful*). There was a time when we couldn't even choose paper weight or anything.

Now, companies like Lulu, BookVault, Mixam, and 48 Hour Books have a million options from gold foil to glow-in-the-dark and much more. Digital printing used to look cheap, but over the last 15 years we've seen incredible advancements in the quality of POD books.

I should mention here that POD wasn't always around. Before the early 2000s, you couldn't even print digitally. The **only** option was an offset print run.

If you've been in indie publishing for fewer than 10 years, it's likely that you don't even know what offset printing is, which is wild to me since it used to be the only way to print books.

Aside from quality, which I think has vastly improved in the last 3-5 years on the POD side, the main reason to choose offset printing instead of digital printing is cost. While it costs more to do an offset print run, as you have to order a minimum of 250 copies, you save significantly when you start printing at higher volumes.

COST DIFFERENCE

Offset printing is printed on a bigger, more complicated machine. They will adjust the color for consistent printing across your entire order. Additionally, when you print more, the cost is less. When you have bigger quantities, like 1,000 copies or above, it saves cost while providing better quality. For offset printing, 100 copies at once is expensive because each process has a lot of waste. We also need to make CTP plates for the big offset machine. All the waste are divided to each copy. So printing more saves more. - Lily Wong

The biggest argument I have with authors is about long-term thinking vs. short-term term thinking and never is this more apparent than when we talk about print runs.

Why? Offset printing costs more upfront than POD, but it's vastly more cost-effective over the long term. I still have books I printed in 2016 that I'm selling today at no additional cost to me.

Yes, it does take longer-term thinking to plan for the next 3-5 years of your life, but if you know you're going to be selling the same books for a long time, then it starts to make sense. The independent publishing industry is traditionally built upon "churn and burn," where you put out a book a month until you burn out, but that model is changing. It was never healthy to begin with, but now we're starting to see how toxic that model is and treating our books with the care they deserve.

If we're focused on maximizing our backlist for years instead of churning and burning our books as fast as possible, an offset run makes more sense. As Lily says above, the more you print during an offset run, the more you save.

This is because almost all the cost of printing an offset run is in the first 500 copies. Why is this? Because it costs a lot to create the plates used to print your books. With digital printing, there are no plates, so the cost is consistent, but with offset printing, they create new plates for every job (which is what Lily means above with there being a lot of waste), so you get economy of scale.

Let's talk numbers for a minute. For a digital print run, a paperback copy of *Ichabod Jones: Monster Hunter* costs about $6 to print through IngramSpark. The print quality is pretty good, but it's not perfect. The color is pretty crappy, actually. Still, for a down-and-dirty print job, it's fine.

A few years ago, I printed 1,000 copies of the same book in hardcover, on beautiful paper, with ribbons and everything. That whole run cost about $4,000. So, for $4/book, I was able to get a higher quality print, on better paper, in hardcover.

That paperback version sells for $20, while the hardcover sells for $30, too. So, yes, if I was printing 100 copies, then it would probably be absurd to print those hardcover books…but that's only if I thought I would never sell those books again.

You see, I still have hundreds of those books in my garage that have been paid off years ago. Every time I did a new volume of Ichabod, I didn't have to print those books again. I already had them. Yes, I had to make that investment upfront, but by printing more I saved more.

And I didn't even print a lot of books. I did the math once, and for every 500 more books I printed, it would have only cost me $750. I found that my best value was around 2,000 books, but that's a lot of books to store at a time. Plus, the more books you have to sell, the fewer books of any one title you seem to sell. I sell roughly the same amount at shows now as I did years ago, but across dozens more books.

UPGRADING YOUR BOOKS ECONOMICALLY

One of the other things that stands out about offset printing is that while it's more expensive to get an initial order, upgrading to better and better options is way more affordable.

For instance, in order to upgrade to hardcover in most POD printers, there is roughly a $4/book upcharge, making hardcover not very economical. Not to mention if you want the binding to be sewn-bound instead of glue-bound. Lily is unequivocal on her preference here.

You need to choose sewn-bound. It is stronger and lays flat. If you do not care about quality, or if you need something like advertising brochures or magazines that are not for long-term use, you can choose glue-bound, not sewn. -Lily Wong

When I went to quote sewn-bound hardcovers from a digital printer, the costs went from $6 to $15, a wild difference, especially since with an offset printer, especially an international printer, it could cost as little as $.83 to upgrade from paperback to sewn-bound hardcover.

That says nothing about the other improvements you can make to books. One day I was trying to find a POD option for spot UV, a process that adds a shine to only certain areas of a cover and found that you had to pay $5/book for that option on a book, whereas I could get it for $.10 or less from an offset printer.

That's not to say there aren't a ton of options when it comes to digital printing, but offset printing becomes way more economical as you start to create premium and then super premium books, especially the ones I see people offering on Kickstarter.

I should mention that in general, this pricing is only true for overseas printers like Alpaca Printing. Companies like Marquis in Canada or ones in the USA tend to vastly overprice these upgrades, which to me is the most compelling reason to look internationally.

GANG PRINTING, GANG BINDING, AND SPLIT RUNS

You can save money if you print several books together because we can put two covers or three covers on the same plate. If your books are the same size, we can bind them together without the need to adjust the machine. If your book uses the same paper, we can also purchase paper together and save costs. -Lily Wong

Often, authors tell me that they could never sell 1,000+ books. I'm not saying it doesn't take a lot of effort, but there is also an ingenious way to break up your print run to take advantage of several marketing strategies. It is called **gang-binding**, or **split runs**.

The general idea is that you can bind a print run in several different ways to service different markets. For instance, let's say you run a Kickstarter and need 50 leatherbound books, 100 hardcover books, and 200 paperback books.

Well, you might go to a POD printer for that order, or you can go to an offset printer and print them together to take advantage of those economies of scale, and since the interiors are the same, you would really be paying for 350 books with what is called a "change fee" of between $50-$250 per new cover.

Comics are notorious for using this trick to produce dozens of variant covers, including show variants and getting people to rebuy the same book multiple times. Any single book could have 10-20 or more variant covers, all with the same interior paper stock. All they are doing is changing the covers and getting their readers to buy the same book multiple times.

This isn't something that independent authors have taken to as much, but it happens all the time in comics and book publishing, and I think we should lean into it. We have:

- Paperback covers
- Mass market covers
- Hardcover
- Limited edition covers
- Book Club covers
- Retailer exclusive covers
- Kickstarter exclusive covers
- Convention covers
- Anniversary covers
- Leather covers

Plus more that I'm probably forgetting, but the point is that if you parcel these covers out then ordering 1,000+ books doesn't seem that bonkers anymore.

If you want to save even more money, then you can order multiple books together, called **gang printing**. This doesn't mean you have to order the books. You could create a little consortium of authors and order 2-5+ books at the same time and save. Maybe consortiums exist for the sole reason of saving on printing costs.

I ordered a book several years ago that cost $10,000 to bring 2,000 copies. When I went to place a second order, I was able to print books 1 and 2 in the series for $12,000, saving me a ton of money. Yes, there are price breaks with POD books, but you're not saving as much as you do with an offset run. ***This is really how you game the publishing system for fun and profit.***

One other thing I want to mention here is that every book size has a different unit of paper they consider their standard measurement. This usually ranges from 12-16 pages and is called a **signature.**

When you print to the signature, meaning you have the exact right page count equal to their unit of measurement, then you save a lot of money. Printing to signature is one of the easiest ways to save money on a print run.

WHEN TO PRINT LOCALLY OR POD

If you print in small quantities, less than 500 copies, it's probably best to print locally. -Lily Wong

I'll be honest. Even though I know all of this, I haven't printed an offset run since 2022. *Why?* Because most of my books are printed in 100-200 unit runs and I have a quick turnaround time.

If you print overseas, you should expect 3-4 months turnaround time. If your order is for a small quantity of paperback books, then people might receive their order in two months. -Lily Wong

The biggest thing that prevents me from printing more books in an offset run, besides space, is that I want to deliver books within a month of a campaign ending, and usually within 2 weeks.

While my longer series could warrant an offset run, printing 12 books is prohibitively expensive, even if I take advantage of all these tricks, especially since people usually only buy 50-100 of any single title during a campaign.

I'm also not offering a lot of filigree or enhancements to my books. They are no-nonsense paperbacks, which is when you see the least value in offset printing. While paperbacks are cheaper when ordered at scale, the delta between them and ordering from a POD printer is nominal compared to hardcover or other enhancements.

BOOK ENHANCEMENTS

Not every printer does every type of enhancement, but these are some of the coolest enhancements I have seen.

Die-cutting means part of the cover is cut out revealing the artwork underneath. If you work in comics, this is an amazing enhancement to your work.

Embossing and debossing allow you to raise or lower parts of the cover, so they stand out more from the rest of the book.

UV Spot allows you to add a pop of gloss to make certain parts of your image shine. I prefer matte covers, so I use them all the time. Another one I use all the time is adding a ribbon to my books.

One I am too scared to do is ***sequential numbering*** as it's hard to make sure somebody gets the right number, but it's a popular one.

Glow-in-the-dark is super popular with fans. I only have one cover that glows, and it's generally regarded as people's favorite cover we've ever done.

You can also add ***glitter, gold foil, silver foil,*** or other types of foil to the cover.

You've probably seen a lot of people adding ***gilded or painted edges*** to their books.

You can also add a ***dust jacket***, though I find them more of a pain than a help, as they often tear leading to complaints. I've seen some people do cool things with half or quarter-dust jackets.

If you have a black-and-white book but want to add some color illustrations, you can create an ***insert*** inside your book that shows off the color images without paying for full color.

You also have some options for cover material, like ***cloth or leather,*** that can make your books feel special.

Finally, you can create a *slipcase* for your book that protects it in a specially made box.

I'm sure there are more, but those are the main ones I've seen that work for indie authors.

WHAT ABOUT SHIPPING BOOKS TO ME?

There are five terms you need to know when shipping books internationally.

- **Free On Board (*FOB*)** is a shipment term that defines the point in the supply chain when a buyer or seller becomes liable for the goods being transported. Purchase orders between buyers and sellers specify the FOB terms and help determine ownership, risk, and transportation costs.
- **Cost, Insurance, and Freight (*CIF*)** is an international shipping agreement, which represents the charges paid by a seller to cover the costs, insurance, and freight of a buyer's order while the cargo is in transit.
- **Delivered Duty Unpaid (*DDU*)** is an international trade term meaning the seller is responsible for ensuring goods arrive safely to a destination; the buyer is responsible for import duties. By contrast, Delivered Duty Paid (DDP) indicates that the seller must cover duties, import clearance, and any taxes.
- **Delivered Duty Paid (*DDP*)** shipping is a type of delivery where the seller takes responsibility for all risk and fees of shipping goods until they reach their destination.

- **EX Works (*EXW*)** is an incoterm whereby the buyer of a shipped product pays for the goods when they are delivered to a specified location. FOB, or Free on Board, instead shifts the responsibility of the goods to the buyer as soon as they are loaded onboard the ship. - Investopedia

In general, I always choose DDP, because I know I won't owe any additional costs once the boats cross the ocean. As Lily has told me many times, this is easily the most expensive option. I know that I'm spending a premium, but I just don't want the hassle.

The number of complaints I've heard from friends who were hit with additional charges when they chose FOB or CIP or had to rent a truck to pick the books up at a port is extensive. Unless you know a freight forwarder or would like to learn all about logistics, I highly recommend you bite the bullet and pay more for DDP.

FULFILLMENT COMPANIES

One of the biggest questions I get asked by authors deals with hassle. They don't want to ship their books or store their books. While you can ship books to a fulfillment company like Merrick Books or Shipbob, there is one big issue with this: *signing the books.*

Luckily, there is a solution for you: tip-in sheets.

A tipped-in page or, if it is an illustration, tipped-in plate, is **a page that is printed separately from the main text of the book, but attached to the book**. A tipped-in page may be glued onto a regular page or even bound along with the other pages. -Wikipedia

When you order tip-ins, the printer sends you a box of paper to sign. Then, you ship them back to the printer and they add them to the book after printing. This is how all big publishers deal with signed books. Brandon Sanderson doesn't get delivered a million books to sign. He gets a million pages to sign and then the printer deals with it.

I want to thank my friend Lily Wong from Alpaca Color Printing. If you want to talk to her about printing your books, then you can email sales@alpacaprinting.com.

The last thing I wanted to do in this section was to provide a glossary of terms you could use for discussion with your printer contacts. These might not be the only terms you need, but they will get you a long way to speaking the same language as your printer.

- **POD** - Print on Demand. It's a printing technology where books or other documents are printed individually as orders come in, rather than in bulk.
- **Offset** - A traditional printing method where ink is transferred from a plate to a rubber blanket and then onto the printing surface.
- **IngramSpark** is a publishing platform that allows authors and publishers to create and distribute print books and ebooks. It's a service provided by Ingram Content Group, one of the largest book distributors in the world. IngramSpark enables users to print on demand, meaning books are printed and shipped when ordered, eliminating the need for large print runs and

storage of inventory. It offers various formats, including hardcover, paperback, and ebooks, and distributes to a wide range of retailers and libraries.

- **Amazon KDP (Kindle Direct Publishing)** is Amazon's self-publishing platform. It allows authors to publish their books in digital format (ebooks) and in print through Amazon's print-on-demand service, formerly known as CreateSpace. With KDP, authors can upload their manuscripts, create book covers, set prices, and make their books available for sale on Amazon's various global marketplaces. KDP also provides various promotional tools and analytics to help authors track their sales and performance.
- **BookVault** - a POD printing company specializing in printing high-end books and providing integrations to direct sales web stores.
- **Lulu** - Lulu Press is a self-publishing platform where authors can create and publish their own books.
- **Mixam** - A printing company that offers various printing services, including book printing.
- **Gang printing** - Printing multiple different projects or copies on the same sheet to optimize paper usage and cost-effectiveness.
- **Gang Binding** - Binding multiple different printed projects together as a batch.
- **Tip-ins** - Additional pages or materials that are inserted into a book after it has been bound.
- **Shipping** - The process of transporting goods (in this case, books) from one place to another.
- **DDP** - Delivered Duty Paid. It refers to a shipping arrangement where the seller is responsible for all costs

and risks associated with transporting goods until they reach the buyer.

- **DDU** - Delivered Duty Unpaid. In this shipping arrangement, the buyer is responsible for the import clearance and any applicable taxes or duties upon arrival.
- **FOB** - Free On Board. It indicates the point at which the seller is no longer responsible for shipping costs or liability for the goods being transported.
- **CIP** - Carriage and Insurance Paid. It's a trade term where the seller pays for transportation and insurance to deliver goods to a specified destination.
- **Signature** - A printed sheet folded to become a part of a book with a certain number of pages. Printing a book to signature will save you money.
- **Register** - The accurate alignment of different colors or elements in printing.
- **Change Fee** - A fee incurred for changing the covers on a book at a printer.
- **Alternate covers** - Different cover designs for the same book.
- **Insert** - Additional materials placed inside a book, such as cards, maps, or other supplemental content.
- **Binding** - The process of fastening or securing the pages of a book together.
- **Paperback** - A book with a flexible paper or cardstock cover.
- **Hardcover** - A book with a rigid cover, usually made of cardboard wrapped in cloth, paper, or leather.
- **Board Book** - A book with thick, durable pages made of cardboard, often designed for young children.

- **Trade** - In the publishing industry, it refers to books that are meant for general retail sale, as opposed to specialized or academic books.
- **Case Binding** - A type of bookbinding where the book block is glued to a cover made of thicker material like cardboard.
- **Die-cutting** - A process of cutting paper or cardboard into specific shapes using a die or mold.
- **Embossing** - Creating a raised design or pattern on paper or cardstock.
- **Gloss** - A shiny and reflective finish applied to printed materials.
- **Matte** - A non-reflective, dull finish applied to printed materials.
- **Lamination** - A thin layer of plastic or similar material applied to the surface of printed materials for protection or enhancement.
- **Paper weight** - The thickness and heaviness of paper, often measured in pounds or grams per square meter (GSM).
- **H/T** - Acronym for High-Touch, referring to a personalized or customized approach in printing or customer service.
- **Sew bound** - Binding pages together by sewing them along the spine.
- **Glow-in-the-dark** - Materials or inks that emit visible light after exposure to light.
- **Spot UV** - A coating applied to specific areas of printed material to create a glossy, raised effect.
- **Bleed** - Printing that extends beyond the trim edge of the sheet, allowing for a margin of error in trimming.

- **CMYK** - Acronym for Cyan, Magenta, Yellow, and Key (Black), the four colors used in color printing.
- **DPI** - Dots Per Inch. It measures the resolution of printed images.
- **Foil** - Metallic or colored material applied to printed materials for a decorative or reflective effect.
- **Overrun** - Producing more copies of a printed item than originally ordered.
- **Ream** - A quantity of paper, usually 500 sheets.
- **Saddle stitch** - A binding method where folded sheets are stapled along the fold line to create a booklet.
- **Scoring** - Creating a crease in paper or cardstock to help it fold cleanly.
- **Spine** - The edge of a book where the pages are bound together.
- **Split run** - Printing different versions of a document in the same print run.
- **GSM** - Grams per Square Meter. It measures the weight or density of paper.
- **Proofing** - The process of reviewing and checking a sample print for errors or quality before final printing.
- **Metal** - In printing, it could refer to metallic inks or foils used for decorative purposes in printing.
- **Slipcase** - a protective box used to keep books or special items safe. It's usually made of strong material like cardboard or wood and helps shield these items from damage, dust, and light. They're often used for collectible books or special editions, adding both protection and a nice look to the collection.

CHAPTER 23

DELIVERY WITHOUT DRAMA

We've gotten all the logistics sorted and we're ready to actually get books into backer's hands. This is the last part of the process before you can claim victory, but there are still pitfalls to avoid and best practices to employ even at this stage.

Let's start by organizing your assembly line.

Before you slap labels on packages, get your workspace and process organized. This will save enormous time and reduce errors. Treat your fulfillment like a mini factory line:

- **Set up a dedicated packing area:** Clear a large table or floor space. You don't want to be hunting for tape under a couch or stepping over clutter. Layout all your supplies within arm's reach.
- **Sort rewards by type:** Group all your books, all your prints, all your bookmarks, etc. Ideally, each item type has its own stack or bin. This way you're not mixing things up.
- **Pre-count and pre-inspect items:** Count how many of each item you need per your backer list (plus a few

extras). Check item quality – do a quick flip through books to ensure no upside-down pages, check posters for misprints, etc. Catch issues now. It's easier to request a handful of replacement prints from a vendor now than deal with multiple backers reporting damage later.

- **Prepare address labels or printouts:** If you haven't already, generate and print address labels or an address list. If using a software to print postage, have that loaded and tested with one or two samples. Print them in small batches so if you find a mistake (like the wrong postage class), you haven't wasted 300 labels.
- **Create a packing order:** Decide the sequence you'll pack in. One approach: go tier by tier, from simplest to most complex reward. For example, Tier 1 just gets a paperback in an envelope – knock those out first. Tier 2 gets paperback + bookmark – do those next, etc. This helps because you get a rhythm, and the easier ones act as warm-up. Alternatively, you might pack by region (domestic vs international) to utilize specific packaging or customs forms in batches. Pick what makes sense for you.

A trick some fulfillers use: **color-code or label piles** for each tier's items. Say Tier 3 backers get 4 items – put a sticky note on each relevant item pile that says, "Tier 3 needs this." As you pack a Tier 3, you go through each pile with a sticky note for Tier 3. This reduces the chance of forgetting an item. You could also print a short packing list for each backer (some pledge managers can do this) that you place with their stuff and check off as you insert items.

PACK SMART AND SECURELY

Now, onto the actual packing:

- **Use appropriate packaging:** Books generally go in padded envelopes or sturdy cardboard mailers. If it's a single book, a bubble mailer works (maybe add an extra piece of cardboard to keep it rigid). For multiple books or books plus merch, consider small boxes. The packaging should protect contents but also not be excessively large (postage often depends on weight and dimensions).
- **Consider weatherproofing:** Particularly for paper goods, seal them in a plastic bag or wrap in plastic inside the envelope. You don't want rain soaking someone's book.
- **Bubble wrap or cushioning:** For delicate items (enamel pins scratching books, etc.), wrap them separately or use bubble wrap. If a box isn't full, pad it with crumpled paper or bubble wrap so things don't rattle around.
- **One backer at a time:** It's tempting to do an assembly style (stuff all envelopes with a book first, then come back and add prints). But that can lead to mis-packaging if different tiers are similar. Instead, for each backer, pull their entry/packing list, assemble all their items, put in package, seal, label. Then move to the next. That way, each package is self-contained and double-checked before you seal. If you do multi-step assembly, triple check before sealing that the right stuff ended up in the right package.

- **Double-check addresses:** This is critical. Ensure you're putting the correct label on the correct package. Many packages will look similar (lots of white bubble mailers!). A system might be to write the backer's name in pencil on the envelope as you pack, then affix the matching label on that envelope. Or keep packages grouped in the same order as your address printout. Attention to this detail can prevent a nightmare of Joe in NY getting Jane in CA's rewards and vice versa.
- **Seal well:** Use quality packing tape. Nobody likes a package that opens in transit. For envelopes, the adhesive might be enough, but adding a strip of tape over the flap is cheap insurance, especially if the package is a bit overstuffed.
- **Add a personal touch:** If you can, drop a short thank-you note in each package, especially for higher-tier backers. Even a small card with "Thank you for your support! – [Your Name]" can leave a great impression. It reminds them this is from a person, not an impersonal warehouse. If volume is huge, you may not manage one per package but consider at least including a printed thank-you message or a signed bookplate as a gesture.

As you pack, keep an eye on your inventory of items and supplies. If you see you're running low on something unexpectedly, pause and address it. For example, if you're using more bubble wrap than thought and might run out, better to get more before continuing. Running out of mailers halfway is a momentum killer, so periodically assess if you need to reorder any supplies mid-fulfillment.

MASTER THE POSTAGE PROCESS

Time to buy postage and get these on their way:

- **Weigh sample packages:** Prepare one of each typical package configuration and weigh it. Use that to buy correct postage. It's fine to round up an ounce or two for safety. If all your packages are very similar (say all single books), you can batch print the same postage for many labels. If they vary, you may need to weigh individually or by group.
- **Choose shipping methods:** For domestic (in the US, for example) Media Mail is very cost-effective for books. Use it for packages that qualify (only books and maybe printed matter like posters – if you added merch like pins or T-shirts, officially those *disqualify* Media Mail, though some still risk it; use your judgment). First Class is good for small lightweight items, Priority for heavier or if you need faster delivery. Most of your backers are fine with slower shipping as long as it's reliable. For international, open a PirateShip account and unlock Simple Export Rate. It will save you lots of money.
- **Print labels with ease:** If using an online service, import the addresses or fill them in. Check that international addresses format correctly (some systems might not validate foreign postal codes; if in doubt, verify the address manually via Google). Print a few and make sure sizes align to your label paper or printer settings. Nothing like printing 100 labels only to find half the address is cut off.

- **Include customs info:** For international labels, fill out the customs form on the site. Again, listing low values (like $10) and marking as "gift" can help backers avoid fees. If it's a book, you can also choose category "printed material" or "documents" which often pass duty-free. Do be truthful enough not to get packages seized (don't list a book as "plastic toy" for example), but within reason, you want to minimize import taxes on your backers. Most books slide through customs easily.
- **Tracking:** Ensure tracking is enabled (most services include it for domestic and some international). Once you purchase labels, you'll have tracking numbers. If possible, share those with backers – some pledge managers automatically email them. If not, consider dropping each backer their number via Kickstarter message or email (this is tedious for large campaigns, so at minimum, keep the numbers in case someone asks). Alternatively, when you do a shipping update, you can say "All packages are now shipped. US backers, you should have gotten an email with tracking (or DM me if you need yours). International, many of your packages have tracking too – reach out if you want the number, though note it may not update once it leaves the US."
- **Schedule pick-ups or drop-off:** Lugging hundreds of packages to the post office is rough. In many places, you can schedule a free USPS pick-up at your door (for Priority or any, sometimes they require at least one Priority package for pickup). Do that if you can – just have them ready by your mailbox or door. If you must

drop off, maybe do it in batches so you're not overwhelming the clerk with 300 scans at once (also, some post offices have a limit or will ask you to come at a less busy time).

- **Keep receipts or proof:** If you physically drop them off, get a receipt for the shipment or at least scan forms. Online label printing often provides a "scan sheet" – a single barcode the postal worker scans that marks all packages as accepted. Very handy! Use that if available, it ensures everything is in the system.

COMMUNICATE DURING DELIVERY

Your role isn't over once you hand packages to the carrier. Now it's time to proactively shepherd your backers through the waiting period:

- **Post a "Shipping Underway" update:** Let everyone know when you've shipped, how you shipped, and what to expect for delivery times. For example: *"All packages were shipped by July 15! US backers, most are via Media Mail – please allow 5-10 days. International backers, shipping times vary by country (usually 2-4 weeks). Keep an eye out!"* Encourage them to post a photo or shout-out when they get it – this not only is fun; it also serves as social proof that packages are arriving.
- **Remind about customs (if relevant):** *"International friends in the UK/EU, note that you may need to pay a VAT or customs fee on delivery as per your local laws."* (If you marked low, it might slip through, but you

should acknowledge the possibility so they aren't surprised).

- **Email confirmation:** If you collected emails and want to go the extra mile, you can send a direct email to each backer saying their reward shipped (with tracking if you have). This personal touch is great customer service. However, for hundreds of backers, it's time-consuming. An alternative is a MailChimp (or similar) mass email BCC with a generic "orders are on the way" and a note on how to request tracking if desired.
- **Stay available:** Check messages daily around delivery time. People might say "My tracking hasn't updated in a week, is that normal?" (Often yes, especially international – you can explain it's likely in customs or in transit). Or someone might say "I realize I moved, and the package is going to my old address!" Try to monitor and respond promptly. Often you can resolve or alleviate concerns with a quick reply.
- **Celebrate publicly:** Share your own excitement as books land. Maybe do a social media post like *"Kickstarter backers are getting their books! My heart is so full seeing your photos. Thank you all once again!"* Tag some who shared (if they're okay with it). This wraps up the campaign story on a high note.

TURN ISSUES INTO OPPORTUNITIES

No matter how well you plan, you'll likely have to handle a few customer service issues. Approach each with a solution-oriented and empathetic mindset:

- **Prompt response:** When a backer emails with a problem, reply as quickly as feasible (ideally within 1-2 days max, even if just to say, "I'm looking into this."). Silence is what frustrates people more than the issue itself.
- **Apologize and assure:** If something went wrong, start with a sincere apology for the inconvenience and assure them you'll make it right. Even if it's not your fault (postal damage), you are taking responsibility for getting them a good product.
- **Replace or refund when necessary:** Almost always, the solution will be sending a replacement item. Do it without making the backer jump through hoops. If they say a book was damaged, you can ask for a photo to confirm (and so you can maybe adjust packaging next time), but then immediately arrange to send a new one. You rarely need the damaged one sent back – that would be an undue burden on the backer. If an item is missing, send it with a note or an extra gift. In extreme cases (lost package and you have no more stock), you might offer a refund or an alternative solution (perhaps a different edition of the book). But refunds are last resort; most backers prefer to get what they pledged for.
- **Be generous:** If one backer's package got lost and you're resending, maybe throw in an extra bookmark or sign the replacement book or something as a goodwill gesture. It costs you little and can actually turn their experience into a positive one ("hey, I got a bonus for the trouble, neat!").
- **Track issues in a log:** Maintain a simple list of who reported what and when you shipped a replacement.

This helps ensure you don't forget to follow up or double-send to the same person.

- **Manage public perception:** If someone posts a complaint in the Kickstarter comments or on social media, respond calmly and helpfully in public, then take it to private messages to resolve specifics. Often showing a public willingness to fix things is enough for others who see it to be reassured. But avoid drawn-out problem-solving in public forums – move it to DM/email after the initial acknowledgment.
- **Learn from issues:** Each problem is data. If a lot of books got dinged corners, maybe improve corner protection next time or use different mailers. If international shipping to a particular country had many lost items, maybe use a different service or partner next time. Document these patterns.

Throughout, maintain the **tone of gratitude**. Even when someone is upset, a phrase like, "I'm so sorry this happened. You trusted me with your pledge, and I want to ensure you get exactly what you were promised. Thank you for your patience while I sort this out for you," can soothe frustration. It shows you value them not just as a customer but as a supporter.

By handling post-campaign customer service well, you often turn people into even bigger fans. They think, "Wow, when something went wrong, the creator jumped on it and fixed it. That's rare!" That trust and goodwill is invaluable going forward.

WRAPPING UP FULFILLMENT

After the majority of backers have their rewards, you might still have a handful who are MIA (no survey, bad address that never got updated, etc.). For these:

- Send final reminder emails/messages. Kickstarter allows you to message all who haven't answered surveys. Do that and maybe mention a deadline (like "If I don't hear back by X date, I'll hold your reward until you contact me."). You want to close the books eventually, but give them ample opportunity.
- Hold on to unclaimed rewards. Some creators state that after a year, unclaimed items are forfeit. But realistically, if a backer comes back even later with a good reason (they had life issues, etc.), it's good karma to still fulfill it if you can. You might not keep inventory forever, but maybe keep a small stash or be willing to print a single POD copy if someone resurfaces.
- **Complete your spreadsheet:** Mark all as shipped that went. Note any refunds or special cases. This is both for your own record and for when you review finances or provide any campaign outcome summary.

Now, do a **big sigh of relief** – you did it. All pledges have been delivered or accounted for. Fulfillment is done. It's a huge milestone.

Don't forget to share that news: a final Kickstarter update or social post to the effect of *"Fulfillment complete! All rewards have been sent. Thank you all for joining me on this journey from idea to book in hand. I couldn't have done it without you.*" This brings official closure to the campaign narrative. It also sets the stage for whatever you announce next (maybe in the conclusion or future communications).

Some creators at this point also send a brief **survey or feedback request** to backers (like "How did we do? Please fill this 3-question survey about your experience."). This is optional, but if you're looking to improve, it can yield insights. Keep it simple and assure it's fine if they ignore it. Alternatively, you can just gauge feedback from how people reacted in comments or messages without a formal survey.

DELIVERING EXCELLENCE

The delivery phase is where you *truly* earn your reputation. How you handle shipping and customer service shows backers what kind of creator you are. By delivering without drama – meaning you handle the challenges competently and kindly – you cement yourself as someone people will happily support again.

A few key takeaways:

- **Preparation and organization** are half the battle in shipping. A little planning prevents a lot of pain.
- **Invest in tools** (labels, software) that scale your one-person operation. Professional-looking labels and tracked packages boost confidence.
- **Take care of your backers** as you would a friend. That might sound cheesy, but it's a helpful mindset. You

wouldn't nickel-and-dime a friend or ghost them if something went wrong; you'd be proactive and generous. Do that for your backers.

- **Expect the unexpected, financially too.** Not every pledge yields profit – some might cost you (that one international package you had to reship three times). Build contingency into your budgeting for these inevitabilities. Better to have a cushion than come up short.
- **Keep communicating until the very end.** Backers will remember that you didn't abandon them after you got funded. Instead, you stuck with them until every last package arrived safely. That's the mark of a creator who cares.
- **Take pride in fulfillment.** It's easy to see it as grunt work, but it's actually the grand finale of your show. Treat it as part of the creative process: the transformation of idea to reality to a delivered dream. There's something deeply satisfying about a fulfilled campaign. Enjoy that feeling.

After going through all these steps, you'll also likely realize you've become much more adept at logistics and customer relations – skills that will serve you in any business endeavor. These are the unglamorous, crucial skills of a successful author-entrepreneur.

In summary, a drama-free delivery is achievable with good planning and even better attitude. You've turned what could be a stressful time into a testament of your reliability and care for your supporters. These backers are now much more than one-time customers – they're your early fanbase, forged through a journey that ended happily in their mailbox.

CHAPTER 24

POST-CAMPAIGN SUCCESS

You've done a hard thing and delivered a great book to your amazing backers. They are thrilled and they love what you've done. All the work you did on this campaign has paid off. Now, let's talk about where to go next.

First off, make sure to heap love on your backers not just today, but often. Remember, your Kickstarter backers are now your **most engaged readers**. They've been through a journey with you, and you've likely built rapport via updates and fulfillment. Don't let that relationship fizzle out now that the campaign is over. Instead, treat them as a VIP inner circle for your author career going forward.

How to nurture this:

- **Move them to your mailing list or community:** Hopefully you collected emails (either via surveys or via a sign-up prompt during the campaign). If you haven't yet, ask them to join your author newsletter or Facebook reader group, etc. Better to ask them the question during the survey, but if you didn't, then this is your best shot. Emphasize they'll get exclusives and first looks if they do. Most will happily stay connected.

If you already have their emails (Kickstarter gives you a list of backer emails unless they opt out), send a welcome message after fulfillment that essentially says *"Thank you for being part of my first Kickstarter – I'd love to keep you updated on my future books and projects. Here's what to expect from my periodic newsletter..."*. Of course, give them an opt-out, but expect low opt-outs if you frame it warmly and relevantly.

- **Show continued appreciation:** Consider doing a special backer-only content drop after everything. For example, an exclusive bonus short story PDF emailed to backers a month after fulfillment, or a discount code for your online store as a "thank you for being a superfan." This unexpected extra surprise can delight people and makes them feel valued beyond the campaign.
- **Engage them in future decisions:** You have this group of true fans – involve them! Maybe poll them on what your next project might be or show them a sneak peek of a new cover and ask for opinions. When people feel involved, they invest deeper in your success. And practically, their feedback can be gold. Just as they helped shape some campaign elements, they can help guide what offerings might excite them down the road.
- **Personal touches for high-tiers:** If you had high-tier backers (like someone who paid a lot for a character name or just a big bundle), consider reaching out individually down the line to check in. "Hey, I just wanted to personally thank you again. I'm working on a sequel, and as one of my top backers, I'd love to send

you an early draft if you're interested." That level of personal recognition can turn someone into a lifelong ambassador for you.

The idea is to **keep the flame alive**. Don't vanish for a year and then pop up only when you need something (like another campaign or book launch). Regular, authentic communication will turn that Kickstarter one-time crowd into a foundational community. Many authors find that after a successful Kickstarter, their readership multiplies because those backers bring friends for the next book, leave reviews, and hype you up – if you continue to cultivate them.

SELL BEYOND THE CAMPAIGN

Kickstarter shouldn't be the only time you sell those books. Now that the campaign is done, you likely have extra stock (you printed in bulk, remember). It's time to make the most of it:

- **Open an online store:** This could be as simple as adding a page on your author website with a PayPal "Buy Now" button for signed copies, or as elaborate as a Shopify store. You can list any leftover inventory – "Missed the Kickstarter? You can still get the book here!" Charge a bit more than the campaign price (backers got the best deal). Many curious readers who see the post-campaign buzz might come looking to buy. Be ready to capture those sales. Some authors use Etsy for selling signed books and swag, others use Gumroad or Shopify. Choose what you're comfortable with.

- **Use BackerKit or Indiegogo InDemand:** If you want a hassle-free way, some keep their project open for late pledges. BackerKit's pre-order store or Indiegogo InDemand can essentially act as a shop for a period after. This works well if there's considerable demand from people who missed out. It's good especially for special editions you might not put on Amazon, etc. Just ensure you fulfill these orders promptly and don't let it distract from original backers (which if you followed earlier advice, you've finished that or mostly so).
- **Amazon and retail channels:** If your project was, say, a special edition hardcover, you might still publish a regular edition on Amazon or other retailers for the wider audience. Don't undercut your backers (perhaps release it later, or in a different format). But distributing on Amazon Kindle, paperback, etc., can bring in a steady stream of royalties beyond the campaign. The Kickstarter success might itself be a selling point; mention in the book description, "Funded in 48 hours on Kickstarter" or such, which adds social proof. Traditional store distribution is also possible if you have ISBNs and want to reach bookstores or libraries – your successful Kickstarter stats (like X copies sold, $Y raised) can help convince some indie bookstores to carry copies, because it shows demand.
- **Upsell to backers:** Now that backers have Book 1, perhaps some will want your other work. In your communication (like a thank-you email or an insert in the package), gently mention what else you have available. *"If you enjoyed this book, you might also like my earlier novel [Title]. Backers can use code*

THANKYOU for 20% off on my website." This can spur immediate extra sales. Also, if you plan a sequel or related book, start teasing it. *"Stay tuned – this story continues in [Next Book], coming next year. As a backer, you'll be the first to know!"* That keeps them on the hook (in a good way).

- **Special Editions & Merchandise:** If during the campaign you unlocked or created special items (like art prints or pins), consider offering those on your store too, or bundling them. Some folks who got just a book might later wish they'd grabbed that poster – give them a chance to. Or if you have extra Kickstarter-exclusive editions, decide how/if to sell them. Some create a "collector's bundle" on their shop at a premium price – appealing to latecomers who really want the fancy version. Just be mindful if you promised exclusivity to backers; maybe limit availability or timeframe to keep it special.

- **Events and Cons:** With physical copies on hand, you can also sell at conventions, book fairs, or launch parties. Use the Kickstarter as a story to draw interest: *"This book was launched on Kickstarter and raised X amount."* People find that intriguing. It might even get you local media coverage or speaking invites ("Author crowdfunds her book successfully…"). Realize that Kickstarter essentially gave you a supply of books *and* a great story to tell in marketing.

One big note: **Pricing**. Know your costs and price your post-campaign sales to ensure profit. On Kickstarter, you might have given discounts or free swag. In regular sales, you don't need to. Often, authors price signed copies higher than retail because they're special (and because shipping is often built into the price). Don't undervalue your work – the Kickstarter proved people will pay for it. I sell my Kickstarter-born books at premium pricing on my site, because they come with signature or extras, and fans are willing. Meanwhile, the mass market edition might be cheaper on Amazon for the casual buyer. That tiered approach can work well.

Also consider **formats**: If you haven't yet, releasing an ebook or audiobook version can open more sales channels. Some backers who got a hardcover might even buy the ebook to have on the go. Or if you produce an audiobook later, you can market it to them: *"You've read the book, now hear it performed – backers get a discount code…"* Essentially, one successful Kickstarter project can spawn multiple product formats that each bring income.

CAPITALIZE ON CREDIBILITY

Don't be shy about touting your Kickstarter success as you move forward. It's a badge of honor and a signal to others that you have an audience and you deliver:

- **Press releases and media pitches:** Now that you've fulfilled, you have a concrete success story. Send a press release to local media or niche industry blogs: "Local author raises $15,000 on Kickstarter to publish novel" – these human-interest or business stories often get picked up. Even months later, you can frame it as "what happened after – community rallies to fund book, now available in stores." That exposure can lead to more sales and opportunities.

- **Bio and website update:** Include a line like "Successful Kickstarter creator" or "My last crowdfunding campaign raised 300% of its goal" on your author bio. It sets you apart. Also, maybe put some photos of the campaign journey or backer testimonials on your site. Show the world you have passionate readers already – success begets success.

- **Publishers or Partners:** If you ever seek a publisher or collaborate with others (like getting your book into a bundle or an event), mention your campaign stats. Publishers perk up at someone who can move hundreds of copies on their own – it indicates a platform. You effectively proved market demand, which is extremely valuable data. Some authors have even landed book deals or distribution partnerships on the back of a strong Kickstarter performance, because it de-risks you in the eyes of the industry.

- **Speaking or teaching gigs:** If you're inclined, your experience makes you somewhat of an expert in crowdfunding now. You could write a blog post or give a talk about "How I crowdfunded my novel." Many author conferences or podcasts are interested in that content. That can raise your profile and indirectly sell more books or at least build your personal brand. It also plugs you into networks of other creators, which can lead to future collaborations or cross-promotions.

- **Plan the next Kickstarter (if relevant):** Perhaps the best use of the credibility is rolling it into the next launch. When you announce a second Kickstarter, you can bet many of the first backers will return, *and* new people will see "Oh, their last one was successful and delivered. I trust this." There's a snowball effect. Many creators find their second campaigns raise significantly more because of this compounding trust and audience growth.

One caution: staying humble and genuine is important when leveraging success. It's one thing to say, "Thanks to 300 amazing backers, we made this happen, and I'm excited to share it with even more readers" versus "I made 15K on Kickstarter, I'm kind of a big deal." Always frame it in terms of community achievement and quality of the work. That way people see it as a sign of the book's value and your reliability, not ego.

CONTINUE INVOLVING YOUR AUDIENCE

The best long-term strategy after a Kickstarter is to keep creating and to keep your audience involved in that journey. Use the momentum:

- **Start the next book or project:** Channel the energy and confidence you've gained into writing your next work. You now have an audience waiting. This can be incredibly motivating (and a bit of pressure, but mostly in a good way). You might even share progress updates with backers to make them feel like insiders. E.g., a year later, email them *"Remember the character you helped bring to life? She's returning in a sequel I'm drafting now. Can't wait to share more soon!"*

- **Consider future crowdfunding or hybrid approaches:** Perhaps you'll do Kickstarter for special editions and use traditional publishing for standard editions. Or crowdfund the launch and then go straight to Amazon for ongoing sales. There's no one way – experiment. Some successful authors alternate: one book on Kickstarter, next directly to retail, etc. See what sustains your income and growth best. But rest assured, you've unlocked crowdfunding as a viable, powerful path for you – a repeatable one.
- **Build long-term fan engagement:** Nurture an "ecosystem" around your work. Maybe start a Patreon for monthly support, or a Discord server for fans to chat. The folks from your Kickstarter can be the seed of a larger fan community. Long-term, this is how you graduate from one-off transactions to a stable author career. Your Kickstarter backers can turn into superfans who not only buy everything but recruit others. Treat them like VIPs and they'll reward you with loyalty.
- **Keep learning and iterating:** Post-mortem your Kickstarter experience (what worked, what didn't) and adjust strategies for future endeavors. Maybe you realized you could have offered a certain add-on that people wanted – next time you will. Maybe you saw a lull in communication at one point – next time, plan for more updates. Continuous improvement is key to long-term success. Crowdfunding and publishing landscapes evolve; stay informed (listen to podcasts, follow crowdfunding news) so you can adapt and capitalize on new opportunities.

Above all, **stay grateful and connected**. It's the theme from start to finish: gratitude. In success, some people forget those who got them there. Don't be that person. Keep thanking your readers, keep delivering quality stories to them, and they will stick with you.

Kickstarter is not a one-off cash grab, but the cornerstone of a sustainable, direct-to-reader business model. You've now seen how that can work, first-hand. As an author in this modern era, having control and direct access to your audience is a huge advantage. You're not beholden to the whims of Amazon algorithms or publisher budgets – you have readers who will literally fund your art because they want it. That's powerful. Cherish that and build on it.

CROWDFUNDING IS A LAUNCHPAD

Your Kickstarter was a success – congratulations! Now, the real magic is in how you amplify that success into something bigger:

- **Think beyond one campaign:** Use it as a catalyst for an ongoing relationship with fans and for future projects. Don't view it as a one-and-done. The skills and audience you gained are assets for life.
- **Keep the buzz going:** After delivering, ride the wave of excitement. Backers posting positive things? Share those (with permission). Use that momentum in marketing your book broadly. You might even compile a short case study on your blog: "How 300 readers helped me launch [Book]." It's content that can engage new folks.

- **Monetize smartly:** You have multiple avenues now – direct sales, retail, events. Plan a mix that fits your career. Don't be afraid to sell – remember, you're providing value and people are happy to pay for it when asked appropriately.
- **Value your community above all:** A core tenet of post-campaign success is remembering that the community is more important than the dollar amount. If you nurture the community, the dollars will follow (repeat pledges, sales, etc.). If you focus only on the money and neglect the community, you'll see diminishing returns. Fortunately, your genuine engagement and delivering on promises has probably endeared you to them.
- **Stay adaptable and open:** Crowdfunding and indie publishing reward creativity and flexibility. Maybe next time, you'll try offering a subscription model, or team up with other authors for a joint campaign. Who knows? Keep an open mind and watch what others do successfully (like Kickstarter anthologies, or campaigns for audiobooks, etc.). Continual innovation keeps your career dynamic.

A wonderful thing to realize is that you have turned casual readers into invested patrons of your art. They are not just readers – they feel like stakeholders in your success because they were there early. That feeling can last years if you cultivate it. Many backers will proudly say, "I backed them when they were starting out!" They become advocates.

So, take care of those people. And welcome new ones warmly as your circle grows. Over time, you may go from 100 backers to 1,000 to 10,000 fans. The principles remain: respect, gratitude, quality, communication.

In essence, Kickstarter was the launchpad, but your journey as an author continues upward from here. You've proven to yourself that your stories have value and that readers will support you. Carry that confidence forward. Set bigger goals, knowing you have a process and a support network to reach them.

As we conclude this chapter – and this book – think about how far you've come. From perhaps being unsure if Kickstarter could work for you, to planning meticulously, to executing a campaign, fulfilling it, and now leveraging it for long-term success. It's an arc of growth, and you should be proud.

CONCLUSION

A NEW CHAPTER BEGINS

You started this book as an author curious (and maybe a bit nervous) about Kickstarter. Now, you stand at the end of these chapters armed with knowledge, a blueprint, and hopefully a healthy dose of confidence. We've journeyed together from the first inklings of an idea, through planning and promotion, into the thrilling live campaign and the hard work of fulfillment, and finally to envisioning a long-term strategy beyond the campaign. Take a moment to appreciate how far you've come.

RECAP OF CORE THEMES

Throughout, a few key themes echoed:

- **Community is Everything:** Time and again, we emphasized that *crowdfunding is not about "the crowd," it's about the people.* Your backers aren't anonymous ATM machines – they're readers who share your vision. By involving them, listening to them, and appreciating them, you turned a funding exercise into a community-building experience. That community will continue to fuel your success beyond the campaign.

- **Preparation and Professionalism Pay Off:** From setting clear goals and budgets to crafting your page and updates, your meticulous preparation sets you up for a win. We championed a no-nonsense, professional approach – and you saw how it delivered results. You treated your campaign like a serious launch, and backers responded with serious support. That blend of passion and professionalism is now a hallmark of your brand.
- **Bold, Candid Authenticity:** You likely noticed how being candid and bold – in your outreach, in your story, in your asks – rallied people to your side. There was no room for fear or half-measures. You owned your role as the campaign leader, communicated with heart and clarity, and it resonated. Authenticity is magnetic; when you show genuine enthusiasm and even vulnerability ("this means so much to me, and I won't lie – it's nerve-wracking but exciting"), it draws people in. Keep that authenticity in all your endeavors; it's your superpower.
- **Adaptability and Perseverance:** Your journey had highs (like a big Day 1 surge) and likely some lows (maybe a mid-campaign slump or a hiccup in fulfillment). But you adapted and pushed through. We laid out plans for challenges, and you met them head-on. This flexibility – adjusting marketing when pledges slowed, extending deadlines if needed, finding solutions on the fly – is what separates successful creators from those who falter. You've proven you can handle the rollercoaster. Future challenges in publishing or

business won't faze you as easily, because you'll recall, *"I navigated tougher on Kickstarter."*

- **Value Beyond Money:** Yes, funding your book was goal #1, but along the way you gained so much more. You've built an engaged mailing list, garnered reviews and testimonials, maybe attracted media attention, and certainly gained confidence in yourself. We said Kickstarter offers fringe benefits – buzz, community, credibility – and here you are with all those in hand. You're leaving this campaign not just with money in the bank, but with a stronger foundation for your author career.

INSPIRE YOUR CONTINUED SUCCESS

So, what's next? The beauty of this journey is that it's just the beginning. Now you know, deep in your bones, that you have the power to mobilize readers and bring a project to life. That knowledge is liberating.

Maybe you'll launch a sequel or a whole series through Kickstarter. Maybe you'll venture into new genres or formats (a board game of your novel? an audiobook project?). The playbook might differ slightly, but the fundamental approach remains: understand your audience, present a compelling vision, and work tirelessly and transparently to achieve it.

As you move forward:

- **Stay fearless and entrepreneurial:** You didn't wait for permission or an agent's approval to pursue this project; you took charge. Keep that entrepreneurial spirit alive. Whether it's Kickstarter or some other innovative strategy, don't be afraid to blaze your own path. The publishing world is changing, and you are riding the wave rather than being drowned by it.

- **Keep learning and leveling up:** Crowdfunding and marketing are dynamic fields. There are advanced tactics you may explore next – perhaps Facebook Ads retargeting for your next launch, or hiring collaborators to magnify your reach, or tapping into international backer markets. Stay curious. Each campaign (or book launch) is a chance to apply past lessons and experiment with new ideas. Over time, you'll build an enviable toolkit of skills.

- **Believe in the value of your work:** One of the biggest mental shifts many creators experience after a successful Kickstarter is a new level of confidence. You set a price on your work and people paid it – happily. Remember that feeling when imposter syndrome creeps in. You have concrete proof that your writing matters to readers. Use that as fuel when writing the next book or pitching to a new opportunity. You're not just hoping people will care; you *know* they do.

And on tough days (they'll still come – perhaps a slower sales month, or a creative block), recall the enthusiasm of your backers. Re-read some positive comments or unboxing posts. Let their excitement rekindle yours. In a way, your crowd is like a co-author of your motivation; their energy can lift you when yours ebbs.

NEXT STEPS AND STAYING CONNECTED

As we wrap up, here are some practical next steps to consider:

- **Join the Creator Community:** If you haven't already, plug into communities of fellow Kickstarter creators or indie authors. There are Facebook groups, subreddits, and forums where people share tips and support each other. Being part of such a community can provide ongoing ideas and camaraderie. (For example, the "Kickstarter Best Practices for Authors" group on Facebook is a great resource).

- **Further Resources:** We touched on many topics in this book, but if you want to dive deeper, consider exploring additional resources. Podcasts like *Comics Launch* or *The Creative Penn* have episodes on crowdfunding that might spark new insights. The learning never stops.

- **Mentorship or Coaching:** Perhaps now that you've seen success, you feel compelled to help others or maybe even formalize your knowledge. Conversely, if there were aspects you struggled with, you might seek out a mentor for that specific area (be it Facebook ads or public speaking at launch events). Many creators become mentors to newcomers – it's a wonderful way to pay it forward and also solidify your own expertise.

- **Plan Your Career Moves:** Treat this moment as a springboard. Draft a one-year and five-year vision. For instance: *"In one year, I want Book 2 funded and delivered, an audiobook produced, and my mailing list doubled. In five years, I aim to have a sustainable* *income purely from my books and related products, perhaps with three successful Kickstarters under my belt and a fanbase that can support even larger projects (like a special edition omnibus or a creative spin-off)."* Don't hold back – dream big. You've seen that big dreams can be realized step by step.

- **Stay in Touch:** Share your successes – it makes my day to hear that this book played a part in someone smashing their goals. And if you ever stumble, reach out; often a quick piece of advice or even just encouragement from those who've been there can get you back on track.

If you loved this book, I hope you go check out *The Author Stack,* my weekly newsletter that goes into even more depth about how to build your creator career.

https://www.theauthorstack.com/

As a paid member, you get access to a ton of my previous work, including fiction, non-fiction, courses, and more.

RESOURCES:

- *How to Build Your Creative Career*
- *How to Become a Successful Author*
- *Advanced Growth Tactics for Authors*
- Create Profitable Facebook Ads course
- Fund Your Book with Kickstarter course
- How to set up and run an awesome anthology course
- How to run a viral giveaway to build your mailing list
- Write a Great Novel course
- How to Build an Audience from Scratch minicourse
- 10x your productivity course
- Lessons and lectures

- Interview archive
- Complete Creative data archive
- Income reports since 2018
- Script library

There's probably even more now since I update it every couple of months.

You can also find my work at www.russellnohelty.com

LET'S END WITH A BIT OF HEART

Thank you for allowing us to accompany you on this journey. Your passion for your project shone through every step you took. In a world where creative work can sometimes feel undervalued, you proved that stories – *your* stories – are worth something, both emotionally and monetarily. That's huge.

Kickstarter wasn't a magic wand or a lottery ticket; it was a mirror reflecting the effort and heart you put in. You looked into that mirror and saw hundreds of people standing behind you, cheering you on and holding up your book. That's the image I want you to carry with you. On days when writing is hard or marketing feels like a slog, remember that there's a crowd of readers out there who literally invested in you. They want your words. They're waiting for the next chapter, in your book and in your journey.

You've crushed it on Kickstarter, and now, you're poised to crush it in whatever you set your sights on next. The skills and confidence you've gained are yours to keep. The audience you've gathered is yours to nurture. The momentum is yours to channel.

So go forth and continue this adventure. Write the stories that excite you. Build on the platform you've created. Try new things, make a splash, maybe even break some conventions. You have the tools, you have the supporters, and you have the drive.

Whenever you need a reminder of your capability, flip through these pages again or look at your campaign page – see that funded bar, those positive comments, that book in your hand that once was just a dream. That's tangible evidence of your ability to set a goal and achieve it despite challenges.

Your Kickstarter campaign has concluded, but your author career is just opening onto new horizons. From all of us who contributed to this guide and from the community of creators cheering you on: Congratulations on what you've accomplished, and here's to your continuing success.

The story of your book's journey is just beginning a new chapter – and thanks to your courage and hard work, it's looking like a bestseller. Now, go out there and keep crushing it – on Kickstarter, in bookstores, and beyond. The world needs your stories, and you've shown you have what it takes to deliver them.

Onward to your next adventure!

www.ingramcontent.com/pod-product-compliance
Lightning Source LLC
Chambersburg PA
CBHW062130040426
42335CB00039B/1858